Two Chefs in the Garden is pac[ked with]
recipes inspired by country living, growing vegetables,
and a desire to eat more plants. From the endless bounty of
their garden—sweet cherry tomatoes, spicy arugula, earthy
leeks, zucchini, eggplant, pumpkins, potatoes, and more—
chefs and vegetable farmers Crawford and Kirk's stunning
collection of over 150 recipes coax the most out of vibrant
seasonal produce in unique and exciting dishes: Pan-Roasted
Asparagus with Sage, Shallot Cream, and Crispy Parmesan;
Tempura Eggplant Tacos; Garden Ratatouille Pasta Salad;
End-of-Summer Tomato Risotto, Celery Root Soup with
Brown Butter Sunflower Seed Pesto and Hickory Sticks;
Sweet Corn, Potato, and Leek Chowder; Spaghetti Squash
Gratin with Leeks and Spinach; Beet Falafel with Lemony
Tzatziki; Pumpkin Mac and Cheese; Apple Brown Sugar
Pancake; Ginger Rhubarb Custard Tarts; Cherry Ruffled Milk
Pie; and Summer Berry Spoon Cake with Vanilla Sauce.

Crawford and Kirk take readers on a culinary tour through
an outstanding array of recipes, showcasing the abundant
rewards of their garden throughout the seasons. You'll
discover new and approachable ways to cook with vegetables
and make plant-based foods the central part of your meals.
Featuring beautiful photography throughout, *Two Chefs in
the Garden* celebrates the ease and versatility of cooking
with vegetables that will satisfy everyone.

Two Chefs in the Garden

Two Chefs in the Garden

Over 150 Garden-Inspired Vegetarian Recipes

Lynn Crawford
Lora Kirk

PENGUIN
an imprint of Penguin Canada,
a division of Penguin Random
House Canada Limited

Canada • USA • UK • Ireland •
Australia • New Zealand • India •
South Africa • China

First published 2024

www.penguinrandomhouse.ca

LIBRARY AND ARCHIVES CANADA CATALOGUING IN PUBLICATION

Title: Two chefs in the garden : over 150 garden-inspired vegetarian recipes /
     Lynn Crawford and Lora Kirk.
Names: Crawford, Lynn, 1964- author. | Kirk, Lora, author.
Description: Includes index.
Identifiers: Canadiana (print) 2023056836X | Canadiana (ebook) 20230568378 |
     ISBN 9780735245624 (hardcover) | ISBN 9780735245631 (EPUB)
Subjects: LCSH: Vegetarian cooking. | LCSH: Cooking (Vegetables) |
     LCSH: Seasonal cooking. | LCGFT: Cookbooks.
Classification: LCC TX837 .C73 2024 | DDC 641.5/636—dc23

Cover and interior design by Terri Nimmo
Typeset by Sean Tai
Food and prop styling by Lynn Crawford and Lora Kirk
Photography by Ash Nayler

Printed in China

0 9 8 7 6 5 4 3 2 1

Penguin
Random House
PENGUIN CANADA

For our daughters, Addie Pepper and Gemma Jet Aubergine.

May you always run wild and free through the garden, and feel the warmth of the sun on your beautiful faces. May you continue to learn patience, love, and respect for the food that we grow, cook, and share together.

Contents

The Recipes

Pasta

Bucatini al Limone with Green Beans, Olives, and Pine Nuts | 215
Pumpkin Mac and Cheese | 216
Penne Peperonata | 219
Pici Pasta with Broccoli Almond Pesto | 220
Whole Wheat Spaghetti with Roasted Cauliflower, Caramelized Onions, and Brown Butter Parmesan Croutons | 223
Orecchiette with Cherry Tomatoes and Rosé Sauce | 224
Fettuccine Sweet Corn Alfredo | 227

Mains

Spinach Ricotta Gnudi with Chive Butter Sauce | 231
Eggplant Katsu with Caramelized Onion Tonkatsu Sauce and Red Cabbage and Green Onion Slaw | 233
Onion Bourguignon with Buttery Mashed Parsnips | 235
End-of-Summer Tomato Risotto | 239
Harissa and Maple Roasted Carrot Tart with Carrot-Top Dill Cream Cheese | 240
Savoy Cabbage with Borscht Trimmings | 243
Lentil Mushroom Shepherd's Pie with Buttery Rutabaga Potato Mash | 245
Potato, Kale, and Chickpea Korma | 247
Spicy Orange Sesame Cauliflower | 249
Moroccan-Spiced Pumpkin Tagine with Pumpkin Yogurt | 251
Sweet Potato and Black Bean Chili | 252
Sweet Potato and Spinach Enchiladas | 255
Chili Oil | 257
Celery Stir-Fry with Crispy Tofu and Sesame Honey Chili Sauce | 259
Beet Falafel with Lemony Tzatziki | 260
Celery Root Steaks with Sautéed Mushrooms and Café de Paris Butter | 263
Grilled Cajun Zucchini and Summer Corn Salad with Avocado | 264
Butternut Squash Scallopini with Apples, Sage, and Hazelnut Dukkha | 267
Buffalo Fried Cauliflower | 268

Sides

Sweet Corn on the Cob with Coconut and Lime | 273
Braised New Potatoes with Shallots, Garlic, Rosemary, and Thyme | 274
Spaghetti Squash Gratin with Leeks and Spinach | 277
Pan-Roasted Asparagus with Sage, Shallot Cream, and Crispy Parmesan | 278
Roasted Cauliflower and Tomatoes with Mint Chimichurri Sauce | 281
Curried Acorn Squash with Golden Raisins, Honey, and Pine Nuts | 282
Charred Broccoli Spears with Confit Garlic Butter, Chickpeas, and Kale | 285
Roasted Rainbow Carrots with Honey Miso Glaze and Carrot-Top Green Goddess Dip | 286
Thai Green Bean Curry | 289
Sweet-and-Sour Glazed Golden Beets with Walnuts and Black Pepper Mascarpone | 290
Sesame Cucumber Salad with Lime, Cilantro, and Pickled Shallots | 293
Savoury Bread Pudding with Swiss Chard and Cheddar | 294
Butternut Squash Bravas with Basil Aioli | 297
Spice Market Fried Rice | 298
Fondant Potatoes | 300
Cheesy Corn Casserole | 303
Cauliflower Gratin with Caramelized Onions and Gruyère | 304
Roasted Brussels Sprouts with Maple Cashew Caramel | 307
Orange-Braised Leeks with Horseradish and Pine Nuts | 308
Confit Garlic Potato Cakes | 311

Desserts

Sweet Potato Pie with Maple Meringue | 315
Summer Berry Spoon Cake with Vanilla Sauce | 316
Almond Coconut Plum Cake with Coconut Whipped Cream | 318
Chocolate Sheet Cake with Raspberries and Buttercream Frosting | 321
Toffee Pecan Peach Crisp | 322
Ginger Rhubarb Custard Tarts | 325
Apple Turnovers | 327
Pumpkin Cheesecake with Chai Caramel Sauce | 330
Cherry Ruffled Milk Pie | 333
Chocolate Swirl Meringue with Strawberries, Hazelnuts, and Sweet Cream | 334
Chocolate Almond Tart with Pears | 337

Introduction

NEW CHAPTERS IN OUR LIVES ARE INEVITABLE. They are often necessary, sometimes unexpected or potentially scary, but hopefully most are exciting, rejuvenating, and simply the best changes. Moving out to the country in 2020 was life-changing for us, and I never regretted leaving the big city. I am finally home and feel like I truly belong. The calm and peaceful life in the countryside has allowed me to slow down. One of the best things about a slower pace is that I can observe more and align my priorities. Sunrises and sunsets have more meaning now than ever before, and family is everything. My days in this new chapter of life are filled with watching and experiencing in pure amazement the cherished moments as our daughters Addie and Gemma grow up.

We started building our family garden together the first year we moved to the country. Kids and gardens are a natural partnership partly because the garden is about being outside and partly because things are always changing in the garden. Addie and Gemma helped Lora and me build the containers and fill them with dirt. The girls helped sow the seeds and water each row as they patiently watched the vegetables grow. They harvested our first radishes. Farmers at heart, those girls could dig up potatoes all day long, and eat every bean, cucumber, and cherry tomato in sight! Moments like these are new opportunities to make incredible memories together and encourage both girls to be their best unique selves.

While discovering the farmer side of our new life in the country, we have developed a deeper love of vegetables and have been so energized to find new and exciting ways to pack them into our diet in as many ways as possible. Through this book, our intention is to inspire you to cook with vegetables and make plant-based foods the central part of your meals. All our recipes were created with the vegetables we grew in our family garden. But you don't need to grow your own to make these recipes taste great. All the ingredients are easy to find. Just shop in the season, and make sure you hit the farmers' market first. Our recipes are delicious, incredibly nutritious, easy to prepare, and, for the record, every one is Addie and Gemma approved!

Good food is real food, and we must all eat with intention. See food like you have never seen it before and rethink your relationship with food.

Eating plant-based or plant-forward is not a fad. It is ages old, and it is the perfect lasting, sustainable lifestyle that can and will transform your life.

—Lynn

WHEN I WAS GROWING UP I COULD NOT wait to move to the big city to be part of the hustle and bustle. The draw of the bright lights, tall sky-scrapers, different restaurants, large supermarkets, and people everywhere.

That changed when I got a bit older and had a family of my own. I looked back and reflected on the adventures of my childhood. From these reflections I wanted to teach and share with our daughters the life adventures that helped make me who I am today.

Some of the best parts of my childhood were the times I spent on my grandparents' farm during summer vacation. I could also not get enough of working in my family's vegetable garden and then pickling and preserving everything we harvested. Our family meals were based around the food we grew in the garden, not what was at the store.

I have so many amazing memories of exploring in the woods with my siblings, picking raspberries along the back lane, being able to run wild and free until the sun set. The best was just being able to be outside all day long and truly experience nature. There were so many life lessons to be learned and shared.

My Babka means the world to me, and as a child (and still to this day) I loved spending all of my days with her. It didn't matter what was in store for us on any given day, she always made it special. I would help Babka take care of her honeybees, and what a gift that was for me. I've learned so much from her and keep her bee and garden journal that she gave to me close to my heart. I would help her cut the grass, change the oil in the rototiller, forage for mushrooms, and climb up her apple tree (apparently since the age of three) to pick ripe, juicy fruit that together we magically turned into the most delicious strudel I've ever tasted.

These fond childhood memories, my family, the kinds of outdoor adventures I experienced, the appreciation I have of growing our own food, living in a place where children grow up in a hands-on environment that puts them in touch with Mother Nature—these were just a few of the reasons why I wanted to move back to where I grew up to raise our children.

I wanted to teach our daughters Addie and Gemma how to garden, to give them immeasurable life skills of independence and sustainability—while encouraging them to eat more vegetables as well. Building our family garden has been a rewarding bonding experience. Planting the seeds, nurturing them, and watching them grow gives us such a feeling of accomplishment that's hard to describe. It's fun work that helps you nourish your family and maintain your health. Caring for the garden is also a perfect way to teach the girls about nature and give them a great sense of pride. Eating fresh spring peas from the garden or a sun-kissed cherry tomato are magical moments to share with the girls. Watching them explore and taste what we grow as a family in the garden is an experience we will always remember.

From our little garden that we grew, we started cooking more plant-based meals. We were inspired by the excitement and the sense of pride that came from watching a tiny seed transform into a beautiful vegetable. Maybe I am biased, but our little garden grew the sweetest cherry tomatoes, the spiciest arugula, the zestiest dill, and the crunchiest cucumbers. Not to mention all the other wonderful produce, the zucchini, carrots, red beets, onions, broccoli, eggplant, pumpkins, potatoes. I swear in our first year we grew it all! We grew produce in raised beds, large pots, small pots, raised rows, directly in the ground. We started seeds, and we were given some seedlings. Not everything was successful, but it was all part of the learning curve. And when the garden started to flourish, it was such an inspiration for us to start dreaming of the dishes we wanted to cook.

We hope that these plant-based recipes help inspire you and your family to try vegetables in different ways. And while it's not necessary in order to cook our recipes, hopefully this book will inspire you to grow your own vegetables, whether in a garden on your property or in large pots on a balcony. You just need some good soil, sunshine, and time. You will be surprised at how rewarding and tasty the food you grow will be.

Now back to the garden we go!

—**Lora**

Morning Baking

Strawberry Cornmeal Muffins

When it's peak season for strawberries we grab the kids and head up to our berry patch to start picking—or should I say eating! It's hard to get the girls (and us) to stop eating them all and put those just-picked berries in the basket. But we have the perfect incentive: the promise to bake them one of their favourite treats, strawberry cornmeal muffins. Yes, call it a bribe, but it works every time!

MAKES 12 MUFFINS

2 cups all-purpose flour

2 cups cornmeal

¼ cup granulated sugar

2 tablespoons baking powder

½ teaspoon salt

4 eggs

2 cups whole milk

⅔ cup liquid honey

8 tablespoons unsalted butter, melted

¼ cup vegetable oil

1½ teaspoons pure vanilla extract

1½ cups diced hulled fresh strawberries, divided

Turbinado sugar, for sprinkling (optional)

1. Preheat the oven to 425°F (220°C). Line a standard muffin tin with 12 paper liners.

2. In a large bowl, sift together the flour, cornmeal, granulated sugar, baking powder, and salt.

3. In a medium bowl, whisk together the eggs, milk, honey, melted butter, vegetable oil, and vanilla. Add the wet ingredients to the dry ingredients and stir until just combined. Gently fold in 1¼ cups of the strawberries to avoid overmixing.

4. Using a spoon, divide the batter evenly between the prepared muffin cups, filling two-thirds full. Top the muffins with the remaining ¼ cup strawberries and sprinkle with the turbinado sugar, if using.

5. Bake until a cake tester inserted into the centre of a muffin comes out clean and the tops are nicely browned, 15 to 18 minutes. Let the muffins cool in the pan set on a rack for 5 minutes, then turn them out onto the rack to cool completely. Store in an airtight container at room temperature for up to 3 days.

NOTE: We use this recipe all through the summer berry season. You can replace the strawberries with raspberries, blueberries, or blackberries, or if you can't decide, a mixture will be a hit too!

Blueberry Muffins with Lavender Streusel

MAKES 16 MUFFINS

LAVENDER STREUSEL TOPPING

¾ cup all-purpose flour

⅔ cup granulated sugar

¾ teaspoon dried lavender buds

4 tablespoons unsalted butter, diced, at room temperature

BLUEBERRY MUFFINS

2¾ cups all-purpose flour

1½ teaspoons baking soda

½ teaspoon salt

1 teaspoon cinnamon

3 eggs

½ cup granulated sugar

½ cup lightly packed brown sugar

¾ cup vegetable oil

1 cup fresh apple cider or pure apple juice

¾ cup plain full-fat yogurt

1 teaspoon pure vanilla extract

1½ cups fresh or frozen blueberries (see Note)

These perfectly domed muffins are bursting with fresh, plump, juicy blueberries and have a wonderful lavender crumb crust. Lavender works so beautifully with summer fruits, especially blueberries, bringing an exciting sweet and floral aroma and dimension to your morning baking.

1. Preheat the oven to 350°F (180°C). Line a standard muffin tin with 12 paper liners.

2. **Make the lavender streusel topping:** In a medium bowl, whisk together the flour, granulated sugar, and lavender buds. Add the butter and use a wooden spoon to mix it into the dry ingredients. Then rub together with your hands until the mixture has the texture of crumbs. Set aside.

3. **Make the muffins:** In a large bowl, sift together the flour, baking soda, salt, and cinnamon.

4. In a separate large bowl, whisk together the eggs, granulated sugar, brown sugar, and vegetable oil until fluffy, about 5 minutes, scraping down the sides of the bowl as needed. Add the apple cider, yogurt, and vanilla. Whisk until smooth, about 2 minutes.

5. Add the wet ingredients to the dry ingredients and stir until just combined. The batter will be very thick. Using a rubber spatula, fold in the blueberries until evenly distributed.

6. Spoon about 1½ tablespoons of the batter into each prepared muffin cup. Sprinkle half of the streusel over the batter. Divide the remaining batter evenly over the streusel, filling the cups two-thirds full. Evenly sprinkle the remaining streusel over the batter, gently pressing the crumbs into the batter so they stay on the muffins.

7. Bake until a cake tester inserted into the centre of a muffin comes out clean and the tops are nicely browned, 20 to 25 minutes. Let the muffins cool in the pan set on a rack for 5 minutes, then turn them out onto the rack to cool completely. Store in an airtight container at room temperature for up to 3 days.

NOTE: Tossing the fresh or frozen berries in a little flour before stirring them into the batter helps keep them suspended so that each muffin is evenly studded with blueberries.

Spiced Apple Muffins with Butter Pecan Crumble

These apple muffins are packed with apples and lots of warm spices. The butter pecan topping is so irresistible and gives these muffins that perfect nutty crunch. Your kitchen will smell amazing once these are baking in your oven. Better make a double batch because no one will be able to resist them.

1. Preheat the oven to 375°F (190°C). Line a standard muffin tin with 12 paper liners.

2. **Make the butter pecan crumble:** In a small bowl, mix together the flour, melted butter, demerara sugar, pecans, and cinnamon. The mixture will be quite wet. Set aside.

3. **Make the spiced apple muffins:** In a medium bowl, sift together the all-purpose flour, whole wheat flour, baking powder, baking soda, salt, cinnamon, nutmeg, and cloves.

4. In the bowl of a stand mixer fitted with the paddle attachment, beat the butter, granulated sugar, and brown sugar on medium speed until fluffy, 1 to 2 minutes. Scrape down the sides of the bowl with a rubber spatula. Add the egg and yogurt and mix well, stopping to scrape down the sides of the bowl as needed. Add the dry ingredients and mix on low speed until just combined. Add the chopped apples and mix until just combined.

5. Using a spoon, divide the batter evenly between the prepared muffin cups. Spoon the butter pecan crumble evenly over the batter.

6. Bake until a cake tester inserted into the centre of a muffin comes out clean and the tops are nicely browned, 25 to 30 minutes. Let the muffins cool in the pan set on a rack for 5 minutes, then turn them out onto the rack to cool completely. Store in an airtight container at room temperature for up to 3 days.

MAKES 12 MUFFINS

BUTTER PECAN CRUMBLE

⅓ cup all-purpose flour
5 tablespoons unsalted butter, melted
⅓ cup demerara or turbinado sugar
¾ cup chopped pecans
¼ teaspoon cinnamon

SPICED APPLE MUFFINS

1 cup all-purpose flour
1 cup whole wheat flour
1 teaspoon baking powder
1 teaspoon baking soda
½ teaspoon salt
1½ teaspoons cinnamon
½ teaspoon ground nutmeg
¼ teaspoon ground cloves
8 tablespoons unsalted butter, at room temperature
½ cup granulated sugar
¼ cup packed brown sugar
1 large egg
1 cup plain full-fat yogurt or Greek yogurt
2 cups peeled, cored, and finely chopped apples (see Note)

NOTE: So many wonderful varieties of apples can be used in baking. Here are the ones we love that'll really help your baking shine: Cortland, Fuji, Granny Smith, Winesap, Honeycrisp, Empire, and Gala.

Autumn Morning Glory Muffins

MAKES 12 MUFFINS

2 cups all-purpose flour

1 teaspoon baking soda

½ teaspoon salt

2 teaspoons cinnamon

½ teaspoon ground ginger

1 cup packed light brown sugar

1 cup grated peeled carrots

1 cup grated peeled butternut squash

1 large apple (any variety), peeled
   and grated

½ cup golden raisins

½ cup unsweetened shredded
   coconut

½ cup chopped toasted walnuts

⅓ cup sunflower seeds

2 tablespoons hemp seeds (optional)

3 large eggs

⅔ cup vegetable oil

¼ cup fresh orange juice

1 teaspoon pure vanilla extract

The famous Morning Glory muffin just got a well-deserved makeover. These muffins are fluffy, moist, and filled with hearty fall ingredients—autumn squash, carrots, apples, and lots of healthy seeds and nuts. They are easy to make and are a glorious way to start your day.

1. Preheat the oven to 375°F (190°C). Line a standard muffin tin with 12 paper liners.

2. In a large bowl, sift together the flour, baking soda, salt, cinnamon, and ginger. Mix in the brown sugar until combined. Stir in the carrots, butternut squash, apple, raisins, coconut, walnuts, sunflower seeds, and hemp seeds, if using.

3. In a medium bowl, whisk together the eggs, vegetable oil, orange juice, and vanilla. Add the wet ingredients to the dry ingredients and stir until evenly moistened.

4. Using a spoon, divide the batter evenly between the prepared muffin cups. Bake until a cake tester inserted into the centre of a muffin comes out clean and the tops are nicely browned, 22 to 25 minutes. Let the muffins cool in the pan set on a rack for 5 minutes, then turn them out onto the rack to cool completely. Store in an airtight container at room temperature for up to 3 days or in the freezer for up to 3 months. If frozen, thaw on the counter for 2 to 3 hours before serving. To reheat, wrap individual muffins in foil and heat in a 350°F (180°C) oven until warm.

Chocolate Zucchini Bread

This recipe always amazes us, every time we make it! How can a simple vegetable from our garden be transformed into such a rich, chocolaty treat? We make this delicious bread to enjoy any time of the day—a special breakfast, a fabulous afternoon snack when those chocolate cravings hit, or we serve it up for dessert with a scoop of ice cream. A great way for everyone to get their veggies in.

1. Preheat the oven to 350°F (180°C). Spray a 9 × 5-inch loaf pan with non-stick cooking spray.

2. In a medium bowl, whisk together the flour, cocoa powder, salt, baking soda, baking powder, and cinnamon.

3. In a large bowl, whisk together the eggs, vegetable oil, sugar, and vanilla until smooth. Using a rubber spatula, stir the dry ingredients into the wet ingredients until just combined. Do not overmix. Fold in the zucchini and ¾ cup of the chocolate chips.

4. Scrape the batter into the prepared loaf pan and smooth the top. Evenly sprinkle the remaining ¼ cup chocolate chips over the top.

5. Bake until a cake tester inserted into the centre of the bread comes out clean, 50 to 60 minutes. Let the bread cool in the pan set on a rack for 15 minutes. Run a knife around the edges of the bread and carefully remove from the pan. Let the bread cool on the rack until slightly warm before slicing. Store the cooled loaf in an airtight container at room temperature for up to 3 days or in the freezer for up to 3 months.

MAKES ONE 9 × 5-INCH LOAF

2½ cups all-purpose flour

½ cup unsweetened cocoa powder

1 teaspoon salt

1 teaspoon baking soda

¼ teaspoon baking powder

1 teaspoon cinnamon

3 eggs

1 cup vegetable oil

1½ cups granulated sugar

1 tablespoon pure vanilla extract

2 cups grated zucchini

1 cup semisweet chocolate chips, divided

NOTE: For extra flavour and texture, you can add up to 1 cup of dried fruit or nuts (chopped if they're large) to this loaf. A combination of raisins and walnuts or sun-dried cherries and almonds are both so good.

Cardamom-Spiced Carrot Date Loaf with Sunflower Seed Butter and Plum Jam

Cardamom brings a warm, herbal, citrusy aromatic brilliance to baking. This beautiful carrot loaf makes a wonderful addition to any coffee break or afternoon tea. We love to serve it with nutty sunflower seed butter and our homemade plum jam.

MAKES ONE 9 × 5-INCH LOAF

PLUM JAM (MAKES TWO 2-CUP JARS)

2 pounds (900 g) plums (a firm and sweet variety such as prune or damson), pitted and sliced

1½ cups granulated sugar

3 tablespoons grated peeled fresh ginger

1 teaspoon pure vanilla extract

Zest and juice of 2 lemons

SUNFLOWER SEED BUTTER (MAKES 1½ CUPS)

2¼ cups sunflower seeds, toasted

¼ cup lightly packed brown sugar

1 teaspoon salt

CARDAMOM-SPICED CARROT DATE LOAF

2 eggs

1 cup granulated sugar

⅔ cup vegetable oil

1 teaspoon pure vanilla extract

1½ cups all-purpose flour

¾ teaspoon baking soda

½ teaspoon salt

1 teaspoon ground cardamom

½ teaspoon cinnamon

1½ cups grated peeled carrots

1 cup Medjool dates, pitted and roughly chopped

1 tablespoon grated peeled fresh ginger

1. **Make the plum jam:** To sterilize the jars, bring a large pot of water to a boil. Using metal tongs, submerge two 2-cup mason jars into the boiling water, allowing the water to fill the jars. Add the lids and rings and boil for 8 minutes. Turn off the heat. Using tongs, transfer the jars, lids, and rings to a clean kitchen towel; allow to air-dry. Reserve the pot of water.

2. In a large saucepan, combine the plums, sugar, ginger, vanilla, and lemon zest and juice. Cook over medium heat, stirring occasionally, until the plums are soft and the sugar has dissolved, about 20 minutes. Using an immersion blender, blend until smooth. Continue to cook the jam, stirring occasionally, until thick, 5 to 10 minutes. Remove from the heat and let the jam cool slightly.

3. Bring the pot of water back to a slow rolling boil over medium-high heat.

4. Ladle the jam into the sterilized jars leaving ½ inch of headspace. Wipe the rims of the jars. Place a lid on the top of each jar, then screw on the rings just until fingertip tight. Carefully submerge the filled jars in the boiling water and boil for 5 minutes. Remove the jars from the water bath and place on a clean kitchen towel. Let cool for about 30 minutes. While cooling, the jar lids will pop, creating a vacuum seal, letting you know that the jars are properly sealed. Store sealed jars at room temperature for up to 1 year. Once opened, store the jam in the refrigerator for up to 2 months.

5. **Make the sunflower seed butter:** In a food processor, pulse the sunflower seeds until finely chopped, then blend continuously for 1 minute. Stop the processor and scrape down the sides of the bowl, then blend until creamy and smooth, 1 to 2 minutes. Add the brown sugar and salt and process until blended. Set aside or store in a sealed jar in the refrigerator for up to 1 month.

6. **Make the cardamom-spiced carrot date loaf:** Preheat the oven to 350°F (180°C). Spray a 9 × 5-inch loaf pan with nonstick cooking spray or line with parchment paper.

7. In a large bowl, whisk together the eggs, granulated sugar, vegetable oil, and vanilla until combined.

8. In a medium bowl, sift together the flour, baking soda, salt, cardamom, and cinnamon. Add the dry ingredients to the wet ingredients and mix well. Fold in the carrots, dates, and ginger.

9. Scrape the batter into the prepared loaf pan. Bake for 1 hour or until a cake tester inserted into the centre of the loaf comes out clean. Let cool on a rack. Once the loaf is fully cooled, turn out of the pan. Wrap the loaf in plastic wrap and store in the refrigerator for up to 4 days or in the freezer for up to 1 month.

10. Serve the loaf with sunflower seed butter and plum jam on the side.

NOTE: Parsnips are an exceptional substitution for carrots. They are a cousin of the carrot and have a sweet, nutty flavour with some peppery and earthy notes. Parsnips become sweeter when you cook or bake with them.

Honey Buttermilk Biscuits with Strawberry Jam

MAKES 12 BISCUITS

STRAWBERRY JAM (MAKES ABOUT 1½ CUPS)

2 cups sliced hulled fresh strawberries
¾ cup granulated sugar
2 teaspoons fresh lemon juice

HONEY BUTTERMILK BISCUITS

3 cups all-purpose flour
2½ teaspoons baking powder
¾ teaspoon salt
½ teaspoon baking soda
¾ cup cold unsalted butter, cut into
    small cubes (see Note)
1 large egg
1 cup buttermilk
¼ cup wildflower honey
1 teaspoon pure vanilla extract

EGG WASH

1 egg
1 tablespoon whole milk

NOTE: For flaky layers, be sure to use cold butter. When you cut in the butter, you get coarse crumbs of butter coated with flour. During baking, the butter will melt, releasing steam and creating pockets of air that result in airy and flaky biscuits.

No one loves honey and everything to do with the harvest of honey more than Lora. Her long love of beekeeping comes from her Babka, who kept beehives in her backyard when Lora was growing up. Babka was passionate and patient (and just as in love with honey as Lora is) and taught Lora everything she needed to know to become an outstanding beekeeper in her own right. The magical results are enjoyed by our family every day. Honey truly is one of the most coveted culinary treats. There is always a jar in our kitchen ready to add delicious flavour and the perfect touch of sweetness to everything we cook or bake. These honey buttermilk biscuits are one of our most favourite recipes using honey. We love making our own strawberry jam, but feel free to use store-bought.

1. **Make the strawberry jam:** In a medium saucepan, stir together the strawberries, sugar, and lemon juice. Heat over high heat, stirring constantly with a heatproof spatula. Once the mixture starts to bubble up, reduce the heat to medium-low and cook, stirring constantly, until the jam is thick, 10 to 15 minutes.

2. Remove the pot from the heat and carefully ladle the jam into a 2-cup heatproof airtight container. Let the jam cool completely at room temperature. Store in the refrigerator for up to 2 months or in the freezer for up to 6 months.

3. **Make the honey buttermilk biscuits:** Preheat the oven to 400°F (200°C). Line a baking sheet with parchment paper.

4. In a large bowl, whisk together the flour, baking powder, salt, and baking soda. Add the cold butter and, using a pastry cutter or fork, cut the butter into the flour mixture until it forms pea-size crumbs and is uniformly mixed.

5. In a medium bowl, whisk together the egg, buttermilk, honey, and vanilla. Make a well in the centre of the flour mixture. Pour the buttermilk mixture into the well and stir together until a moist, slightly tacky dough forms.

6. Transfer the dough to a floured work surface and knead the dough 2 or 3 times, then pat it out into a circle ¾ inch thick. Using a lightly floured 2-inch round cookie cutter, cut out 12 biscuits. (To prevent sticking, dip the cutter lightly in flour before cutting each round.) Do not reroll scraps—simply pat them together and cut into rounds. Transfer the biscuits to the lined baking sheet, evenly spaced.

7. **Prepare the egg wash, brush the biscuits, and bake:** In a small bowl, whisk together the egg and milk. Brush the tops of the biscuits with the egg wash. Bake until golden brown on top, 18 to 20 minutes. Serve hot. Store in an airtight container at room temperature for up to 2 days.

Pumpkin Cinnamon Buns with Maple Cream Cheese Frosting

If you love super-soft and gooey cinnamon buns, wait until you try these pumpkin cinnamon buns. A layer of maple cream cheese frosting melts into the just-baked rolls, making them truly irresistible. Whether you're in charge of ensuring your next brunch is a huge success or you want to make a soul-satisfying any-time-of-the-day treat, bake a tray of these showstoppers. They'll steal the spotlight from whatever else is happening that day!

MAKES 12 BUNS

DOUGH

1 cup whole milk

2¼ teaspoons active dry yeast

1 large egg, lightly beaten

¾ cup pure pumpkin purée

¼ cup lightly packed brown sugar

4 tablespoons unsalted butter, melted

4 cups bread flour, more if needed

1 tablespoon cinnamon

1 tablespoon ground ginger

¾ teaspoon salt

FILLING

4 tablespoons unsalted butter, at room temperature

⅔ cup lightly packed brown sugar

4 teaspoons cinnamon

MAPLE CREAM CHEESE FROSTING

½ cup (4 ounces/115 g) cream cheese, at room temperature

3 tablespoons unsalted butter, at room temperature

¼ cup icing sugar

¼ cup pure maple syrup

Pinch of salt

— continued —

1. **Make the dough:** In a small bowl, combine the milk and yeast and stir a few times. Let sit for 5 minutes or until foamy.

2. Meanwhile, in a large bowl, combine the egg, pumpkin purée, brown sugar, melted butter, bread flour, cinnamon, ginger, and salt. Add the yeast mixture. Using a wooden spoon, stir until the dough forms a soft ball, adding more flour if needed. The dough should be soft and slightly sticky to the touch, not stiff.

3. Turn the dough out onto a floured work surface and knead until smooth and elastic, about 10 minutes. Place the dough in a lightly oiled bowl and cover with a damp kitchen towel (see Note). Let rest in a warm place for 30 minutes or until doubled in size.

4. Preheat the oven to 350°F (180°C). Butter a 13 × 9-inch baking pan.

5. Deflate the dough by pushing it down with your hands. Transfer the dough to a well-floured work surface. Use a rolling pin to roll out the dough into an 18 × 14-inch rectangle, with a long side facing you.

6. **Make the filling, shape the buns, and bake:** Evenly spread the softened butter over the dough.

In a small bowl, stir together the brown sugar and cinnamon. Evenly sprinkle the sugar mixture over the buttered dough. Starting at the long edge closest to you, carefully roll the dough into a tight log. With the seam side down, use a sharp knife to cut the log into 12 equal pieces.

7. Arrange the buns cut side down in the prepared baking pan. Cover with a kitchen towel and let rest in a warm place for 20 minutes or until doubled in size.

8. Bake until the buns are lightly browned, 25 to 30 minutes. Transfer the pan to a rack and let the buns cool for 5 minutes before icing.

9. **Meanwhile, make the maple cream cheese frosting:** In a medium bowl, using a hand-held electric mixer, beat the cream cheese on medium speed until smooth. Add the butter and beat until blended. Add the icing sugar, maple syrup, and salt and beat until fluffy, about 5 minutes.

10. **Frost the buns:** Using an offset spatula or a table knife, evenly spread about one-third of the frosting in a thin layer over the warm buns. Let the buns sit for another 15 to 20 minutes to cool. Spread the remaining frosting over the buns and serve. Store, covered, at room temperature for up 2 days.

NOTE: It is important to place the mixed dough in a clean, slightly oiled bowl for its first rise. This extra step will make the dough easier to remove after proofing and allows the dough to rise higher, since it won't stick against the bowl.

Make a double batch of these tasty cinnamon buns to enjoy later. The dough freezes well once rolled and sliced. Place the buns in a baking pan, and wrap tightly in plastic wrap and store in the freezer for up to 2 months. To use from frozen, thaw in the refrigerator overnight. Bring to room temperature on the counter and allow the dough to rise until doubled in size, about 1 hour. Bake as directed above.

Cranberry Cheddar Scones with Rosemary Orange Glaze

Fresh scones warm from the oven are perfectly simple and perfectly delicious. This recipe is a favourite of ours on weekends when we are guaranteed to have a few impromptu visits from friends or relatives. Time to put the kettle on!

1. **Make the cranberry cheddar scones:** Preheat the oven to 425°F (220°C). Line a baking sheet with parchment paper.

2. In a large bowl, whisk together the whole wheat flour, turbinado sugar, baking powder, and salt.

3. Cut the butter into tiny pieces and mix it into the flour. Add the cranberries, cheddar, and orange zest and gently stir to combine. Gently mix in the yogurt and milk. Use your hands to knead the last bits of the flour into the dough until no dry patches remain. Do not overmix (see Note).

4. Turn the dough out onto a lightly floured work surface. Shape the dough into an 8-inch circle about 1 inch thick. Use a sharp knife to cut the dough into 8 wedges. Arrange the wedges on the lined baking sheet, evenly spaced. Sprinkle the scones with a bit of turbinado sugar.

5. Bake for 15 minutes or until golden brown on top. Let the scones cool slightly on the baking sheet before glazing.

6. **Make the rosemary orange glaze:** In a small bowl, whisk together the icing sugar, melted butter, orange zest, orange juice, rosemary, and vanilla until smooth.

7. When the scones are cooled slightly, drizzle with the glaze. Serve warm. Store in an airtight container at room temperature for up to 2 days.

MAKES 8 SCONES

CRANBERRY CHEDDAR SCONES

2 cups whole wheat flour

3 tablespoons turbinado sugar, plus more for sprinkling

1 tablespoon baking powder

⅛ teaspoon kosher salt

5 tablespoons cold unsalted butter

½ cup sun-dried cranberries

½ cup grated aged cheddar cheese

Zest of 1 orange

½ cup plain full-fat Greek yogurt

½ cup whole milk

ROSEMARY ORANGE GLAZE

1 cup icing sugar, sifted

3 tablespoons unsalted butter, melted

Zest of 1 orange

2 tablespoons fresh orange juice

1 teaspoon chopped fresh rosemary

½ teaspoon pure vanilla extract

NOTE: The best tip we can give is don't overwork the dough! It should have lumps and bumps in it. Overworking the dough will make your scones heavy.

The consistency of the dough is the only tricky thing in making these scones. After making them a few times, you'll know exactly what you're looking for. Too dry and your scones will be dense and crumbly; too wet and sticky, they won't rise and will be tough and chewy.

Cherry Walnut Babka

Babka is made with a rich brioche dough and usually filled with layers of fudgy chocolate or cinnamon. There is an infinite number of variations, from sweet fillings to savoury flavours like goat cheese, bacon, and caramelized onions. While we do love those versions, our ultimate favourite is this babka packed with sweet cherries and toasted walnuts. We pick the cherries from our one and only cherry tree next to our garden. It always gives us just enough fruit to make a batch of jam to make this recipe.

MAKES ONE 9 × 5-INCH LOAF

CHERRY JAM (MAKES ABOUT 4 CUPS)
2 pounds (900 g) sweet or sour cherries (or a mixture), pitted
1 package (1.75 ounces/49 g) fruit pectin powder
Zest and juice of 1 lemon
2½ cups granulated sugar
1 to 2 drops almond extract

DOUGH
2¼ teaspoons active dry yeast
½ cup warm whole milk
1 whole egg
1 egg yolk
¼ cup granulated sugar
2 cups all-purpose flour
½ teaspoon salt
7 tablespoons unsalted butter, at room temperature

CHERRY FILLING
3 tablespoons finely chopped toasted walnuts
3 tablespoons unsalted butter, melted
1 tablespoon granulated sugar
1 tablespoon brown sugar
½ teaspoon cinnamon
¾ cup Cherry Jam (recipe at left)

STREUSEL TOPPING
2 tablespoons brown sugar
1 tablespoon granulated sugar
½ teaspoon cinnamon
Pinch of salt
2 tablespoons unsalted butter, at room temperature
2 tablespoons chopped walnuts

EGG WASH
1 egg
1 tablespoon whole milk

1. **Make the cherry jam:** Put a small plate or saucer in the freezer. In a food processor, working in batches, process the cherries just until finely chopped. Transfer the cherries to a large, heavy pot. Stir in the pectin and lemon zest and juice. Bring to a full rolling boil over high heat, stirring constantly. Stir in the sugar, return to a full rolling boil, and boil, stirring constantly, for 1 minute. Reduce the heat to a simmer and cook, stirring frequently, until the jam thickens, about 10 minutes.

2. Remove the pot from the heat and test the jam. Remove the plate from the freezer and put a small spoonful of jam on it. Return the dish to the freezer for a few minutes until the jam is cool, then run a spoon through it. If the jam is very thick and the spoon leaves a clear path, it's done. If not, return the plate to the freezer, continue to cook the jam for another 5 minutes, then test again. When the jam is done, remove from the heat and stir in the almond extract.

3. Ladle the jam into clean jars. Allow the jam to cool. Screw on the lids and store in the refrigerator for up to 3 months.

4. **Make the dough:** In a small bowl, stir together the yeast and warm milk. Let sit for 5 minutes or until foamy.

5. In a medium bowl, whisk together the egg, egg yolk, and sugar. Whisk in the yeast mixture.

6. In the bowl of a stand mixer fitted with the paddle attachment, combine the flour and salt. Add the egg mixture and mix on low speed until combined. Stop the mixer and switch to the dough hook. With the mixer running on medium speed, slowly incorporate the butter, 1 tablespoon at a time, and knead until the dough is smooth and elastic, 8 to 10 minutes.

7. Turn the dough out onto a lightly floured work surface and shape into a smooth ball. Place the dough in a buttered large bowl, cover with a kitchen towel, and let rest in a warm place for about 2 hours, until it puffs and no longer springs back when pressed with a finger.

8. **Meanwhile, make the cherry filling:** In a food processor, combine the walnuts, melted butter, granulated sugar, brown sugar, and cinnamon. Add the cherry jam and pulse until a smooth paste forms. Set aside.

9. Preheat the oven to 350°F (180°C). Butter a 9 × 5-inch loaf pan.

10. **Fill the dough and shape the loaf:** Transfer the dough to a well-floured work surface. Use a rolling pin to roll out the dough into a 22 × 12-inch rectangle, with a long side facing you.

11. Use an offset spatula to evenly spread a thin layer of the cherry filling over the dough, leaving a 1-inch border of exposed dough around the edges. Starting at the long edge closest to you, roll the dough into a tight log. Pinch the seam to seal.

12. With the seam side down, use a sharp knife to cut the log lengthwise down the centre. Arrange the halves with a short side facing you and the filling facing up. Keeping the filling facing up, lay one half over the other half to form an X. Starting at the centre of the X, take the ends closest to you and twist them around each other twice. Repeat on the other side, for a total of 4 twists. Place a hand on each end of the roll and quickly and firmly push together until the loaf is closer to the size of the pan. Lift the dough and place it in the prepared loaf pan. Cover loosely with a kitchen towel and let sit in a warm place for 30 minutes.

13. **Make the streusel topping:** After 30 minutes, in a small bowl, whisk together the brown sugar, granulated sugar, cinnamon, and salt. Add the butter and use a wooden spoon to mix it into the dry ingredients. Then rub together with your hands until the mixture has the texture of crumbs. Add the walnuts and stir to combine. Set aside.

14. **Prepare the egg wash, finish, and bake:** After 30 minutes, in a small bowl, whisk together the egg and milk. Brush the top of the babka with the egg wash. Evenly sprinkle the streusel over the top. Bake until golden brown, 50 to 60 minutes. Let the babka cool in the pan for 20 minutes. Run a knife around the edges of the pan, invert the loaf onto a rack, turn it right side up, and let cool completely before slicing. Store in an airtight container at room temperature for up to 2 days or in the freezer for up to 2 months. To thaw, let sit at room temperature for 2 hours or overnight in the refrigerator.

NOTE: Leftover babka—should you have any leftovers—makes excellent French toast. We always make a double batch to make sure we have some leftover slices.

Breakfast and Brunch

Berry Beet Blast Smoothie

There is no easier way to give yourself—and others—a morning energy boost than a tasty, nutrient-rich smoothie. Beets are innately sweet, and they bring a slight earthiness to this berry-bright smoothie.

1.   Combine the ingredients in a high-speed blender. Pulse for 1 minute to mix the ingredients, then blend on high speed until smooth. Pour into glasses.

SERVES 2

½ cup chopped peeled raw red beet

½ banana

1 cup fresh or frozen mixed berries (blueberries, strawberries, blackberries)

½ cup milk of choice or water

½ cup plain full-fat Greek yogurt

½ cup pure apple juice

1 tablespoon liquid honey

½ cup ice cubes

NOTE: To make any smoothie a little more filling and nutrient-rich, add a tablespoon of hemp seeds (a complete source of plant-based protein) or chia seeds (for extra fibre and omega-3 fatty acids). We love to add almond butter for healthy fat, fibre, and a delicious nutty taste.

Carrot Pineapple Smoothie

SERVES 2

1 medium carrot, peeled and roughly chopped

1 cup fresh or frozen diced pineapple

1 banana

1 cup full-fat coconut milk or unsweetened vanilla almond or almond milk

2 teaspoons grated peeled fresh ginger

½ teaspoon ground turmeric

2 tablespoons fresh lemon juice

1 tablespoon liquid honey

½ cup ice cubes (if using fresh fruit)

Sweet pineapple and nutritious carrots make a refreshing smoothie. Add a good dose of sunshine with a dash of antioxidant-rich turmeric. After you try this recipe, you may just see smoothies in a different way.

1. Combine the ingredients in a high-speed blender. Pulse for 1 to 2 minutes to mix the ingredients, then blend on high speed until smooth. Pour into glasses.

NOTE: If you are more of a breakfast-on-the-go type, smoothie packs are the way to go. To make a smoothie pack, chop up and portion your favourite fruits and veggies and freeze them in small freezer bags. When you're ready for a smoothie, empty the contents of one bag into your blender, add liquid such as almond milk or water, and blend.

Green Mango Smoothie

Green smoothies are a terrific way to eat more fruits and veggies. They're a perfect pick-me-up any time of the day. Leafy greens and tropical fruit make for a smoothie that even the kids will love.

1. Combine the ingredients in a high-speed blender. Pulse for 1 minute to mix the ingredients, then blend on high speed until smooth. Pour into glasses.

SERVES 2

1 cup unsweetened almond milk or water
½ cup fresh orange juice
1 cup kale or baby spinach, washed and roughly chopped
4 to 6 fresh mint leaves
½ avocado, pitted and peeled
1 frozen banana, roughly chopped
1 cup frozen mango chunks
1 tablespoon hemp seeds
1 tablespoon liquid honey
1 teaspoon fresh lime juice

NOTE: If your smoothie is too thick, add a splash more almond milk.

This smoothie is equally delicious if you swap out the mango for strawberries or pineapple.

Greens such as kale, spinach, Swiss chard, and collard greens are bulky and take up a lot of space in the refrigerator. The best solution is to quickly blanch them right after you bring them home. Store the blanched greens in the refrigerator, or freeze them in small packages for later use.

Summer Berry Yogurt Parfaits with Bee Pollen Granola

SERVES 4

**BEE POLLEN GRANOLA
(MAKES ABOUT 3 CUPS)**

2 cups old-fashioned rolled oats

1 cup unsweetened coconut flakes

¼ cup pumpkin seeds

¼ cup sunflower seeds

1 teaspoon cinnamon

½ teaspoon salt

½ cup wildflower honey

2 tablespoons vegetable oil

1 teaspoon pure vanilla extract

¼ cup bee pollen

SUMMER BERRY YOGURT PARFAITS

2 cups plain full-fat Greek yogurt

1 cup Bee Pollen Granola (recipe
    above)

2 cups mixed fresh berries
    (blackberries, blueberries,
    strawberries)

GARNISHES

Wildflower honey

Fresh mint leaves

Honeybees love wildflowers, and wildflower honey comes from uncultivated fields and is just about the closest thing to all-natural that you will ever taste. This raw honey is removed from the honeycomb and simply strained. It is sweet, floral, and slightly fruity. Forager bees collect granules of flower pollen on their hind legs and take the pollen back to the hive, where it is stored and used as food for the colony. The texture is soft and powdery, with a slightly sweet taste. Bee pollen contains so many vitamins, minerals, and antioxidants. We like to sprinkle it over smoothies, salads, and desserts. Our favourite recipe using bee pollen is Lora's granola.

1. **Make the bee pollen granola:** Preheat the oven to 300°F (150°C). Line a baking sheet with parchment paper.

2. In a medium bowl, stir together the oats, coconut flakes, pumpkin seeds, sunflower seeds, cinnamon, and salt. Drizzle with the honey, vegetable oil, and vanilla and stir until combined. Scoop the granola onto the lined baking sheet and press the mixture into a 1-inch-thick oval.

3. Bake for 15 minutes. Rotate the pan and use a fork to gently break up the granola just a bit. Bake for another 15 minutes or until golden brown. Remove from the oven and sprinkle the bee pollen over the granola. Let cool for 15 minutes before serving. Store completely cooled granola in an airtight container at room temperature for up to 1 month.

4. **Assemble the parfaits:** Spoon ¼ cup of the yogurt into each of 4 small parfait glasses or bowls. Top each with 2 tablespoons of the bee pollen granola, then ¼ cup of berries. Repeat layering one more time with yogurt, granola, and berries. Drizzle with the honey and garnish with mint.

NOTE: We highly recommend buying your honey and bee pollen from a farmers' market and supporting your local beekeepers. You can also purchase bee pollen at health food stores or online.

Quinoa Carrot Oatmeal with Maple Syrup Caramelized Pears

Delicious, nutritious goodness—there is nothing more comforting in the morning than a bowl of oatmeal. Start your day off right with this quinoa carrot oatmeal bursting with beautifully caramelized pears, toasted nuts, coconut, and warm spices. You can even serve this oatmeal for dessert—it's that good!

1. **Make the quinoa carrot oatmeal:** In a medium saucepan, combine the steel-cut oats, quinoa, and vegetable oil. Lightly toast over medium heat, stirring with a wooden spoon until slightly golden, 4 to 5 minutes.

2. Stir in the water, carrots, raisins, maple syrup, orange zest, vanilla, ginger, cinnamon, and salt. Bring to a boil, then reduce the heat to a simmer, cover, and cook until the quinoa is tender and the liquid is absorbed, 15 to 20 minutes. Remove from the heat and let the mixture sit, covered, for another 5 minutes.

3. **Meanwhile, make the maple syrup caramelized pears:** Put the brown sugar in a medium bowl. Add the pear wedges and turn to lightly coat in the sugar.

4. Heat a large nonstick skillet over medium-high heat. Place the pear wedges flat side down in the hot pan and cook until they start to caramelize and brown on the bottom, 1 to 2 minutes. Add the maple syrup, butter, and vanilla, swirl the pan a bit to slide the pears around in the mixture, and cook until golden and caramelized on the bottom, 1 to 2 minutes. Gently turn the wedges over and cook until golden and caramelized on the other side and fork-tender. Immediately transfer the pears to a plate.

5. **Assemble:** Divide the quinoa carrot oatmeal between bowls. Top with the caramelized pears and garnish with a sprinkle of walnuts and coconut.

SERVES 8

QUINOA CARROT OATMEAL

1 cup steel-cut oats
⅓ cup white quinoa, rinsed and drained
1 teaspoon vegetable oil
4 cups water
1 cup grated peeled carrots
⅔ cup golden raisins
2 tablespoons pure maple syrup
1 tablespoon orange zest
1 teaspoon pure vanilla extract
¼ teaspoon ground ginger
¼ teaspoon cinnamon
½ teaspoon salt

MAPLE SYRUP CARAMELIZED PEARS

2 tablespoons brown sugar
2 Bartlett pears, peeled, cored, and cut into wedges
2 tablespoons pure maple syrup
1 tablespoon unsalted butter
1 teaspoon pure vanilla extract

GARNISHES

¼ cup chopped toasted walnuts
¼ cup unsweetened shredded coconut, toasted

NOTE: If you have leftover oatmeal, let cool to room temperature, cover, and store in the refrigerator for up to 3 days. Reheat in the microwave and start another great day.

Raspberry Almond Croissant Bread Pudding

SERVES 6 TO 8

12 mini croissants (or 4 large
    croissants, cut into thirds)
2 cups fresh raspberries
4 eggs
1 cup whole milk
1 cup heavy (35%) cream
1 cup granulated sugar
2 teaspoons orange zest
1½ teaspoons pure vanilla extract
½ teaspoon almond extract
½ teaspoon salt
½ cup sliced almonds
Icing sugar, for dusting

This flaky, buttery, perfectly sweet and creamy croissant bread pudding is loaded with raspberries. It's a stunning breakfast or brunch treat that also works well for dessert any day of the week.

1. Preheat the oven to 350°F (180°C). Butter an 8-inch square baking dish.

2. Layer the croissants in the prepared baking dish. Scatter the raspberries over the croissants.

3. In a large bowl, whisk together the eggs, milk, cream, granulated sugar, orange zest, vanilla, almond extract, and salt. Pour the egg mixture over the croissants and gently press the croissants so they are submerged in the custard. Let sit for 10 minutes so the croissants soak up the custard.

4. Sprinkle the almonds over the bread pudding. Place the baking dish on a baking pan and bake for 45 minutes or until the centre of the pudding is set and puffed up and a fork inserted into the centre comes out clean. Let sit for 15 minutes before serving. Dust with icing sugar just before serving. Store leftovers, covered, in the refrigerator for up to 3 days.

NOTE: Croissants give this bread pudding an irresistible texture, but you can use brioche, challah, or any other bread you have at home.

Lemon Ricotta Pancakes with Blackberry Maple Syrup

These lemon ricotta pancakes have become our go-to recipe when we are all craving pancakes on the weekend. Everyone loves these super-fluffy pancakes that puff up so beautifully and are bursting with lemony vanilla flavour. Serve with maple syrup or go one step further and make our blackberry maple syrup.

1. **Make the blackberry maple syrup:** In a small saucepan, bring the maple syrup to a boil over medium-high heat, then immediately remove from the heat. Gently stir in the blackberries and lemon juice. Set aside to cool slightly while you make the pancakes. You can cool the syrup completely and store in an airtight container in the refrigerator for up to 1 week. Warm before using.

2. **Make the lemon ricotta pancakes:** Preheat the oven to 200°F (100°C). Line a baking sheet with parchment paper.

3. In a large bowl, whisk together the flour, sugar, baking powder, baking soda, and salt.

4. In a medium bowl, whisk together the eggs, milk, ricotta, and vanilla until well blended. Add the lemon zest, lemon juice, and melted butter and whisk until combined. Make a well in the centre of the flour mixture. Pour the ricotta mixture into the well and whisk until just combined and smooth, with no large dry patches of flour remaining.

5. Heat a large nonstick skillet or griddle over medium heat with a little canola oil or butter to lightly coat the pan. Pour ¼ cup of the batter per pancake onto the hot pan and spread it out gently into a circle using the back of a ladle or spoon. Cook the pancakes until bubbles begin to appear on the surface and the bottom is golden brown, about 2 minutes. Flip and cook until golden brown on the other side, 2 to 3 minutes. Transfer to the lined baking sheet and keep warm in the oven while you cook the remaining pancakes.

6. Serve the pancakes with warm blackberry maple syrup.

SERVES 4

**BLACKBERRY MAPLE SYRUP
(MAKES ABOUT 1¼ CUPS)**
½ cup pure maple syrup
2 cups fresh blackberries
1 tablespoon fresh lemon juice

LEMON RICOTTA PANCAKES
1½ cups all-purpose flour
3½ tablespoons granulated sugar
2 teaspoons baking powder
¼ teaspoon baking soda
½ teaspoon salt
3 large eggs
1 cup whole milk
¾ cup ricotta cheese
1 teaspoon pure vanilla extract
2 tablespoons lemon zest
¼ cup fresh lemon juice
1 tablespoon unsalted butter, melted
Canola oil or unsalted butter, for
    frying

NOTE: If you prefer soufflé-like pancakes, separate the whites from the yolks. Beat the egg whites until stiff peaks form. Mix the yolks in with the wet ingredients, combine the wet and dry ingredients as directed, then fold in the beaten egg whites. Cook as directed.

Apple Brown Sugar Pancake

SERVES 4

4 eggs
½ cup heavy (35%) cream
½ cup whole milk
½ teaspoon pure vanilla extract
¾ cup all-purpose flour
1 tablespoon granulated sugar
¼ teaspoon salt
¼ teaspoon cinnamon
4 tablespoons unsalted butter,
    divided
2 medium Gala apples, peeled, cored,
    and thinly sliced
⅓ cup lightly packed brown sugar

This is probably one of the most decadent, over-the-top, and delicious apple treats that you can make: apples caramelized with brown sugar surrounded with a cinnamony eggy batter that puffs up like a popover but has crispy sweet edges. It is incredible.

1.   Preheat the oven to 425°F (220°C).

2.   In a medium bowl, whisk together the eggs, cream, milk, vanilla, flour, granulated sugar, salt, and cinnamon until smooth.

3.   Melt 2 tablespoons of the butter in a 10-inch ovenproof skillet, preferably cast iron, over medium heat. Once the butter is bubbling, add the apple slices and sprinkle with the brown sugar. Cook, tossing frequently, until the apples are coated and softened, about 4 minutes. Transfer the apples to a plate.

4.   Wipe the skillet. Transfer it to the oven and heat until very hot, 8 to 10 minutes.

5.   Carefully remove the hot skillet from the oven. Add the remaining 2 tablespoons butter and swirl to evenly coat the bottom and sides. Spread the apples out evenly in the pan, then pour the batter over them. Bake until the pancake is puffed up and golden brown around the edges and the centre is set but still custardy, 12 to 15 minutes. Place a serving plate upside down over the pan. With the plate and pan firmly pressed together, quickly invert the pancake onto the plate. Serve immediately.

NOTE: We have made many variations of this pancake, changing the fruit depending on what's in season. Try pears, peaches, or a strawberry-rhubarb combination.

Honey Cornbread French Toast with Caramelized Peaches and Basil Sweet Cream

This cornbread, with its crisp golden crust and moist fluffy centre, really can't be beat, except when you slice it up and turn it into the best French toast. It makes for a decadent and delightful version of that much-admired brunch classic. Using basil in the sweet cream adds such a summer flavour when combined with the sweetness of the ripe peaches and buttery cornbread.

SERVES 4 TO 6

**BASIL SWEET CREAM
(MAKES ABOUT 2 CUPS)**
1 cup heavy (35%) cream
½ cup fresh basil leaves, plus sprigs
3 tablespoons icing sugar
¼ teaspoon pure vanilla extract

HONEY CORNBREAD
1 cup cornmeal
1 cup all-purpose flour
⅔ cup granulated sugar
1 tablespoon baking powder
2 teaspoons salt
3 large eggs
1¼ cups whole milk
4 tablespoons unsalted butter, melted
¼ cup liquid honey

**CARAMELIZED PEACHES
(MAKES ABOUT 2 CUPS)**
4 peaches, pitted and thickly sliced
2 tablespoons pure maple syrup
1 tablespoon fresh lemon juice
¼ teaspoon salt
2 tablespoons unsalted butter
½ teaspoon pure vanilla extract

FRENCH TOAST
4 large eggs
1 cup whole milk
1½ teaspoons pure vanilla extract
¼ teaspoon cinnamon
Pinch of salt
1 to 2 tablespoons unsalted butter or
  canola oil, for frying

Pure maple syrup, for serving (optional)

— continued —

1. **Make the basil sweet cream:** In a small saucepan, bring the cream to a simmer over medium heat. Once simmering, remove from the heat and stir in the basil leaves and sprigs. Let sit for 20 minutes, then strain through a fine-mesh sieve into a small bowl. Refrigerate until cold, at least 2 hours. Discard the basil leaves and sprigs.

2. Just before serving, whip the chilled cream until foamy. Gradually add the icing sugar, whipping to form soft peaks. Whisk in the vanilla.

3. **Meanwhile, make the honey cornbread:** Preheat the oven to 375°F (190°C). Line the bottom and sides of a 9 × 5-inch loaf pan with parchment paper.

4. In a large bowl, stir together the cornmeal, flour, sugar, baking powder, and salt until combined.

5. In a medium bowl, whisk together the eggs, milk, melted butter, and honey. Add the wet ingredients to the dry ingredients and stir until just combined.

6. Pour the batter into the prepared loaf pan and smooth the top. Bake for 1 hour or until a cake tester inserted into the centre of the loaf comes out clean. Turn the cornbread out onto a rack and let cool completely, about 30 minutes. Once cooled, trim the ends of the cornbread, then cut four or six 1-inch-thick slices. Set aside.

7. **Make the caramelized peaches:** In a medium bowl, toss the peaches with the maple syrup, lemon juice, and salt to coat.

8. Melt the butter in a large nonstick skillet over medium-high heat. Pour the peach mixture into the skillet and cook, stirring occasionally, until caramelized, about 10 minutes. Stir in the vanilla. Set aside until ready to use.

9. **Make the French toast:** In a shallow medium bowl, whisk together the eggs, milk, vanilla, cinnamon, and salt.

10. Melt the butter in a large nonstick skillet over medium-high heat. Working in batches, dip the cornbread slices, one at a time, into the batter, coating both sides. Place the coated cornbread in the hot skillet and cook until golden, 3 to 4 minutes per side.

11. Serve the French toast hot with the caramelized peaches and basil sweet cream. Drizzle with maple syrup, if using.

Buckwheat Crêpes with Mushrooms, Leafy Greens, and Green Onion Gruyère Béchamel

We have so many fun memories of our visits to Paris, wandering the streets as we love to do, stumbling upon the many crêperies that instantly satisfy our cravings. Whether filled with goat cheese, walnuts and honey, or smothered in salted caramel, these are the very best bites you can enjoy. Our version of this nutty, earthy, and incredibly satisfying crêpe has a creamy Gruyère béchamel sauce that is the perfect complement to the insanely delicious caramelized mushrooms and leafy greens.

SERVES 4

CRÊPE BATTER

1⅔ cups buckwheat flour

3 large eggs

2 cups oat milk

2 tablespoons unsalted butter, melted

2 tablespoons finely chopped fresh flat-leaf parsley

1 tablespoon finely chopped fresh chives

Pinch of salt

MUSHROOMS AND LEAFY GREENS

3 tablespoons unsalted butter, divided

1 tablespoon vegetable oil

4 cups stemmed and sliced cremini mushrooms

1 garlic clove, minced

2 teaspoons soy sauce

2 cups baby spinach or baby kale (or a mixture)

Salt and cracked black pepper

1 tablespoon nutritional yeast

GREEN ONION GRUYÈRE BÉCHAMEL

2 tablespoons unsalted butter

2 tablespoons all-purpose flour

1¼ cups whole milk

2 teaspoons Dijon mustard

½ cup grated Gruyère cheese

Salt and cracked black pepper

2 green onions, finely chopped

— continued —

1. **Make the crêpe batter:** In a blender, combine the buckwheat flour, eggs, oat milk, and melted butter. Blend until smooth. Add the parsley and chives and season with salt. Stir. Cover the batter and let sit in the refrigerator for at least 30 minutes or up to 4 hours.

2. **Meanwhile, sauté the mushrooms and leafy greens:** Melt 2 tablespoons of the butter with the vegetable oil in a large sauté pan over medium-high heat. Once the butter starts to bubble, add the mushrooms and cook, without stirring, for 4 to 5 minutes, allowing the mushrooms to start to caramelize on the bottom, then stir. Add the garlic and cook, stirring occasionally, for 2 to 3 minutes, until softened. Add the soy sauce and stir into the mushrooms until evaporated. Add the remaining 1 tablespoon butter and the spinach and cook for another minute or until wilted. Season with salt and pepper. Remove from the heat and stir in the nutritional yeast. Set aside.

3. **Make the green onion Gruyère béchamel:** Melt the butter in a medium saucepan over medium-high heat. Sprinkle the flour over the butter and cook, whisking constantly, for 1 minute. Whisking constantly, add the milk and mustard and bring to a boil. Once the sauce is thick and creamy, stir in the Gruyère cheese and whisk for another 1 to 2 minutes, until the cheese is melted. Remove from the heat and season to taste with salt and pepper. Stir in the green onions. Keep warm.

4. **Cook the crêpes and assemble:** Heat a 10-inch crêpe pan or nonstick skillet over medium-high heat. Lightly grease the pan with butter or nonstick cooking spray. Pour ¼ cup of batter to thinly coat the bottom of the pan, swirling the pan as you pour the batter to ensure an even coating. Cook for 1 to 2 minutes, until the crêpe is golden brown on the bottom and the sides easily separate from the pan. Using a thin heatproof spatula, gently flip the crêpe and cook for another 1 to 2 minutes, until lightly golden brown. Transfer the crêpe to a plate and cover with a kitchen towel to keep warm. Grease the pan and repeat with the remaining batter, stacking the cooked crêpes on the plate.

5. **Assemble the crêpes:** Reheat the mushrooms and leafy greens. Working with one crêpe at a time, spoon about ½ cup of the mushrooms and leafy greens down one side of the crêpe. Fold the bare side of the crêpe over the filling, then fold the crêpe in half again, creating a triangle. Spoon on more mushroom and leafy greens mixture. Top with the green onion Gruyère béchamel.

NOTE: This is a perfect dish to impress your friends and family when you have them over for brunch. You can prepare the crêpes, filling, and béchamel in advance. Then you only need to assemble and heat just before serving in a baking dish in a 300°F (150°C) oven for 20 minutes.

A terrific way to keep cooked crêpes is to freeze them. Just stack them in an airtight container, placing a sheet of waxed or parchment paper between each crêpe. Store in the freezer for up to 2 months. Thaw before using.

Chili Butter-Basted Fried Egg Sandwiches with Tempeh Bacon, Heirloom Tomatoes, and Deli Mayo

Basting eggs with sizzling hot butter will always give you that perfect sunny-side up egg with a runny yolk and satisfyingly crispy edges. The introduction of some subtle chili heat and savoury notes from our One-Hit Butter will give the flavour boost that takes this sandwich to the next level. We recommend making our Deli Mayo, but in a pinch you can use store-bought plain mayo.

1. **Make the deli mayo:** In a small bowl, whisk together the mayonnaise, capers, cornichons, dill, parsley, and lemon zest and juice. Season to taste with salt and pepper. Set aside or store in an airtight container in the refrigerator for up to 2 weeks.

2. **Make the tempeh bacon:** Preheat the oven to 400°F (200°C). Line a baking sheet with parchment paper.

3. Slice the tempeh into 8 or 12 slices, each about ¼ inch thick. Place the tempeh in a baking dish.

4. In a shallow small bowl, whisk together the soy sauce, maple syrup, olive oil, sriracha, and smoked paprika. Season to taste with pepper. Pour the mixture over the tempeh and let marinate for 10 minutes. Flip the tempeh and marinate for another 10 minutes.

5. Arrange the tempeh in a single layer on the lined baking sheet. Reserve the marinade for brushing. Bake for 10 minutes, then remove from the oven, flip the tempeh slices, and brush generously with the reserved marinade. Bake for another 8 to 10 minutes or until browned and slightly crispy.

6. **Make the chili butter-basted fried eggs:** Melt the one-hit butter in a medium nonstick skillet over medium heat. When the butter foams, crack the eggs into the pan. Season to taste with salt and pepper. As the eggs cook, carefully tilt the pan toward you so the butter pools at the edge closest to you, and use a spoon to baste the egg whites with the hot butter. Baste until the whites are fully cooked, 2 to 3 minutes. Use a spatula to transfer the eggs to a plate, leaving the butter behind in the pan. Continue to cook the butter over medium heat until it is deep golden, about 2 minutes. Pour the browned butter over the eggs.

7. **Assemble the sandwiches:** Place a slice of toast on each plate. Spread the deli mayo on each piece of toast. Layer each with 2 or 3 slices of tomato and 2 or 3 pieces of tempeh bacon. Top each with a fried egg.

SERVES 4

DELI MAYO
(MAKES ABOUT 1 CUP)
1 cup mayonnaise
2 tablespoons minced drained capers
2 tablespoons finely chopped cornichons
2 tablespoons finely chopped fresh dill
2 tablespoons finely chopped fresh flat-leaf parsley
Zest and juice of 2 lemons
Salt and cracked black pepper

TEMPEH BACON
1 (7-ounce/200 g) package tempeh
2 tablespoons soy sauce
2 tablespoons pure maple syrup
1 tablespoon olive oil
1 to 2 teaspoons sriracha sauce (depending how spicy you want it)
1 teaspoon smoked paprika
Cracked black pepper

CHILI BUTTER-BASTED FRIED EGG SANDWICHES
4 tablespoons One-Hit Butter (page 62) or unsalted butter
4 large eggs
Salt and cracked black pepper
4 slices Country Morning Loaf (page 77), toasted
2 heirloom tomatoes, thinly sliced (8 or 12 slices)

NOTE: If you prefer your eggs cooked all the way, after the whites are cooked reduce the heat to low, add a splash of water (just less than 1 tablespoon per egg), cover with a lid, and steam until the yolks are cooked to your liking, just a matter of minutes.

One-Hit Butter

Makes about 2 cups

Espelette pepper originates from the Basque region of France, and it is an amazing little pepper that we both love to cook with. It has a sweet, lightly smoky flavour and is not too over-the-top hot, bringing just enough heat. Understanding that you may not be able to grow them as we do, you can find the dried form of this pepper at your local gourmet food store or online. A good substitute for fresh or dried Espelette pepper is smoked hot paprika, dried Aleppo pepper, or the ever so common red chili flakes.

   3 tablespoons olive oil
   1 cup finely chopped shallots (about 4 shallots)
   1 cup minced garlic (about 2 heads of garlic)
   ½ cup finely diced fresh Espelette pepper (or 1 tablespoon dried
      piment d'Espelette)
   1 pound (450 g) unsalted butter, at room temperature
   2 tablespoons chopped fresh flat-leaf parsley
   2 tablespoons chopped fresh oregano
   Zest and juice of 1 lemon
   1½ teaspoons smoked paprika
   Salt

1. Heat the olive oil in a medium sauté pan over medium-high heat. Add the shallots, garlic, and Espelette pepper and cook, stirring, until soft, 3 to 5 minutes. Remove from the heat and let cool completely.

2. Cut the butter into 8 pieces and put in a food processor. Pulse until the butter is smooth. Add the cooled shallot mixture, parsley, oregano, lemon zest and juice, and smoked paprika. Pulse until well combined, then season to taste with salt. Store in an airtight container in the refrigerator for up to 1 month or in the freezer for up to 6 months.

Smashed Avocado Toast with Whipped Feta, Spring Peas, Radish, and Za'atar

There is a lot of love in our house for this smashed avocado toast. First, our Country Morning Bread is truly the highlight. We don't buy bread anymore because our bread is so fast and easy to make and tastes better than any bread you can buy. Second, we adore how all the flavours and textures intertwine so perfectly. The creaminess and richness of the avocado and feta pair perfectly with the bright citrus notes that the sumac in the za'atar spice brings to the sweet peas and crisp radish. Feel free to use store-bought za'atar.

1. **Make the za'atar spice:** In a small bowl, whisk together the ingredients until well combined. Store in an airtight container for up to 3 months.

2. **Prepare the toppings:** In a small blender or food processor, combine the feta and cream cheese. Blend on medium speed until smooth and creamy, 1 to 2 minutes.

3. In a small bowl, mix together the peas, radishes, green onions, olive oil, za'atar spice, and salt and pepper to taste.

4. In a separate small bowl, mash the avocados with a fork. Stir in the lemon zest and juice, then season to taste with salt and pepper and more lemon juice, if desired.

5. **Assemble:** Place the slices of toast on plates or a platter and spread an even layer of the mashed avocado on each. Spread a spoonful of the feta mixture on top of the avocado. Spoon some pea mixture in the middle. Garnish with pea shoots (if using) and a sprinkle of flaky sea salt.

SERVES 4

ZA'ATAR SPICE
(MAKES ½ CUP)

2 tablespoons dried oregano
2 tablespoons toasted sesame seeds
2 tablespoons sumac
2 tablespoons dried thyme
1 tablespoon ground cumin
1 teaspoon kosher salt

SMASHED AVOCADO TOAST

¼ cup crumbled feta cheese
¼ cup (2 ounces/55 g) cream cheese, at room temperature
1 cup fresh peas, blanched
4 radishes, thinly sliced
2 tablespoons thinly sliced green onions
1 tablespoon olive oil
½ teaspoon Za'atar Spice (recipe above or store-bought)
Salt and cracked black pepper
2 avocados, pitted and peeled
Zest and juice of ½ lemon, more if needed

FOR ASSEMBLY

4 slices Country Morning Loaf (page 77), toasted
Pea shoots (optional)
Flaky sea salt

NOTE: Swap out the peas as soon as tomatoes come in season. Chop the tomatoes and top the mashed avocado with them. Garnish with fresh basil leaves and cracked black pepper.

Sweet Potato Hash with Jammy Eggs and Kimchi

Miso is the secret ingredient in this umami-packed sweet potato hash. Caramelized onions, sweet corn, garlic, and ginger all pair beautifully with miso. This hash is the perfect base for gorgeous jammy seven-minute soft-boiled eggs that have perfectly set whites and dreamy golden yolks.

1. Bring a large saucepan of salted water to a boil. Add the sweet potatoes and simmer for 10 to 12 minutes, until fork-tender. Use a spider or strainer to scoop out the potatoes and transfer to a baking sheet or plate lined with paper towel to dry completely. Turn off the heat but leave the pot of water on the stove.

2. Heat 1 tablespoon of the olive oil in a large nonstick skillet over medium-high heat. Add the onions and cook, stirring occasionally, until just soft and beginning to caramelize, 3 to 4 minutes. Add the butter, miso, garlic, ginger, and corn kernels and sauté until the corn is tender, 3 to 4 minutes. Season to taste with salt and pepper. Transfer the mixture to a large bowl. Wipe the pan and set it aside.

3. Meanwhile, return the pot of water to a boil. Fill a large bowl with ice water. Using a slotted spoon, lower the eggs into the boiling water. Set a timer for 7 minutes. When the timer goes off, use a slotted spoon to transfer the cooked eggs to the ice water. When the eggs are cool enough to handle, remove from the ice water. Tap the wider end of the egg on the side of the bowl (it's the easier part of the egg to peel) and peel the shell off. Cut each peeled egg in half lengthwise.

4. Heat the remaining 2 tablespoons olive oil in the skillet over medium-high heat. Add the sweet potatoes in a single layer and cook, stirring occasionally, until golden and crispy all over, 3 to 4 minutes. Add the corn mixture, green onions, and parsley and sauté until the mixture is hot. Season to taste with salt and pepper.

5. Divide the hash evenly between 4 plates. Top each with 2 halves of the jammy eggs. Serve with the kimchi on the side.

SERVES 4

2 large sweet potatoes, peeled and cut into ½-inch cubes

3 tablespoons olive oil, divided

½ cup finely diced white onion

1 tablespoon unsalted butter

1 tablespoon white or yellow miso

1 garlic clove, minced

2 teaspoons grated peeled fresh ginger

1 cup sweet corn kernels

Salt and cracked black pepper

4 large eggs

2 green onions, finely chopped

2 tablespoons chopped fresh flat-leaf parsley

Kimchi (page 68 or store-bought)

NOTE: Make sure you cut the sweet potato into uniform cubes so it cooks evenly and gets the crisp golden edges that give the hash its great flavour.

Lowering the eggs into already boiling water allows you to precisely track how long they're exposed to the heat. In this recipe, you don't have to wait for the eggs to come to room temperature before cooking them. Just take them out of the refrigerator and lower them carefully into the pot. The eggs will continue to cook if you don't cool them immediately in a bath of ice water. This will also make them easier to peel. The eggs can be cooked and peeled in advance and stored in an airtight container in the refrigerator for up to 3 days.

Kimchi

Makes about 4 cups

Kimchi has a distinctive taste, a spicy, earthy flavour of fermented vegetables. Traditionally, kimchi is left to ferment for weeks, months, or even years. Our version is a lot quicker! Cabbage, ginger, apple, chili, and green onion are pickled in a soy sauce brine, ready to enjoy the next day.

    1 napa cabbage, halved lengthwise, cored, and cut into 1-inch
        chunks (about 10 cups)
    1 small carrot, peeled and thinly sliced diagonally
    ½ red apple, peeled, cored, and julienned
    1 cup seasoned rice vinegar
    2 tablespoons granulated sugar
    1 teaspoon kosher salt
    4 large garlic cloves, roughly chopped
    3 green onions, cut into 1-inch pieces
    ½ Fresno chili, thinly sliced
    5 thin slices peeled fresh ginger
    ½ cup roughly chopped fresh cilantro
    3 tablespoons soy sauce
    1 teaspoon sesame oil

1. Fill a large bowl with ice water. Bring a large pot of salted water to a boil. Add the cabbage and blanch for 1 minute. Drain the cabbage and transfer to the ice bath to stop the cooking process. Drain well.

2. Transfer the blanched cabbage to a large bowl. Add the carrot and apple.

3. In a medium saucepan, combine the rice vinegar, sugar, and salt. Bring to a simmer over medium heat and cook until the sugar dissolves. Add the garlic, green onions, chili, and ginger and cook for another minute. Pour the vinegar mixture over the cabbage mixture. Add the cilantro, soy sauce, and sesame oil and fold gently to combine.

4. Transfer the kimchi to a 4-cup mason jar, screw on the lid, and refrigerate overnight to allow the flavours to meld. Store in the refrigerator for up to 1 month.

Potato Parsnip Latkes with
Sour Cream and Apple Rosemary Mostarda

Potato latkes are one of the most famous of Jewish foods and a specialty at Hanukkah. We think the best latkes are super crispy on the outside. When you bite into these ones you get this awesome crunchy texture, but wait . . . the middle is soft and fluffy! Parsnips don't get much love or credit in a lot of people's kitchens, but in these latkes they add the perfect amount of sweetness and delicious nutty flavour that just might change your mind about them. Apple mostarda is a tasty rich and savoury condiment that is perfect with the sweet crispy potato parsnip latkes.

1. **Make the apple rosemary mostarda:** Melt the butter in a medium saucepan over medium heat. Add the apples and cook, stirring frequently, until softened, about 5 minutes. Stir in the brown sugar and shallot and stir until the sugar dissolves, about 2 minutes. Add the brandy and cook until the alcohol evaporates, about 1 minute. Add the apple cider vinegar, raisins, ginger, orange peel, and lemon peel. Stir to combine. Bring the mixture to a boil, then reduce the heat to low and simmer, stirring occasionally, until the mixture thickens, about 15 minutes. Stir in the Dijon mustard and grainy mustard and cook for another 5 minutes. Stir in the rosemary and season with salt and pepper. Remove from the heat and set aside.

2. **Make the potato parsnip latkes:** In a large bowl, toss together the potatoes and parsnips. Add the onions and mix. Mix in the flour and eggs, then season to taste with salt and pepper.

3. Heat about ¼ inch of vegetable oil in a large nonstick skillet over medium-high heat. Working in batches of 4 or 5 latkes at a time to avoid crowding the pan, drop ¼ cup of the batter per latke into the hot pan and flatten with a spatula. Reduce the heat to medium and cook until golden and crisp on the bottom, about 4 minutes. To prevent oil from splattering, use a spatula and a large spoon to carefully flip the latkes. Fry until crisp and golden on the other side, about 4 minutes. Transfer to a plate lined with paper towel to absorb excess oil.

4. Just before serving, reheat the apple rosemary mostarda. Serve the latkes with the mostarda and sour cream.

MAKES ABOUT 12 LATKES

APPLE ROSEMARY MOSTARDA

3 tablespoons unsalted butter

2 Gala apples, peeled, cored, and diced

¼ cup lightly packed brown sugar

1 shallot, minced

2 tablespoons brandy

¼ cup apple cider vinegar

¼ cup golden raisins

1 tablespoon grated peeled fresh ginger

2 strips of orange peel

2 strips of lemon peel

1 tablespoon Dijon mustard

1 tablespoon grainy mustard

2 teaspoons chopped fresh rosemary

Salt and cracked black pepper

POTATO PARSNIP LATKES

2 cups grated peeled russet potatoes

2 cups grated peeled parsnips

1 medium yellow onion, finely diced

¼ cup all-purpose flour

2 eggs, lightly beaten

Salt and cracked black pepper

Vegetable oil, for frying

Sour cream, for serving

NOTE: If needed, you can keep the latkes warm before serving. Place drained latkes in a single layer on a rack set on a baking sheet in a 200°F (100°C) oven until ready to serve. Alternatively, the latkes can be made in advance, cooled, and refrigerated for up to 3 days. Simply place in a single layer on a rack set on a baking sheet and reheat in an oven set at 325°F (160°C) for 5 minutes or until hot.

Shakshuka with Herb Cream Cheese and Sesame Bagels

SERVES 4 TO 6

HERB CREAM CHEESE

½ cup (4 ounces/115 g) cream
    cheese, at room temperature
2 tablespoons finely chopped fresh
    herbs (parsley, dill, or basil)
Salt and cracked black pepper

SHAKSHUKA

2 tablespoons olive oil
2 red, yellow, or orange bell peppers,
    thinly sliced (about 4 cups)
1 medium yellow onion, diced
2 garlic cloves, minced
1 teaspoon smoked paprika
½ teaspoon ground cumin
½ teaspoon cinnamon
¼ teaspoon cayenne pepper
Salt and cracked black pepper
2 cups tomato sauce
1½ cups roughly chopped Swiss chard
1 cup mixed red and yellow cherry
    tomatoes, halved
6 eggs
Chopped fresh dill, for garnish

Sesame Bagels (page 81),
    for serving

Shakshuka is recognized as a breakfast dish that has stood the test of time. It is one of the most popular dishes in the Middle East, in a variety of versions from spicy to sweet, and featuring vegetables or meat. It is the ultimate egg skillet casserole dish to start your day and will become your go-to impressive brunch or lunch dish when cooking for friends or family. There is so much flavour in our spiced-up tomato pepper sauce that the eggs cook in. Serve it right from the skillet with your very own warm sesame bagels.

1.   Preheat the oven to 375°F (190°C).

2.   **Make the herb cream cheese:** In a small bowl, mix together the cream cheese and fresh herbs. Season to taste with salt and black pepper. Set aside.

3.   **Make the shakshuka:** Heat the olive oil in a large skillet over medium heat. Add the bell peppers, onions, garlic, smoked paprika, cumin, cinnamon, and cayenne pepper. Season well with salt and black pepper. Cook, stirring occasionally, until the vegetables have softened, about 5 minutes. Stir in the tomato sauce, cover, and simmer for about 15 minutes. Uncover, add the Swiss chard and tomatoes, stir together, and cook for another 3 to 4 minutes, until the Swiss chard has wilted. Season to taste with salt and pepper.

4.   Use a wooden spoon to make 6 wells in the tomato mixture. Carefully crack an egg into each well. Drop spoonfuls of the herb cream cheese into the tomato sauce around the eggs. Transfer to the oven and bake for 8 to 10 minutes or until the egg whites are just set. Remove from the oven and garnish with the dill. Serve with sesame bagels.

NOTE: You can cook and serve this in one large skillet or casserole, but it's also a fun presentation to serve in individual skillets.

We like to use herb cream cheese in this recipe, but feel free to explore your love of cheese and top with some wonderful melting cheeses like burrata, goat cheese, feta, or a simple fresh mozzarella.

Bread

Country Morning Loaf

Nothing compares to that delightful culinary experience of tearing into a warm fresh loaf of homemade bread. Making bread from scratch is one of those simple pleasures in life that provides a great sense of satisfaction. With just a few pantry staples and taking the time to get into the groove, you too will be amazed at just how easy and satisfying it is to make your own bread. We have shared this no-knead recipe with so many of our friends and family, and everyone agrees wholeheartedly, homemade tastes the best. So put on your favourite tunes and roll up your sleeves.

1. In a large bowl, stir together the warm water, honey, and yeast. Let sit for 5 minutes or until foamy.

2. Add the salt, bread flour, pumpkin seeds, sesame seeds, and chia seeds to the yeast mixture. Mix together until the dough comes together as a ball. Cover the bowl with a kitchen towel and let the dough rest in a warm, draft-free place for 2 hours or until doubled in size.

3. Once the dough has doubled in size, cut a 9-inch square of parchment paper. Lay the parchment on a work surface and sprinkle with the cornmeal.

4. Sprinkle the risen dough with a dusting of bread flour. Use a rubber spatula to fold the dough in half, turn the bowl, and again fold the dough in half. Repeat turning and folding until the dough is folded into a ball. Gently transfer the dough seam side down onto the cornmeal-dusted parchment paper. Sprinkle extra seeds on top. Let the dough rise, uncovered, for 45 minutes, until about doubled in size.

5. Meanwhile, remove the top rack from the oven and put a large round Dutch oven, with its lid, on the middle rack. Preheat the oven to 450°F (230°C) so that the pot heats up along with the oven. Set a timer for 45 minutes.

6. After 45 minutes, carefully remove the hot Dutch oven from the oven and place it on the stovetop. Remove the lid. Lift the parchment paper with the dough on it and drop it into the pot, being careful not to touch the hot pot. Cover with the lid and bake for 30 minutes. Remove the lid and bake for another 3 to 4 minutes, until the top is golden brown. Transfer the bread to a rack and let cool before slicing. Store, covered, at room temperature for up to 3 days or in a resealable bag in the freezer for up to 1 month.

MAKES 1 LARGE ROUND LOAF

1½ cups warm water

2 tablespoons wildflower honey

2¼ teaspoons active dry yeast

1 teaspoon salt

3 cups bread flour, plus more for dusting the dough

2 tablespoons pumpkin seeds, plus more for sprinkling

2 tablespoons sesame seeds, plus more for sprinkling

1 tablespoon chia seeds, plus more for sprinkling

1 tablespoon cornmeal, for dusting the parchment paper

NOTE: When you make your own bread, you have control over what ingredients go into the loaf. Herbs, fruits, nuts, and seeds can transform the flavour of your bread.

Aunt Lucy's Milk Buns

MAKES 2 DOZEN BUNS

1¼ cups warm whole milk, divided

¼ cup + ¼ teaspoon granulated sugar

¾ teaspoon active dry yeast

¾ teaspoon salt

¼ cup vegetable oil

1 egg

3 cups all-purpose flour

We must thank our aunt Lucy for the inspiration for this recipe. There is not a single special family gathering that doesn't feature these buns. By far the number one requested item at any potluck dinner, these easy-to-make buns are super soft, airy, moist, and slightly sweet. You might think two dozen is a lot of buns to make at one time, but it's not. You might just have to make a double batch, they are that good!

1. In a small bowl, stir together ¼ cup of the warm milk, ¼ teaspoon of the sugar, and the yeast. Let sit for 5 minutes or until foamy.

2. In a large bowl, combine the remaining ¼ cup sugar, salt, vegetable oil, egg, and the remaining 1 cup warm milk. Whisk until well combined.

3. Stir in the yeast mixture, then add the flour and stir with a wooden spoon until a rough or shaggy dough forms.

4. Turn the dough out onto a lightly floured work surface and knead the dough until it forms a smooth ball, 4 to 5 minutes. Place the dough in a greased large bowl, cover with a kitchen towel, and let rest in a warm, draft-free place for 2 hours or until doubled in size.

5. Once the dough has doubled in size, punch it down to release the gases, cover it again, and let it rise again for 1½ hours or until doubled in size.

6. Line two 9-inch round cake pans with parchment paper.

7. Once the dough has doubled in size, punch it down again and turn it out onto a lightly floured work surface. Divide the dough into 2 equal portions, then cut each portion into 12 equal pieces. Working with one piece of dough at a time, tuck the dough into itself by pinching the dough from all sides into the centre using your fingers, creating a tight ball. Place the dough seam side down on the work surface and roll it in a circular motion under the palm of your hand until it forms a round ball. Arrange the dough balls evenly spaced in the lined cake pans (12 buns per pan). Cover the buns with a kitchen towel and let rest on the counter for about 1 hour.

8. Meanwhile, position the racks in the upper and lower thirds of the oven and preheat to 400°F (200°C).

9. Bake the buns until golden brown, 12 to 16 minutes. Serve warm or transfer the buns to a rack and let cool.

NOTE: These milk buns taste best the day they're made. But they will stay soft and moist if you store them in a resealable bag at room temperature for a day or in the freezer for up to 2 months.

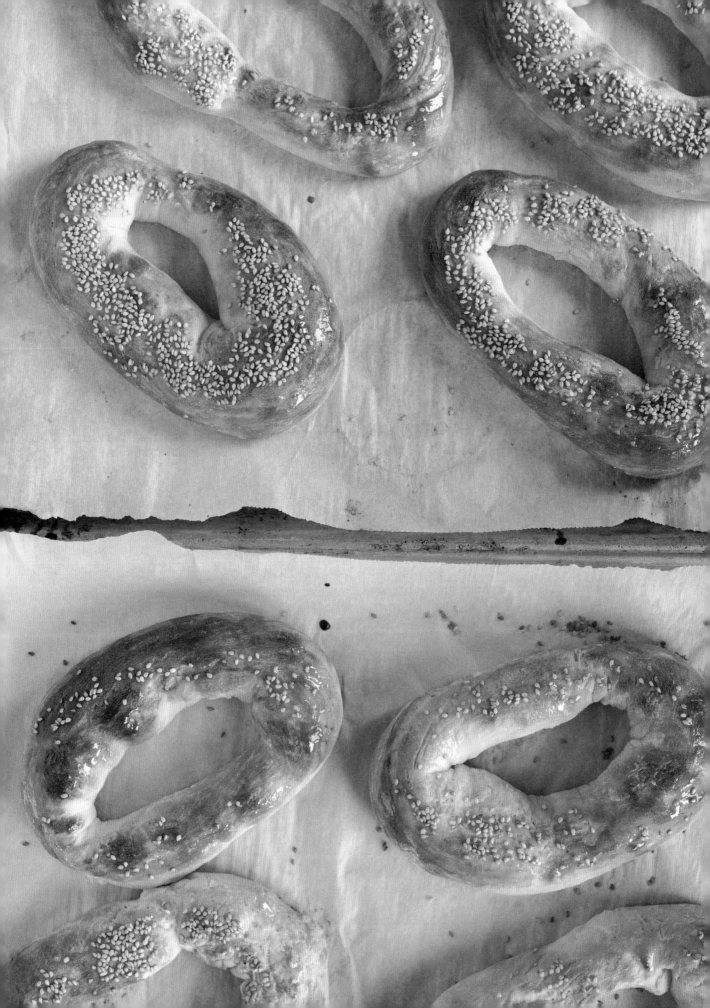

Sesame Bagels

These bucket-list-worthy Jerusalem bagels are not boiled like their Montreal-style cousins, and you'll find their texture and flavour quite different. While a Montreal bagel is heavy, dense, and chewier, the Jerusalem bagel is melt-in-your-mouth tender and fluffy while crisp on the outside—perfect to serve with dips, soups, and anything saucy.

1. **Mix the dough:** In a small bowl, stir together the warm milk and yeast. Let sit for 5 minutes or until foamy.

2. In the bowl of a stand mixer fitted with the dough hook, combine the yeast mixture, flour, sugar, salt, and baking powder. Mix on medium speed until the dough forms a smooth ball, about 2 minutes.

3. Remove the bowl from the mixer. Rub a little olive oil over the top of the dough. Cover with a kitchen towel and let rest in a warm, draft-free place until doubled in size, about 1 hour.

4. **Once the dough is nearly done proofing, prepare the sesame topping:** In a shallow dish, stir together the sesame seeds, honey, and hot water. The seeds should be damp and sticky but not clumpy. Add a bit more water if needed to reach the right consistency.

5. **Shape the bagels and bake:** When the dough has doubled in size, punch it down to release the gases. Turn the dough out onto a lightly floured work surface. Divide the dough into 6 equal pieces. Working with one piece of dough at a time, use your hands to gently shape the dough into a ball on the work surface. Do not overwork the dough. Poke both thumbs through the centre of the ball to create a hole, then stretch the dough outward to make an oval ring about 6 inches long, using your fingers to pull and stretch the dough so the hole is as large as you can make it without breaking the ring. As you form each ring, place it back on the work surface. Once all the dough rings are formed, let rest, uncovered, for 15 minutes until the dough relaxes.

6. Meanwhile, position the racks in the upper and lower thirds of the oven and preheat to 450°F (230°C). Line 2 baking sheets with parchment paper.

7. Working with one ring of dough at a time, press the top into the sesame mixture, then give the dough another tug and pull, coaxing the centre hole even larger. Arrange the rings seed side up on the lined baking sheets (3 per sheet), evenly spaced and let rest for another 10 minutes.

8. Bake the bagels until deep golden brown, 15 to 18 minutes, rotating the sheets front to back and top to bottom halfway through. Transfer to racks and let cool.

MAKES 6 LARGE BAGELS

DOUGH

1½ cups warm whole milk
1 tablespoon active dry yeast
4½ cups all-purpose flour
2 tablespoons granulated sugar
2 teaspoons salt
1 teaspoon baking powder
Olive oil, for coating the dough

SESAME TOPPING

½ cup sesame seeds
1 tablespoon liquid honey
2 tablespoons hot water

NOTE: The bagels are best eaten the day they are made. You can store them in a plastic bag at room temperature for up to 3 days, but toast or warm them in the oven before eating. You can also store them in a resealable plastic bag in the freezer for up to 2 months.

Pita Bread

MAKES 8 PITA

1 cup warm water
2¼ teaspoons active dry yeast
1 teaspoon wildflower honey
3 cups all-purpose flour, divided
1 tablespoon extra-virgin olive oil
1½ teaspoons salt

Pita has been a staple of Middle Eastern and Mediterranean cuisine for over 4000 years. Homemade pita bread has so much more flavour than store-bought and is easier to make than you might think. There is a bit of magic that happens when you make your own pita: in the hot oven the dough puffs up like inflating balloons. Fresh from the oven and torn apart, you will see the steam escape and instantly smell the beautiful aroma of just-made culinary magic.

1. In a large bowl, stir together the warm water, yeast, and honey. Stir in ½ cup of the flour and let sit for 15 minutes, until the mixture foams.

2. Add 2 cups of the flour, the olive oil, and salt and use a wooden spoon to stir until a shaggy dough forms with no dry patches.

3. Dust a work surface with some of the remaining ½ cup flour. Turn the dough out onto the work surface and knead the dough until smooth and elastic, about 7 minutes. The dough should be soft and moist. If it is too sticky, dust the work surface and the dough with more of the remaining flour. Place the dough in a large bowl, cover with plastic wrap, and let rest in a warm, draft-free place until doubled in size, about 1 hour.

4. Meanwhile, put a pizza stone or large cast-iron skillet in the oven and preheat to 500°F (260°C).

5. Once the dough has doubled in size, punch it down to release the gases. Turn the dough out onto a lightly floured work surface and divide it into 8 equal pieces. Roll each piece into a ball. Cover with a kitchen towel or plastic wrap and let rest for 10 minutes.

6. Working with one ball of dough at a time, use a lightly floured rolling pin to roll out the dough into an 8-inch circle, about ¼ inch thick. If the dough starts to stick, sprinkle it with more flour.

7. Working quickly to avoid losing heat, open the oven door and place as many pitas as will fit without touching the hot surface. Bake until the pita are puffed up and the bottoms are golden brown, 3 to 5 minutes (do not flip them). Remove the pita from the oven and cover with a kitchen towel to keep warm while you bake the remaining pita.

NOTE: The pita are best eaten the day they are baked. To freeze them, layer them with parchment, then wrap in foil and plastic wrap. Store in the freezer for up to 2 months. Defrost, then toast in a skillet or on a pizza stone.

This recipe can easily be doubled.

Herb Lavosh Crackers

These unleavened flatbreads originate in the Middle East. These dramatic crispy, crunchy crackers are perfect to serve alongside your favourite cheeses or dips. The best part? This recipe turns out lavosh far more amazing than the store-bought ones, and they are so simple to make.

1. In a large bowl, combine the bread flour, butter, salt, sugar, water, and chopped herbs. Mix until the dough comes together as a smooth ball, about 8 minutes. Cover the bowl with plastic wrap and let the dough rest in the refrigerator for 1 hour.

2. Position the racks in the upper and lower thirds of the oven and preheat to 375°F (190°C). Line 2 baking sheets with parchment paper.

3. Turn the dough out onto a lightly floured work surface and knead the dough a few times until smooth. Divide the dough into 4 equal pieces. Working with one piece of dough at a time, use a rolling pin to roll it out as thin as possible into a large oval. Place on a lined baking sheet (2 ovals per sheet). Brush the dough with the egg wash. Repeat rolling out the remaining dough.

4. Bake the flatbreads until golden brown, 10 to 12 minutes (no need to rotate the pans). Let cool completely on the baking sheets. Once cooled, break them into crackers. Store in an airtight container at room temperature for up to 4 days.

SERVES 4 TO 6

1½ cups bread flour
1 tablespoon unsalted butter, at room temperature
½ teaspoon kosher salt
Pinch of granulated sugar
¼ cup water
2 tablespoons chopped fresh herbs (dill, parsley, chives, thyme)
1 egg, beaten, for brushing

NOTE: Your love of flavours will come in handy in this recipe because you can jazz these crackers up by sprinkling with different toppings before you bake them—think sesame or poppy seeds, Parmesan cheese, sea salt, your favourite spice mix, or red chili flakes.

Garlic Herb Naan

MAKES 6

NAAN

2 cups all-purpose flour
1 teaspoon granulated sugar
¾ teaspoon baking powder
¾ teaspoon baking soda
¾ teaspoon kosher salt
¼ cup thinly sliced green onions
1 tablespoon finely chopped fresh
    flat-leaf parsley
½ cup plain full-fat yogurt
½ teaspoon vegetable oil
½ cup warm whole milk
Sea salt, for sprinkling

LEMON GARLIC BUTTER

3 tablespoons unsalted butter
1 tablespoon olive oil
2 tablespoons Confit Garlic Purée
    (page 89) (or 2 teaspoons grated
    fresh garlic)
Zest and juice of 1 large lemon
Salt and cracked black pepper

We have been using this naan recipe for years. Melt some butter in a saucepan and stir in some garlic and lemon and you will have the best garlic bread you've ever tasted.

1. **Make the dough:** In a large bowl, stir together the flour, sugar, baking powder, baking soda, kosher salt, green onions, and parsley. Make a well in the centre of the flour mixture. Pour the yogurt, vegetable oil, and milk into the well and stir together until the dough forms a ball.

2. Turn the dough out onto a lightly floured work surface and knead the dough until it is smooth, about 5 minutes. Place the dough in an oiled bowl, cover with a kitchen towel and let rest in a warm, draft-free place until doubled in size, 1½ to 2 hours.

3. **Meanwhile, make the lemon garlic butter:** Melt the butter with the olive oil in a small saucepan over medium heat. Add the confit garlic purée and lemon zest and juice and stir together. Season to taste with salt and pepper. Remove from the heat and set aside.

4. **Shape and bake the naan:** Once the dough has doubled in size, turn it out onto a lightly floured work surface. Divide it into 6 equal portions and shape each portion into a ball. Use a rolling pin to roll out each ball of dough into an oval about ¼ inch thick.

5. Heat a large cast-iron or heavy skillet over medium-high heat.

6. Working in batches, place the naan in the hot skillet and cook, turning once, until golden brown, about 2 minutes per side. Transfer to a plate, brush with some lemon garlic butter and sprinkle with sea salt.

NOTE: The naan is best eaten on the day it is baked but can be stored in an airtight container in the refrigerator for up to 2 days.

Don't leave out the yogurt! Naan gets its pleasing chewy texture from the addition of full-fat yogurt. Without it, your finished naan won't have the proper consistency.

Make sure you let the dough rise for at least an hour in a warm place. The warmer the location, the faster the dough will rise. You'll be rewarded with big, airy pockets.

Confit Garlic Purée

Makes about 1 cup

Cooking garlic slow and low in oil until it's soft deepens the sweetness and removes the harsh bitterness you will recognize from eating it raw. Cook up a batch bigger than you think you will need, because once you start using this, you will use it with abandon. You can substitute confit garlic pureé for the garlic in any recipe.

    1 cup peeled garlic cloves
    ½ cup canola oil
    ½ cup olive oil
    ½ teaspoon kosher salt

1. Preheat the oven to 300°F (150°C).

2. Put the garlic cloves in a heavy medium ovenproof pot. Pour the canola oil and olive oil over the garlic, adding more oil if needed to cover the cloves, then add the salt. Cover with a lid, transfer to the oven, and bake until the garlic cloves are pale gold and tender, about 50 minutes. Let cool to room temperature.

3. Using a slotted spoon, transfer the garlic cloves to a small food processor and process until smooth. Alternatively, transfer the cloves to a bowl and mash with the side of a fork. Store in an airtight container in the refrigerator for up to 1 month or in the freezer for up to 3 months.

Olive Rosemary Focaccia

MAKES ONE 13 × 9-INCH SLAB

2½ cups lukewarm water

2¼ teaspoons active dry yeast

2 teaspoons liquid honey

5 cups all-purpose flour

1 tablespoon kosher salt

6 tablespoons extra-virgin olive oil, divided, plus more for brushing

4 tablespoons unsalted butter, at room temperature

Flaky sea salt

2 teaspoons fresh rosemary leaves

½ cup pitted Kalamata or Picholine olives

This focaccia recipe is the only one that you will ever need. So easy to make, and you can add whatever toppings you like. Olives, confit garlic, fresh herbs, cherry tomatoes, caramelized leeks or onions, Parmesan cheese—the possibilities are endless, but the final result will always be an incredibly soft and airy centre with a perfectly crispy golden-brown crust.

1. In a medium bowl, whisk together the lukewarm water, yeast, and honey. Let sit for 5 minutes or until foamy.

2. Add the flour and kosher salt and mix with a rubber spatula until a shaggy dough forms and no dry patches remain.

3. Pour 4 tablespoons of the olive oil into a large bowl. Transfer the dough to the bowl and turn it to completely coat in the oil. Cover with plastic wrap and let rest at room temperature until doubled in size, 2 to 3 hours.

4. Generously butter a 13 × 9-inch baking pan, using all the butter. Pour 1 tablespoon of the olive oil into the middle of the pan.

5. Once the dough has doubled in size, gather up the edges and lift it up and over into the centre of the bowl. Give the bowl a quarter turn and repeat the process. Repeat 2 more times; you want to deflate the dough by releasing the gases while you form it into a rough ball. Transfer the dough to the prepared pan. Pour any oil left in the bottom of the bowl over the dough and turn it to coat. Let the dough rise, uncovered, in a warm, draft-free place until doubled in size, 1½ to 2 hours.

6. When the dough is almost doubled, preheat the oven to 450°F (230°C).

7. When the dough is doubled in size, drizzle with the remaining 1 tablespoon olive oil, then dimple the focaccia all over with your fingers, pressing deeply into the dough. Sprinkle with the flaky sea salt, rosemary, and olives. Bake until puffed up and golden brown all over, 20 to 30 minutes. Remove from the oven and brush 2 to 3 tablespoons olive oil all over the focaccia. Let cool in the pan for 5 minutes, then turn out onto a rack. Serve warm or at room temperature.

NOTE: To store, wrap in parchment and then keep in an airtight bag or container at room temperature for up to 2 days or in the freezer for up to 2 months. Gently toast or reheat the focaccia before serving.

The traditional dimples you see on focaccia are there for a reason: they reduce the air in the dough and prevent the bread from rising too quickly.

If you add extra toppings, you can push these into the dimples so that the bread swallows them up as it bakes.

Black Pepper Parmesan Crackers

These Parmesan crackers are crisp, buttery, and absolutely addictive. Perfect to serve with soups, dips, or on their own as a perfect cheesy snack.

1. In a large bowl, combine the Parmesan, flour, butter, salt, pepper, and smoked paprika. Using a wooden spoon, mix until a ball of dough forms. Wrap the dough with plastic wrap and let rest in the refrigerator for 20 minutes.

2. On a lightly floured work surface, use your hands to roll the dough into a 12-inch log, 2½ inches wide. Wrap the log in plastic wrap and place in the freezer for 20 minutes.

3. Meanwhile, preheat the oven to 350°F (180°C). Line a baking sheet with parchment paper.

4. Cut the log crosswise into ½-inch-thick slices. (You should have about 24 crackers.) Arrange the slices on the lined baking sheet, evenly spaced. Bake until golden brown, 12 to 14 minutes. Let the crackers cool completely on the baking sheet. Once cooled, store in an airtight container at room temperature for up to 4 days.

MAKES ABOUT 24 CRACKERS

2 cups finely grated Parmesan cheese

1½ cups all-purpose flour

8 tablespoons unsalted butter, at room temperature

¾ teaspoon salt

¼ teaspoon cracked black pepper

¼ teaspoon smoked paprika

Grissini

MAKES ABOUT 2 DOZEN BREADSTICKS

½ cup whole wheat flour
¾ cup warm water
1 teaspoon liquid honey
1 tablespoon active dry yeast
1½ cups all-purpose flour
3 tablespoons olive oil, plus more
     for brushing the dough
1½ teaspoons salt

Long, thin, crispy homemade Italian breadsticks are the perfect centrepiece for your antipasti platter or dinner table.

1. **Mix the dough:** In the bowl of a stand mixer, combine the whole wheat flour, warm water, honey, and yeast. Stir with a wooden spoon and let sit for 10 minutes or until foamy.

2. Fit the stand mixer with the dough hook. Add the all-purpose flour, olive oil, and salt. Mix on low speed until combined, then increase to medium speed and mix until the dough is smooth and shiny, 5 to 7 minutes. Transfer the dough to a medium bowl. Drizzle a bit of olive oil over the dough and roll it around until completely coated. Cover with a kitchen towel and let rest in a warm, draft-free place for 1 hour or until doubled in size.

3. Once the dough has doubled in size, position the racks in the upper and lower thirds of the oven and preheat to 425°F (220°C). Line 2 or 3 baking sheets with parchment paper.

4. **Shape the grissini and bake:** Turn the dough out onto a lightly floured work surface. Shape the dough into a rough flat rectangle about 24 inches long and 12 inches wide. With a long side of the dough facing you, use a sharp knife or bench knife to cut the dough crosswise into about 24 strips, each about 1 inch wide.

5. Working with one strip at a time, use your hands to roll the dough into a rope about 12 inches long and ½ inch wide. Transfer each rope to the lined baking sheets, ½ inch apart. Let rest, uncovered, until puffed up a bit, about 15 minutes.

6. Bake for 5 minutes, then rotate the pans back to front and top to bottom. Bake for another 5 to 10 minutes, until golden brown. Let the breadsticks cool completely on the baking sheets. Once cooled, store in an airtight container at room temperature for up to 4 days.

Rye Crackers

Lots of wholesome ingredients go into our version of Swedish rye crispbread. A lovely base for nut butters or whipped ricotta and a good drizzle of honey.

1. Preheat the oven to 375°F (190°C). Line a baking sheet with parchment paper.

2. In a large bowl, stir together the all-purpose flour, rye flour, baking powder, kosher salt, and mixed seeds and spices. Make a well in the centre of the flour mixture. Pour the olive oil, water, and honey into the well. Using your hands, knead briefly to bring the dough together, adding a little more water if the dough is too dry. The dough should just come together and be relatively smooth.

3. Turn the dough out onto a lightly floured work surface and knead briefly. Divide the dough into 6 equal pieces. Working with one piece at a time, use a rolling pin to roll out the dough as thin as possible. Use a sharp knife to cut the dough into 2 large triangles. Transfer the triangles to the lined baking sheet.

4. Lightly brush the dough with olive oil and sprinkle with sea salt and pepper to taste. Bake until golden brown all over, 7 to 8 minutes. Transfer the crackers to a rack and let cool completely. Store in an airtight container at room temperature for up to 1 week.

MAKES 12 CRACKERS

1¼ cups all-purpose flour

1¼ cups rye flour

1 teaspoon baking powder

1 teaspoon kosher salt

3 tablespoons mixed seeds and spices (such as sesame seeds, pumpkin seeds, fennel seeds, coriander seeds)

¼ cup olive oil, plus more for brushing

3 tablespoons water

1 tablespoon liquid honey

Sea salt and cracked black pepper

Appetizers

Labneh with Beet Sumac Marmalade and Pita Bread

We can get carried away with this tasty combo. The beets are super interesting, becoming sweet and tangy with bright citrus notes as they cook down with the orange and sumac. This savoury condiment is served with a creamy dollop of lemony labneh that you can then swirl together, becoming mesmerized by the eye-popping magenta colour and irresistible aroma of this dip.

1. **Make the beet sumac marmalade:** In a medium saucepan, combine the beets, water, apple cider vinegar, orange zest and juice, and honey. Bring to a simmer over medium heat and cook, stirring occasionally, until the beets are tender and the liquid has reduced to a glaze, 15 to 20 minutes. Stir in the coriander, sumac, and chili flakes and cook, stirring, for 2 to 3 minutes, until the marmalade has thickened. Season well with kosher salt and pepper. Remove from the heat and let cool. Set aside or store in an airtight container in the refrigerator for up to 2 weeks.

2. **Assemble:** Spoon the labneh into a shallow serving bowl. Make a well in the centre of the labneh. Spoon a generous scoop of the beet sumac marmalade into the well. Garnish with a sprinkle of sumac, dill, and flaky sea salt. Serve with sliced cucumbers and warm pita.

SERVES 4 TO 6

**BEET SUMAC MARMALADE
(MAKES ABOUT 2½ CUPS)**

2 cups grated peeled red beets

1 cup water

½ cup apple cider vinegar

Zest and juice of 1 orange

2 tablespoons liquid honey

1 teaspoon ground coriander

1 teaspoon sumac, plus more for garnish

½ teaspoon red chili flakes

Kosher salt and cracked black pepper

FOR ASSEMBLY

1 cup labneh

Chopped fresh dill and/or dill flowers, for garnish

Flaky sea salt

Sliced cucumbers (any variety)

Pita Bread (page 82 or store-bought), warm, for serving

NOTE: This beet sumac marmalade is a delicious condiment for Potato Parsnip Latkes (page 71). It is also a beautiful addition to our Lemon Dill Vinaigrette (page 178); just add 1 or 2 tablespoons to ½ cup of the vinaigrette and stir together.

Green Garden Hummus with Herb Lavosh Crackers

MAKES ABOUT 2 CUPS

1 can (19 ounces/540 mL) white
  beans, rinsed and drained
1 cup fresh green peas, blanched
¼ cup fresh dill, roughly chopped
¼ cup fresh mint leaves
¼ cup fresh flat-leaf parsley leaves
2 garlic cloves, minced
3 tablespoons almond butter or
  tahini
½ teaspoon ground cumin
Zest and juice of 1 lemon
¼ cup extra-virgin olive oil
3 tablespoons water, as needed for
  thinning
Salt and cracked black pepper

GARNISHES (OPTIONAL)
Wasabi peas
Baby kale
Mint sprigs

Your favourite cut raw vegetables,
  for serving
Herb Lavosh Crackers (page 85)
  and/or Rye Crackers (page 97),
  for serving

We adore the classic chickpea dip, but we love our spin on everyone's favourite hummus even more. We add lots of herbs and sweet, tender peas from our garden to make this a new meze appetizer star. Make-ahead dips and freshly cut veggies to lay out for your guests when they arrive is called super-easy entertaining, and it's the only way to go.

1. In a food processor or high-speed blender, combine the white beans, peas, dill, mint, parsley, garlic, almond butter, cumin, lemon zest and juice, and olive oil. Blend until smooth, 3 to 4 minutes, scraping down the sides as needed. If the hummus is too thick, add up to 3 tablespoons of water to make the hummus creamier. Season to taste with salt and pepper. The hummus can be stored in an airtight container in the refrigerator for up to 1 week.

2. To serve, transfer the hummus to a small bowl and place it on a large platter. Garnish with some wasabi peas, kale, and mint, if using. Arrange the raw vegetables and herb lavosh crackers and/or rye crackers on the platter.

NOTE: This dip is also incredible with grilled veggies or used as a spread in a wrap or sandwich.

Pastrami-Spiced Roasted Carrot Hummus with Rye Crackers

Roasting sweetens carrots, and pastrami spices make these ones super delicious. That distinctive combination of coriander, mustard, black pepper, smoky paprika, and brown sugar is just so comforting. This hummus is a wonderful staple to have in your refrigerator. You can add it to salads and bowls, have it on a healthy cracker, or simply dip some raw vegetables into it for lunch or a snack. You will never find our refrigerator without this hummus in it.

1. **Make the pastrami spice blend:** In a spice blender, combine the brown sugar, black pepper, coriander seeds, mustard seeds, smoked paprika, kosher salt, garlic powder, and cloves. Grind into a powder. Set aside or store in a sealed jar at room temperature for up to 3 months.

2. **Make the hummus:** Preheat the oven to 400°F (200°C). Line a baking sheet with parchment paper.

3. Put the carrots, garlic, and shallots on the lined baking sheet. Drizzle with 2 tablespoons of the olive oil, sprinkle with the pastrami spice blend, and mix well to completely coat. Evenly spread the vegetables on the baking sheet and roast for 30 minutes or until golden brown, stirring halfway through. Remove from the oven and let cool for 10 minutes.

4. In a small bowl, whisk together the tahini, the remaining 2 tablespoons olive oil, lemon zest and juice, and water until smooth.

5. Transfer the roasted vegetables to a food processor or high-speed blender. Add the chickpeas and pulse 4 to 5 times, scraping down the sides as needed. With the processor running, drizzle in the tahini mixture and blend until the hummus is creamy, adding more water if needed. Season to taste with salt and pepper. The hummus, without the cashews, can be stored in an airtight container in the refrigerator for up to 1 week.

6. Scrape the hummus into a serving bowl. Top with toasted cashews and drizzle with olive oil. Serve with the rye crackers.

SERVES 4 TO 6

PASTRAMI SPICE BLEND

2 tablespoons brown sugar

2 tablespoons cracked black pepper

2 tablespoons coriander seeds

2 tablespoons mustard seeds

1 tablespoon smoked paprika

1 teaspoon kosher salt

½ teaspoon garlic powder

⅛ teaspoon ground cloves

HUMMUS

3 cups roughly chopped peeled carrots (reserve green tops for garnish)

3 garlic cloves, peeled

2 shallots, roughly chopped

4 tablespoons olive oil, divided, plus more for drizzling

2 teaspoons Pastrami Spice Blend (recipe above)

¼ cup tahini

Zest and juice of 1 lemon

2 tablespoons water, plus more as needed

1 cup canned chickpeas, rinsed and drained

Salt and cracked black pepper

¼ cup cashews, toasted and roughly chopped

Rye Crackers (page 97), for serving

Eggplant Caponata

SERVES 4 TO 6

2 medium globe eggplants, cut into
    ½-inch cubes (about 6 cups)
4 tablespoons olive oil, divided
½ teaspoon salt
3 tablespoons golden raisins
¼ cup pitted green olives, chopped
3 tablespoons sherry vinegar
2 tablespoons drained capers,
    roughly chopped
¼ cup finely chopped red onion
1 celery stalk, diced
1 yellow bell pepper, diced
Salt and cracked black pepper
1 tablespoon tomato paste
3 garlic cloves, grated
1 pound (450 g) tomatoes (about
    4 medium tomatoes), cored and
    diced
½ teaspoon brown sugar
¼ cup chopped fresh flat-leaf parsley
¼ cup pine nuts, toasted
Fresh basil leaves, for garnish

Herb Lavosh Crackers (page 85) or
    Olive Rosemary Focaccia
    (page 90), for serving

A traditional antipasto from Sicily, eggplant caponata is a versatile dish. It is often served as an appetizer on toasted bread, stirred into pasta, or spooned over polenta. If you have the time, prepare this in advance—it's even better on the second day.

1. Preheat the oven to 425°F (220°C). Line a baking sheet with parchment paper.

2. Put the eggplant on the lined baking sheet and toss with 2 tablespoons of the olive oil and the salt. Evenly spread the eggplant on the lined baking sheet and roast until tender and brown around the edges, 25 to 35 minutes, stirring halfway through.

3. In a small bowl, combine the raisins, olives, sherry vinegar, and capers. Set aside for the raisins to soften while you prepare the caponata.

4. Heat the remaining 2 tablespoons olive oil in a large skillet over medium heat. Add the red onion and celery and cook, stirring occasionally, for 8 minutes or until the vegetables have softened. Add the bell pepper and season to taste with salt and pepper. Cook until tender, about 8 minutes. Add the tomato paste, garlic, tomatoes, and brown sugar and continue cooking, stirring often, for about 8 minutes, until the tomatoes have cooked down and become saucy.

5. Add the roasted eggplant, the raisin and caper mixture (with any liquid), and several grinds of pepper. Cook, stirring, for another 5 minutes. Stir in the parsley and the pine nuts.

6. Serve warm or at room temperature, garnished with basil leaves. Serve with herb lavosh crackers or olive rosemary focaccia.

NOTE: If you can't find fabulous fresh, ripe tomatoes, use good-quality canned ones like San Marzano.

Roasted Red Pepper Dip with Feta and Walnuts with Grilled Flatbread

This dip is loosely inspired by the traditional Middle Eastern dip muhammara, but ours is much easier to make. We've made a few tweaks, simplifying things but holding on to that amazingly smoky, tangy flavour.

1. Preheat the oven to 475°F (240°C). Line a baking sheet with parchment paper.

2. Put the bell peppers, tomatoes, red onion, and garlic on the lined baking sheet. Drizzle with 2 tablespoons of the olive oil and season to taste with salt. Roast for 10 minutes, then stir well. Continue roasting for another 15 to 20 minutes, until the vegetables are caramelized and soft. Remove from the oven and let cool.

3. Transfer the cooled vegetables to a food processor and blend until chunky. Add the walnuts, pomegranate molasses, Aleppo pepper, cumin, and smoked paprika. Pulse until smooth. Scrape down the sides of the bowl. With the processor running, slowly add the remaining 2 tablespoons olive oil and blend until the oil is completely incorporated. Season to taste with salt and black pepper.

4. Transfer the dip to a serving bowl and garnish with the crumbled feta and the reserved toasted walnuts. Serve with warm grilled bread.

SERVES 4 TO 6

4 red bell peppers, roughly chopped

2 Roma tomatoes, each cut into 6 wedges

½ cup roughly chopped red onion

6 garlic cloves, peeled

4 tablespoons olive oil, divided, plus more for drizzling

Salt

½ cup walnuts, toasted and chopped (reserve a few whole nuts for garnish)

2 tablespoons pomegranate molasses

1½ teaspoons Aleppo pepper or ancho chili powder (see Note)

1 teaspoon ground cumin

1 teaspoon smoked paprika

Cracked black pepper

¼ cup crumbled feta cheese

Grilled flatbread, warm, for serving

NOTE: If you can't find Aleppo pepper, mix 4 parts sweet paprika with 1 part cayenne pepper, or use ancho chili powder with a little cayenne to boost the heat.

Tomatillo Pico de Gallo with Chili-Dusted Corn Chips

SERVES 4 TO 6

TOMATILLO PICO DE GALLO

¾ pound (340 g) tomatillos, husks and stems removed, rinsed and diced (about 1½ cups; see Note)

½ cup mixed red and yellow cherry tomatoes, diced

½ cup diced white onion

½ cup chopped fresh cilantro leaves

2 garlic cloves, minced

1 jalapeño pepper, seeded if desired and thinly sliced

¼ cup fresh lime juice

2 tablespoons olive oil

Salt and cracked black pepper

CHILI-DUSTED CORN CHIPS

2 tablespoons salt

1 tablespoon cayenne pepper

1½ teaspoons chipotle chili powder

4 cups canola oil, for deep-frying

24 Corn Tortillas (page 124 or store-bought), cut into quarters

Tomatillos look like small green tomatoes with sticky, papery husks. Tart and fresh tasting, this chunky salsa is a great addition to your summer barbecue party.

1. **Make the tomatillo pico de gallo:** In a medium bowl, combine the tomatillos, tomatoes, onion, cilantro, garlic, jalapeño, lime juice, and olive oil. Season to taste with salt and black pepper. Stir to combine. Store in the refrigerator until ready to use.

2. **Make the chili-dusted corn chips:** In a small bowl, stir together the salt, cayenne pepper, and chipotle chili powder. Set aside.

3. Heat the canola oil in a large, heavy pot until it reaches 350°F (180°C) on a deep-fry thermometer. Working in batches, drop 3 or 4 tortillas into the hot oil and fry until golden, 1 to 2 minutes. Using tongs, turn the tortillas and fry for another minute or until golden brown and crisp. Transfer the tortillas to a plate lined with paper towel to absorb excess oil. Sprinkle with some spice mixture. Serve the corn chips with the tomatillo pico de gallo.

NOTE: Rinse the tomatillos well with warm water to remove the naturally sticky coating, which is bitter.

For a smokier flavour, first pan-roast the diced tomatillos in a large, dry pan over medium-high heat until they are slightly charred.

Herb Cashew Cream Cheese Crostini with Strawberries and Balsamic Glaze

This is a delightfully simple bite and lightning fast to whip up. Aged balsamic vinegar adds to ripe strawberries that have been kissed with a hint of basil and honey.

1. **Make the herb cashew cream cheese:** Put the cashews in a medium bowl and add enough hot water to cover. Cover the bowl with a kitchen towel and soak for at least 2 hours or up to 8 hours. Drain before using.

2. In a high-speed blender, combine the drained cashews, nutritional yeast, olive oil, and lemon juice. Blend until smooth, 3 to 5 minutes, scraping down the sides a couple of times. If the mixture is too thick, add up to ¼ cup hot water as needed and blend.

3. Scrape the cashew cream cheese into a medium bowl. Add the herbs and stir well. Season to taste with salt and pepper. Set aside or store in an airtight container in the refrigerator for up to 2 weeks.

4. **Prepare the strawberries and balsamic glaze:** In a small bowl, combine the strawberries, basil, honey, ginger, lime zest and juice, and pepper. Stir together and let sit for 10 minutes.

5. Meanwhile, in a small saucepan, bring the balsamic vinegar to a boil and cook for a minute or so, until reduced to a syrupy consistency. Remove from the heat and let cool.

6. **Assemble the crostini:** Spread the herb cashew cream cheese evenly on the crostini. Make a small well in the centre of the cream cheese. Fill each well with a spoonful of the strawberry mixture. Garnish with the chopped walnuts, mint, and a drizzle of the balsamic glaze.

SERVES 4 TO 6

HERB CASHEW CREAM CHEESE (MAKES ABOUT 1 CUP)

1½ cups cashews
2 tablespoons nutritional yeast
1 tablespoon olive oil
1 tablespoon fresh lemon juice
½ cup chopped fresh herbs (such as basil, chives, dill, parsley)
Kosher salt and cracked black pepper

STRAWBERRIES AND BALSAMIC GLAZE

1 cup diced hulled fresh strawberries
2 tablespoons chopped fresh basil
2 teaspoons liquid honey
1 teaspoon grated peeled fresh ginger
Zest and juice of 1 lime
¼ teaspoon cracked black pepper
2 tablespoons aged balsamic vinegar

FOR THE CROSTINI

1 baguette, cut into ½-inch-thick slices and toasted
¼ cup walnuts, toasted and chopped
Fresh mint leaves, for garnish

Pimento Cheese Dip with
Black Pepper Parmesan Crackers

MAKES ABOUT 2 DOZEN CRACKERS

2 medium red bell peppers

1 cup (8 ounces/225 g) cream cheese,
    at room temperature

2 cups grated aged cheddar cheese

2 tablespoons mayonnaise

2 garlic cloves, minced

1 shallot, finely minced

1 teaspoon finely chopped seeded
    jalapeño pepper

1 teaspoon Worcestershire sauce

¼ teaspoon cayenne pepper

Salt and cracked black pepper

Black Pepper Parmesan Crackers
    (page 93), for serving

Pimento cheese is a classic Southern dip. It's affectionately referred to as pâté du Sud, or Southern pâté. Every mom has her own version and many just use a jar of diced pimientos to give it that distinctly pinkish hue. We make a big batch of it and use leftovers for the perfect topping on burgers or to make an over-the-top grilled cheese sandwich.

1. Char one of the bell peppers over the flame of a gas burner or under a broiler, turning with tongs, until the skin is blackened all over, 10 to 12 minutes. Place the charred pepper in a bowl, cover with plastic wrap, and let steam for 10 minutes. (The steam will make it easier to peel.)

2. Use your hands to peel the charred pepper. Slice off the stem and remove the seeds. Finely chop the pepper. Set aside.

3. Remove the stem and seeds from the raw bell pepper and finely dice. Set aside.

4. In a medium bowl using a hand-held electric mixer, or in a stand mixer fitted with the paddle attachment, combine the cream cheese, cheddar, mayonnaise, garlic, shallot, jalapeño, Worcestershire sauce, and cayenne pepper. Beat until the mixture is thoroughly combined. Stir in the roasted and raw peppers. Season to taste with salt and black pepper.

5. Scrape the dip into a serving bowl. Serve with black pepper Parmesan crackers.

Baked Caprese Feta

This baked feta appetizer comes together in just minutes with only a handful of ingredients—olives, fresh tomatoes, garlic, olive oil, lemon, and fresh herbs. Bake it all together until the cheese is warm and creamy. Enjoy with focaccia to sop up the scrumptious oil with the lavish warm feta. Add a glass of chilled white wine and you have the perfect supper.

1. Preheat the oven to 400°F (200°C).

2. Place the feta in a small casserole dish. Scatter the green onions, black olives, lemon slices, garlic, tomatoes, chili, basil, dill, and mint over the feta. Pour the olive oil over top. Bake until the feta is light golden and the oil is sizzling, 15 to 20 minutes. Serve immediately with warm olive rosemary focaccia or crusty bread.

SERVES 4 TO 6

1 block (8 ounces/225 g) feta cheese
2 green onions, finely chopped
¼ cup black olives, pitted and halved
2 to 3 slices of lemon
2 garlic cloves, thinly sliced
1 bunch red cherry tomatoes on the vine (or 1 cup cherry tomatoes)
1 fresh red serrano chili, thinly sliced
2 sprigs fresh basil
2 sprigs fresh dill
2 sprigs fresh mint
⅓ cup olive oil, plus more for drizzling if desired
Olive Rosemary Focaccia (page 90) or crusty bread, warm, for serving

NOTE: This baked feta can be prepped in advance, which makes it one of our favourite foods to serve at a party. Prep the feta as directed and store, covered, overnight in the refrigerator. Let the feta come to room temperature before baking. When your guests arrive, pop it in the oven for a warm appetizer that everyone will love.

This recipe is amazing using fruits such as peaches, apricots, or cherries instead of the savoury tomatoes, garlic, olives, and green onions.

Warm Brie with Pears, Fennel, Honey, and Pistachios

SERVES 4 TO 6

½ fennel bulb, cored and thinly
 sliced crosswise
1 pear, cored and thinly sliced
Leaves from 2 sprigs fresh
 rosemary, divided
1 tablespoon olive oil, plus more
 for drizzling
1 small bunch seedless red grapes,
 broken into small clusters
2 tablespoons balsamic vinegar
1 (8-ounce/225 g) Brie wheel

FOR SERVING

Wildflower honey, for drizzling
2 tablespoons chopped pistachios
2 teaspoons bee pollen (optional)
Grissini (page 94), Rye Crackers
 (page 97), or grilled bread

This is classic bistro fare at its finest, with a stunning presentation. Better yet, it's ready in no time at all. The combination of warm, rich melted Brie with sweet honeyed pears and the anise flavour of the fennel is divine.

1. Preheat the oven to 375°F (190°C). Line 2 baking sheets with parchment paper.

2. In a small bowl, toss the fennel, pear, and half of the rosemary leaves with the olive oil. Evenly spread the mixture on a lined baking sheet and roast until the fennel starts to caramelize around the edges and the pear is just fork-tender, 12 to 15 minutes. Remove from the oven. Lay the grape clusters over the roasted mixture and drizzle with the balsamic vinegar. Set aside. Leave the oven on.

3. Place the Brie wheel on the second lined baking sheet. Use a small knife to cut diagonal slashes in the top of the cheese. Nestle the remaining rosemary leaves in the slashes and drizzle with a little olive oil. Bake until the cheese is warm and melted, 10 to 12 minutes.

4. When the cheese is almost ready, warm the fennel and pear mixture in the oven for 2 minutes.

5. Carefully transfer the baked cheese with the parchment paper to a serving platter. Top with the roasted fennel, pears, and grapes. Drizzle with the honey. Sprinkle with pistachios and bee pollen, if using. Serve with grissini, rye crackers, or grilled bread.

NOTE: Baked Brie is best served straight from the oven. Be sure to bake it on a sheet of parchment paper so that you can easily transfer it from the hot baking sheet to a serving platter.

Try different seasonal fruit or jams instead of the roasted pear and fennel combination.

NOTE: When serving these corn tortillas during your meal, keep them wrapped in a kitchen towel or in a tortilla warmer until ready to eat, so that they do not dry out.

Tempura Eggplant Tacos with Baja Sauce and Cabbage Cilantro Slaw

Homemade corn tortillas make the best-tasting tacos, and there is no excuse not to make them from scratch given how easy they are to make. The crunchy, crispy tempura eggplant batons cook up beautifully in a light batter that is quick and easy to pull together. The eggplant lies on a bed of perfectly seasoned slaw and is topped off with pickled jalapeños and a creamy Baja sauce spiked with fresh lime.

1. **Make the Baja sauce:** In a small bowl, combine the mayonnaise, garlic, lime zest, lime juice, and sriracha. Stir until smooth. Season to taste with salt and pepper. Cover and refrigerate for at least 1 hour before serving to allow the flavours to meld. Store in an airtight container in the refrigerator for up to 1 week.

2. **Start the cabbage cilantro slaw:** In a large bowl, mix together the green cabbage, red cabbage, cilantro, carrot, red onion, bell pepper, and jalapeño. Set aside.

3. In a separate small bowl, stir together the lemon juice, lime juice, rice vinegar, olive oil, and salt. Set aside.

4. **Make the tempura eggplant:** Slice the eggplant in half lengthwise, then cut into 2-inch-long batons, about 1 inch thick. Place the batons in a medium bowl and toss with the salt. Set aside for 20 minutes to draw out excess moisture so the eggplant has a stronger flavour and a more tender texture.

5. After 20 minutes, sprinkle ⅓ cup of the flour over the eggplant and toss to coat completely.

6. In a large bowl, stir together the remaining 1⅓ cups flour and the baking powder. Slowly pour in the sparkling water and fold in gently with a rubber spatula until the batter is smooth. Season to taste with salt and pepper.

7. Heat 1 inch of vegetable oil in a deep medium skillet over medium heat until it reaches 350°F (180°C) on a deep-fry thermometer. Once the oil is hot, working with a few pieces of eggplant at a time so you don't crowd the pan, dip the eggplant in the batter and then gently lay it in the hot oil. Fry until golden brown, 1 to 2 minutes per side. Using tongs, transfer the eggplant to a plate lined with paper towel to absorb excess oil. Repeat to fry the remaining eggplant.

8. **Finish the slaw and assemble the tacos:** Give the lemon-lime dressing a stir, pour it over the slaw, and toss to combine. Fill the warm tortillas with the cabbage cilantro slaw, a few batons of eggplant, Baja sauce, pickled jalapeños, and cilantro. Serve with lime wedges on the side.

MAKES 16 TACOS

BAJA SAUCE

¾ cup mayonnaise
1 garlic clove, minced
½ teaspoon lime zest
2 tablespoons fresh lime juice
1 tablespoon sriracha sauce
Salt and cracked black pepper

CABBAGE CILANTRO SLAW (MAKES 5 CUPS)

3 cups thinly sliced green cabbage
1 cup thinly sliced red cabbage
1 bunch fresh cilantro, chopped
    (about ½ cup)
½ cup grated peeled carrot
½ cup minced red onion
2 tablespoons minced red bell pepper
½ jalapeño pepper, seeded if desired
    and minced (about 1 tablespoon)
2 tablespoons fresh lemon juice
1 tablespoon fresh lime juice
2 tablespoons seasoned rice vinegar
2 tablespoons olive oil
½ teaspoon salt

TEMPURA EGGPLANT

1 globe eggplant
½ teaspoon salt
1⅔ cups all-purpose flour, divided
1 teaspoon baking powder
1 cup cold sparkling water or club soda
Salt and cracked black pepper
Vegetable oil, for frying

FOR SERVING

16 Corn Tortillas (page 124 or
    store-bought), warmed
Pickled Jalapeños (page 202)
Fresh cilantro sprigs
Lime wedges

Corn Tortillas

Makes 16 (6-inch) tortillas

There is absolutely no reason to buy store-bought corn tortillas when you can make them from scratch so easily in your very own kitchen. With just a few simple ingredients, a tortilla press, and a comal (a smooth, flat Mexican griddle) or cast-iron skillet, you will have delicious, fragrant, pillowy tortillas.

2 cups masa harina (corn flour)
½ teaspoon salt
1 cup + 2 tablespoons water, more as needed

1. Cut 2 circles of plastic wrap about the size of your tortilla press plate. Heat a comal or cast-iron skillet over medium heat.

2. In a large bowl, combine the masa harina, salt, and water and mix well for about 4 minutes, until a smooth and thick dough forms. If the dough doesn't come together, add more water, 1 tablespoon at a time, and mix some more.

3. Divide the dough into 16 equal portions. Roll into balls and press down slightly on each. Keep the masa covered with a kitchen towel so it does not dry out while you make the tortillas.

4. Lay a circle of plastic wrap on the bottom of the tortilla press. Place a ball of masa on top of the plastic and cover with the second circle of plastic. Close the press and firmly press down on the handle to flatten the dough into a disc about ¼ inch thick. Open the press and remove the top circle of plastic. Holding the tortilla in one hand, peel off the other circle of plastic.

5. Place the tortilla on the hot surface and cook for about 30 seconds, until browned and slightly puffy. Flip the tortilla and cook for about 30 seconds more, until browned in spots and the surface looks slightly dry. Transfer the cooked tortilla to a tortilla warmer or a basket lined with a kitchen towel and cover with another towel to keep warm while you make the rest of the tortillas.

6. Corn tortillas are best served within a few hours of being made. Leftover tortillas can be wrapped in plastic wrap or in a resealable plastic bag and stored in the refrigerator for up to 3 days. Any leftover masa dough can be tightly wrapped in plastic wrap and refrigerated for up to 5 days. To freeze cooked corn tortillas, place a piece of parchment paper between each tortilla to prevent them from sticking together, and place them in a resealable plastic bag. Store in the freezer for up to 2 months.

Sweet Corn Fritters with Rosemary Hot Honey and Lime Sour Cream

This appetizer is one of our favourite ways to savour sweet summer corn. When you bite into these fritters, the melted cheddar and hit of miso is a delicious surprise. These little fritters get jazzed up with sweet honey and fiery red pepper flakes and gently mellowed with the lime sour cream. Each one is a perfect tasty bite.

1. **Make the rosemary hot honey:** In a small saucepan, gently heat the honey, chili flakes, and rosemary over medium heat until small bubbles form around the edges of the pan. Remove from the heat and let the honey infuse for 5 minutes. Stir in the apple cider vinegar. Strain the honey through a fine-mesh sieve into a glass jar. Once cooled, store tightly sealed in the refrigerator for up to 1 month.

2. **Make the lime sour cream:** In a small bowl, combine the sour cream, lime zest and juice, garlic, and salt. Stir until smooth and creamy. Set aside.

3. **Make the sweet corn fritters:** In a large bowl, combine the corn kernels, zucchini, yellow onions, flour, sugar, baking powder, salt, and pepper. Stir well. Add the eggs, milk, and miso and stir until a thick batter forms. Add the green onions and cheddar and gently stir to combine.

4. Heat the canola oil in a deep large skillet over medium-high heat.

5. Working in batches, drop 2 tablespoons of batter per fritter into the hot skillet. Spread the batter with the back of a spoon to form a 3-inch fritter and fry until golden and crispy, about 3 minutes per side. Transfer to a plate lined with paper towel to absorb excess oil. Repeat with the remaining batter, adding more oil to the skillet if necessary.

6. To serve, spoon a dollop of lime sour cream onto each fritter and drizzle with rosemary hot honey. Garnish with basil leaves and marigold petals, if using.

MAKES ABOUT 12 FRITTERS

ROSEMARY HOT HONEY (MAKES 1 CUP)

1 cup liquid honey
2 tablespoons red chili flakes
1 sprig fresh rosemary
2 teaspoons apple cider vinegar

LIME SOUR CREAM (MAKES 1 CUP)

1 cup full-fat sour cream
Zest and juice of 1 lime
1 garlic clove, minced
¼ teaspoon salt

SWEET CORN FRITTERS

1 cup fresh sweet corn kernels
1 cup finely diced green zucchini
1 cup finely diced yellow onion
1 cup all-purpose flour
1 teaspoon granulated sugar
1 teaspoon baking powder
1 teaspoon kosher salt
¼ teaspoon black pepper
2 eggs, lightly beaten
½ cup whole milk
1 tablespoon white or yellow miso
2 green onions, finely chopped
½ cup grated aged cheddar cheese
3 to 4 tablespoons canola oil, for frying

Fresh basil leaves and marigold petals, for garnish (optional)

NOTE: Fritters are best served immediately, but leftovers can be stored in an airtight container in the refrigerator for up to 2 days.

Bao with Gochujang and Sesame Glazed Carrots

MAKES 12 BAO

1 batch Bao (page 129) or 12 store-bought bao

GOCHUJANG AND SESAME GLAZED CARROTS

1 pound (450 g) carrots, peeled and cut into ¾-inch-thick batons

1 tablespoon vegetable oil

1 tablespoon sesame oil

1 tablespoon soy sauce

1 tablespoon liquid honey

1 tablespoon rice vinegar

1 tablespoon fresh lime juice

1 tablespoon brown sugar

1 tablespoon gochujang

2 teaspoons grated peeled fresh ginger

1 tablespoon sesame seeds, toasted

2 green onions, finely chopped

TOPPINGS

Lettuce leaves, such as romaine hearts or Bibb

Mini cucumbers, sliced

Fresh cilantro sprigs

Limes, for squeezing

Gua bao are an iconic Taiwanese snack consisting of a clamshell-shaped bun traditionally filled with braised pork belly. We have finally perfected our recipe for the fluffiest bao we've ever had and have swapped the pork belly for veggies—Korean BBQ-inspired gochujang and sesame glazed carrots. We are big fans of sharing the experience of building your own bao, so this is a terrific appetizer to share with a group of friends. Have the toppings ready, then fill the buns as soon as they come out of the steamer. Top the bao with these glazed carrots, crisp lettuce leaves, cucumber, and a big squeeze of lime juice, and sit back and watch your friends have a blast!

1. **Make the gochujang and sesame glazed carrots:** Preheat the oven to 400°F (200°C). Line a baking sheet with parchment paper.

2. Bring a large pot of salted water to a boil. Add the carrots and cook until al dente, about 5 minutes. Drain the carrots and let sit until cool enough to handle.

3. In a large bowl, whisk together the vegetable oil, sesame oil, soy sauce, honey, rice vinegar, lime juice, brown sugar, gochujang, and ginger. Add the carrots and toss to evenly coat. Evenly spread the carrots on the lined baking sheet and roast for 20 minutes or until they are tender in the middle and caramelized around the edges, turning halfway through. Remove from the oven and sprinkle with the sesame seeds and green onions.

4. **Assemble the bao:** Partially open the bao. Add the lettuce, glazed carrots, cucumber, cilantro, and a squeeze of lime juice.

NOTE: We love the caramelized roasted carrots, but parsnip, eggplant, turnip, and sweet potatoes will also drink up that umami-packed sauce.

Bao

Makes 12 buns

Bao—the word means "bun"—originated in Northern China. Hugely popular, these steamed buns can be many different shapes and can be served on their own or stuffed with your favourite savoury or sweet filling.

⅓ cup warm water

½ cup warm whole milk

4 tablespoons granulated
   sugar, divided

1 tablespoon active dry yeast

2 tablespoons vegetable oil

2½ cups all-purpose flour,
   plus more for dusting

½ teaspoon baking powder

¼ teaspoon salt

1. In a large bowl, combine the warm water, warm milk, 3 tablespoons of the sugar, yeast, and vegetable oil. Whisk to dissolve the yeast and sugar. Let sit for 5 to 10 minutes or until foamy.

2. In a stand mixer fitted with the dough hook, combine the flour, the remaining 1 tablespoon sugar, baking powder, and salt. Pour the wet ingredients into the dry ingredients. Starting on low speed and slowly increasing to medium, knead until the dough forms a firm ball, about 4 minutes. Remove the dough hook, cover the bowl with a kitchen towel , and let rest in a warm, draft-free place until doubled in size, about 1 hour.

3. Cut twelve 4-inch squares of parchment paper.

4. Once the dough has doubled in size, punch it down gently with your hands to release the gases. Turn the dough out onto a very lightly floured work surface and knead for another 2 minutes. Cut the dough into 12 equal portions and roll into balls. Cover the dough balls with a kitchen towel so they don't dry out. Working with one ball of dough at a time, use a rolling pin to roll out the dough into a 2½ × 5-inch oval, about ¼ inch thick. Lightly brush the surface of the oval with vegetable oil, then fold the dough in half to form a clamshell. Place on a square of parchment paper. Repeat with the remaining dough balls.

5. Place the bao in a bamboo steamer, leaving space between them as they will expand. You may need multiple trays. Place the lid on the steamer and let the bao rise in a warm place for 30 to 60 minutes, until 1½ times larger. To check if the dough is ready, gently press a bun with a finger. If the dough slowly returns to its original shape, it is ready to steam.

6. Fill a pot that will fit your steamer about a third of the way with water. Bring to a boil over high heat. Place the steamer on top of the pot of water. (Make sure the water is not touching the steamer.) Steam for 8 to 12 minutes, until the bao are cooked through. Turn off the heat, open the lid slightly, and let the bao rest for 2 to 3 minutes before removing the lid.

7. Remove the bao from the steamer. You can use the bao immediately or let them cool completely before storing. Arrange the bao on a baking sheet lined with parchment paper and place in the freezer until frozen, at least 2 hours. Transfer the bao to a resealable plastic bag and store in the freezer for up to 1 month. When ready to use, defrost the bao overnight in the refrigerator. Place the defrosted buns in a bamboo steamer lined with a steamer liner or perforated parchment paper and steam for 10 minutes.

Cabbage and Apple Gyoza with Lemon Chili Garlic Butter and Tamari Green Onion Dipping Sauce

Crispy on the bottom and juicy on the inside, these gyoza are very delicious and very addictive. Traditional Japanese gyoza, dumplings stuffed with a savoury filling of ground meat and veggies, are balanced in flavour and ingredients. Nothing overpowering, and so easy to eat and enjoy. Our garden-inspired gyoza are fun and easy to make. The filling is all about the flavours of the caramelized mushrooms, cabbage, ginger, sesame, and apples, and the finished dumplings get a wonderful slathering of lemon chili garlic butter. Get your family and friends involved in a production line to turn out as many dumplings as you all can . . . many hands make many dumplings!

MAKES ABOUT 2 DOZEN DUMPLINGS

LEMON CHILI GARLIC BUTTER

8 tablespoons unsalted butter, at
    room temperature
½ fresh serrano chili, finely chopped
1 garlic clove, minced
Zest and juice of ½ lemon
Salt and cracked black pepper

CABBAGE AND APPLE GYOZA

4 tablespoons vegetable oil, divided,
    plus more as needed for frying
1 cup finely chopped shiitake
    mushrooms
¼ cup finely diced white onion
2 cups finely chopped savoy or green
    cabbage
1½ cups grated peeled Gala apple
3 garlic cloves, minced
1 tablespoon grated peeled fresh
    ginger
2 tablespoons tamari
1 tablespoon yellow miso
1 tablespoon seasoned rice vinegar
1 tablespoon toasted sesame oil
½ cup finely minced green onions
1 package gyoza wrappers (25 to
    30 wrappers)

TAMARI GREEN ONION
DIPPING SAUCE
(MAKES ABOUT ½ CUP)

¼ cup tamari
¼ cup seasoned rice vinegar
1 teaspoon sriracha sauce
2 tablespoons thinly sliced green
    onions

1. **Make the lemon chili garlic butter:** In a small bowl, mix together the butter, chili, garlic, and lemon zest and juice until smooth. Season well with salt and pepper. Set aside or store in an airtight container in the refrigerator for up to 2 weeks.

2. **Make the cabbage and apple filling:** Heat 2 tablespoons of the the vegetable oil in a large non-stick skillet over medium heat. Add the mushrooms and white onion and cook, stirring occasionally, until the mushrooms are soft and slightly caramelized, about 5 minutes. Add the cabbage, apple, garlic, and ginger. Cook, stirring, until the vegetables are soft, about 10 minutes.

3. In a small bowl, whisk together the tamari, miso, rice vinegar, and sesame oil. Add the tamari mixture and green onions to the vegetable mixture and stir to combine. Remove from the heat and let cool.

4. **Fold the dumplings:** Have ready a small bowl of water. Lightly dust a baking sheet with flour (to prevent the dumplings from sticking). Spoon 1 tablespoon of the filling in the centre of a gyoza wrapper. Using your finger or a pastry brush, brush a little water over the top half of the wrapper, fold it over the filling, and pinch it closed to seal, making 3 to 5 pleats. Place the dumpling on the floured baking sheet. Repeat with the remaining wrappers and filling. (You can freeze the dumplings on the baking sheet until frozen, then transfer to a resealable plastic bag and store in the freezer for up to 2 months.)

5. **Cook the dumplings:** Wipe the skillet clean and in it heat the remaining 2 tablespoons vegetable oil over medium-high heat. Working in batches of about 12 dumplings at a time to avoid crowding the pan, place the dumplings in the pan and cook, without stirring, for 2 minutes. Pour ¼ cup of water into the pan, cover with a lid, reduce the heat to low, and steam the dumplings for 2 to 3 minutes, until the water has evaporated.

6. Remove the lid, increase the heat to high, and continue cooking until the bottoms of the dumplings are golden and crisp, about 2 minutes. Add 1 to 2 teaspoons of the lemon chili garlic butter, let it melt, then toss the gyoza in the butter. Transfer the dumplings to a plate and pour the melted butter over them. Wipe the pan clean with paper towel and repeat to fry the remaining dumplings, adding more vegetable oil as needed between batches, and tossing with more lemon chili garlic butter.

7. **Meanwhile, make the tamari green onion dipping sauce:** In a small bowl, stir together the tamari, rice vinegar, sriracha, and green onions until combined.

8. Serve the dumplings with the tamari green onion sauce for dipping.

NOTE: This recipe is a great one for batch cooking. The dumplings freeze well and can be cooked from frozen for a quick dinner or starter.

Fried Green Tomato Sliders with Zucchini Relish and Spicy Rémoulade Sauce

Frying green tomatoes was originally a way to use up tomatoes that hadn't ripened by season's end. We like to use a firmer heirloom variety, Green Zebra, all season long. Its flesh is bright green, sweet but with a sharp bite. It has the perfect texture when fried and tastes that much better all dressed up with this zippy zucchini relish and creamy rémoulade mayonnaise.

MAKES 12 SLIDERS

ZUCCHINI RELISH
(MAKES ABOUT 2 CUPS)

2½ cups grated zucchini

½ cup thinly sliced red onion

¼ cup thinly sliced red bell pepper

1 tablespoon salt

½ cup granulated sugar

¼ teaspoon ground turmeric

¼ teaspoon dry mustard

¼ teaspoon mustard seeds

¼ teaspoon cracked black pepper

¼ teaspoon celery seeds

½ cup apple cider vinegar

SPICY RÉMOULADE SAUCE
(MAKES ABOUT 1 CUP)

1 cup mayonnaise

1 tablespoon sriracha sauce

2 tablespoons minced drained capers

2 tablespoons chopped gherkins

1 tablespoon chopped fresh dill

1 tablespoon chopped fresh flat-leaf parsley

Zest and juice of 2 lemons

Kosher salt and cracked black pepper

FRIED GREEN TOMATOES

⅓ cup all-purpose flour

2 large eggs

½ cup buttermilk or whole milk

1½ cups panko breadcrumbs

⅓ cup cornmeal

1 teaspoon nutritional yeast

1 teaspoon garlic powder

1 teaspoon dry mustard

½ teaspoon chili powder

¼ teaspoon smoked paprika

2 teaspoons kosher salt, plus more for seasoning

½ teaspoon cracked black pepper, plus more for seasoning

4 small Green Zebra tomatoes or unripe green tomatoes, sliced into rounds (you need 12 slices)

½ cup vegetable oil, for frying

FOR THE SLIDERS

12 Aunt Lucy's Milk Buns (½ batch; page 78) or store-bought slider buns

4 tablespoons unsalted butter, melted, for brushing

Iceberg lettuce, thinly sliced

1. **Make the zucchini relish:** Place the grated zucchini, red onion, and bell pepper in a large bowl. Sprinkle with the salt and mix well. Let sit at room temperature until the zucchini softens and releases some of its juices, 30 to 45 minutes. Rinse thoroughly in a large strainer and drain well. Use the back of a spoon to push the mixture against the strainer to release as much liquid as you can.

2. Transfer the zucchini mixture to a large stock pot. Add the sugar, turmeric, dry mustard, mustard seeds, black pepper, celery seeds, and apple cider vinegar. Stir to incorporate. Bring to a boil, then reduce the heat to a simmer and cook, uncovered and stirring occasionally, for 30 minutes or until the relish has thickened. Remove from the heat and let cool before using. Set aside or store in an airtight container in the refrigerator for up to 1 month.

3. **Make the spicy rémoulade sauce:** In a small bowl, whisk together the mayonnaise, sriracha, capers, gherkins, dill, parsley, and lemon zest and juice. Season to taste with salt and pepper. Set aside or store in an airtight container for up to 2 weeks.

4. **Make the fried green tomatoes:** Set out 3 shallow medium bowls. In the first bowl, stir together the flour and salt and pepper to taste. In the second bowl, whisk together the eggs and buttermilk. In the third bowl, stir together the panko, cornmeal, nutritional yeast, garlic power, dry mustard, chili powder, smoked paprika, salt, and pepper.

5. Working with one slice at a time, dredge the tomato in the flour, turning to lightly coat. Dip the tomato in the egg mixture, turning to completely coat. Dredge in the seasoned panko, coating both sides. Transfer to a plate.

6. Heat the vegetable oil in a large heavy skillet over medium-high heat. When the oil is hot, working in batches to avoid crowding the pan, fry the tomatoes until golden brown, about 3 minutes per side. Transfer to a plate lined with paper towel to absorb excess oil.

7. Heat a large nonstick skillet over medium heat. Slice the buns in half horizontally. Brush some melted butter on both cut sides. Working in batches, place the buns buttered side down in the pan and toast until golden brown.

8. **Assemble the sliders:** Arrange the bottoms of the buns on a large serving platter. Spread some of the spicy rémoulade sauce on each of the bottoms, then top each with lettuce, a fried green tomato, and some zucchini relish. Finish the sliders with the tops.

Deep-Dish Cheesy Pan Pizza with Tomatoes, Olives, and Basil

A deep-dish pizza is exactly what it sounds like—a deep, deliciously chewy base to hold your favourite toppings. That perfect deep crust allows the pie to hold a lot of sauce, cheese, and toppings, making the entire pizza so incredibly satisfying. You can customize the toppings to your heart's content.

1. **Make the dough:** In the bowl of a stand mixer fitted with the dough hook, stir together the all-purpose flour, semolina flour, yeast, and salt. Pour the warm water and olive oil into the bowl. Starting on low speed, mix for 2 minutes, then increase speed to medium and mix for another 3 minutes, until the dough forms a ball. Transfer the dough to a large oiled bowl and cover with plastic wrap. Let rest in a warm, draft-free place until doubled in size, 45 to 60 minutes.

2. Once the dough has doubled in size, you are ready to make your pizza. (Alternatively, you can wrap the dough tightly in plastic wrap and store in the refrigerator for up to 3 days. Bring to room temperature before using.) Preheat the oven to 425°F (220°C). Generously grease the base and sides of a 12-inch deep-dish pizza pan or cast-iron skillet.

3. Transfer the dough to the prepared pan and stretch it toward the edges until it starts to shrink back. Cover the dough with plastic wrap and let rest for 15 minutes.

4. Once again stretch the dough to cover the bottom of the pan, then gently push the dough up the sides of the pan. Cover again and let the dough rest for another 15 minutes.

5. Uncover and bake the crust for 10 minutes or until golden brown. Remove from the oven. (You are not cooking it completely at this point.)

6. **Assemble and bake the pizza:** In a large bowl, combine the tomatoes, ¾ cup of the pizza sauce, olives, garlic, oregano, and basil and mix well. Season to taste with salt and pepper.

7. Evenly scatter 1 cup of the mozzarella over the base of the dough. Spread the remaining ¾ cup pizza sauce over the cheese, then scatter the remaining 1 cup mozzarella over top. Spread the tomato mixture over the mozzarella. Sprinkle with the Parmesan and drizzle with olive oil.

8. Bake until the filling is bubbly and the cheese is golden brown, about 25 minutes. Carefully lift the pizza out of the pan and onto a rack. Let the pizza cool for about 15 minutes before slicing. Garnish with the basil.

MAKES ONE 12-INCH DEEP-DISH PIZZA, SERVES 4 TO 6

DOUGH

4 cups all-purpose flour

⅓ cup semolina flour

1 tablespoon active dry yeast

1¾ teaspoons salt

1½ cups warm water

⅓ cup olive oil

FILLING

3 cups cherry tomatoes, halved

1½ cups Pizza Sauce (page 142), divided

¼ cup green olives, pitted and halved

2 garlic cloves, minced

1 teaspoon finely chopped fresh oregano

1 teaspoon finely chopped fresh basil

Salt and cracked black pepper

2 cups grated mozzarella cheese, divided

1 cup grated Parmesan cheese

2 tablespoons olive oil

¼ cup fresh basil leaves, for garnish

NOTE: A cast-iron skillet or a springform pan are excellent for making deep-dish pizzas, as they allow the bottom and sides of the crust to crisp and reach a perfect golden brown.

Pizza Sauce

Makes about 3 cups

This simple from-scratch pizza sauce is astoundingly easy and inexpensive to make, yet it tastes like you just came back from making it in Italy! Definitely a keeper according to our daughters Addie and Gemma, who are both the pizza aficionados of the family.

2 tablespoons extra-virgin olive oil
1 sweet onion, minced
3 garlic cloves, minced
1 can (5.5 ounces/156 mL) tomato paste
1 can (28 ounces/796 mL) crushed tomatoes
1 tablespoon chopped fresh oregano
Salt and cracked black pepper

1. Heat the olive oil in a medium pot over medium heat. Add the onions and cook, stirring, until soft and translucent, 4 to 5 minutes. Add the garlic and cook until fragrant, 1 minute more.

2. Reduce the heat to medium-low. Add the tomato paste and stir until it darkens slightly. Stir in the crushed tomatoes and bring the mixture to a simmer. Stir in the oregano and simmer until the sauce develops good flavour, 20 to 25 minutes. Season to taste with salt and pepper. Remove from the heat and let cool. If not using soon, store in an airtight container in the refrigerator for up to 1 week.

Vegetarian Spring Rolls with Ginger Plum Sauce

These flaky spring rolls are one of the most iconic foods in Chinese cuisine. This is our take on the classic, packed with our garden's vegetables. They never fail to tantalize our taste buds, especially because the ginger plum sauce is homemade!

MAKES 12 SPRING ROLLS

**GINGER PLUM SAUCE
(MAKES ABOUT 2 CUPS)**

1 pound (450 g) plums (any variety), pitted and chopped

¼ cup lightly packed brown sugar

¼ cup apple cider vinegar

1 tablespoon soy sauce

1 garlic clove, minced

1 tablespoon minced peeled fresh ginger

1 teaspoon five-spice powder

¼ teaspoon red chili flakes

VEGETARIAN SPRING ROLLS

2 tablespoons soy sauce

2 teaspoons cornstarch

2 tablespoons vegetable oil, plus about 4 cups for deep-frying

1 cup thinly sliced shiitake mushrooms

2 garlic cloves, finely chopped

1 tablespoon finely chopped peeled fresh ginger

2 cups finely shredded green cabbage

1 large carrot, peeled and julienned

1 celery stalk, julienned

1 cup bean sprouts

3 green onions, finely chopped

12 (6-inch) spring roll wrappers

2 egg whites, lightly beaten

— continued —

1. **Make the ginger plum sauce:** In a medium saucepan, stir together the plums, brown sugar, apple cider vinegar, soy sauce, garlic, ginger, five-spice powder, and chili flakes. Bring to a boil over medium heat, then reduce the heat to low and simmer, stirring occasionally, for 20 minutes or until the plums are soft and the sauce has thickened slightly. Remove from the heat and let cool slightly.

2. Pour the sauce into a food processor or high-speed blender and purée until smooth. (Be careful; it will be hot.) Return the sauce to the saucepan and bring to a simmer over medium heat, stirring often to prevent sticking. Cook until the sauce is thick and jammy, about 10 minutes. Remove from the heat and let cool. Set aside or store in an airtight container in the refrigerator for up to 3 weeks.

3. **Make the spring roll filling:** In a measuring cup, stir together the soy sauce and cornstarch until there are no lumps. Set aside.

4. Heat the vegetable oil in a large sauté pan over medium-high heat. Add the mushrooms, garlic, and ginger and sauté until the mushrooms are caramelized, 2 minutes. Add the cabbage, carrot, and celery and sauté until the vegetables have softened, another 3 to 4 minutes. Add the bean sprouts and green onions and stir for 1 minute.

5. Give the soy sauce mixture a stir and pour it over the vegetables. Stir together for 1 minute. Scrape the filling into a large bowl. Refrigerate until completely cool. Drain any excess liquid.

6. **Assemble the spring rolls:** On a work surface, arrange a spring roll wrapper with one corner facing you. Brush some of the egg white along all the edges. Place about 3 tablespoons of the filling on the lower third of the wrapper. Bring the bottom corner of the wrapper up and over the filling. Fold in the sides of the wrapper and roll tightly into a spring roll. Make sure to maintain the tension as you roll so it's tight. Brush egg white along the seal. Repeat with the remaining wrappers and filling. At this stage, the spring rolls can be stored, layered between parchment paper and wrapped in plastic wrap, in the refrigerator for up to 4 hours before deep-frying.

7. **Deep-fry the spring rolls:** Preheat the oven to 200°F (100°C). Line a baking sheet with parchment paper.

8. Heat 4 cups of vegetable oil in a deep medium saucepan until it reaches 375°F (190°C) on a deep-fry thermometer. Once the oil is hot, working in batches of 6, deep-fry the spring rolls, turning often, until crispy all over, 4 to 5 minutes. Briefly drain on paper towel, then place on the lined baking sheet and keep warm in the oven while you fry the remaining spring rolls.

9. Serve the spring rolls immediately with the ginger plum sauce for dipping.

NOTE: Controlling the heat during deep-frying is important to ensure that the spring rolls fry to an even golden-brown colour and don't soak up too much oil. The spring rolls will darken slightly as they cool, so do not overcook them.

Uncooked spring rolls can be frozen in a single layer on a baking sheet lined with parchment paper. Once frozen, transfer them to a resealable freezer bag and store in the freezer for up to 4 months. Fry the spring rolls from frozen.

Potato Perogies with Beet Sauerkraut, Caramelized Onions, and Sour Cream

Lora and her Babka hands-down make the best perogies! Years of cooking alongside her Babka has taught Lora so much about her grandmother's life, her stories, her Polish-Ukrainian heritage, and the recipes that have been family favourites for generations. Watching and listening to the banter and laughs these two incredible women share while spending precious time together is simply amazing. Some of our fondest memories of cooking in our kitchen are those times cooking with Babka.

MAKES 4 DOZEN PEROGIES

**BEET SAUERKRAUT
(MAKES 3 CUPS)**

3 cups finely chopped green
    cabbage (reserve 1 whole leaf)
1 cup grated peeled red beets
¼ cup thinly sliced red onion
1 teaspoon kosher salt

PEROGY DOUGH

3 cups all-purpose flour, plus more for
    dusting
1 cup cold water
1 tablespoon vegetable oil
1 egg
Pinch of salt

**CARAMELIZED ONIONS
(MAKES ABOUT 2 CUPS)**

3 tablespoons unsalted butter
3 cups thinly sliced white onions
Salt and cracked black pepper

PEROGY FILLING

4 russet potatoes, peeled and cubed
3 tablespoons unsalted butter, at
    room temperature
1 tablespoon chopped fresh dill
Salt and cracked black pepper

FOR FINISHING

2 to 4 tablespoons unsalted butter,
    for frying
Sour cream, for serving
¼ cup chopped fresh dill, for garnish

— continued —

1. **Make the beet sauerkraut:** Place the cabbage, beets, and red onion in a large bowl. Sprinkle with the kosher salt and massage it into the vegetables. Cover with plastic wrap and let sit on the counter, mixing occasionally, until the cabbage has wilted and released a little juice, 1 to 2 hours. Transfer the cabbage mixture and any juices to a clean 4-cup mason jar and pack it down with a tamper or the end of a wooden spoon. Top with the whole cabbage leaf and gently push it down to submerge the mixture in its juices. The mixture should be covered with liquid, with at least 1 inch of headspace. Loosely cover with the lid, place the jar on a small baking sheet, and let sit in a cool (65° to 72°F/18° to 22°C), dark place for 3 to 5 days.

2. After 3 or 4 days, check for activity. When you tap the jar, tiny bubbles should rise to the top, indicating it is fermenting. The longer it ferments, the more sour it will taste. Once fermented to the desired sourness, discard the cabbage leaf, seal the jar, and chill the sauerkraut in the refrigerator for at least 8 hours or overnight before using. Once opened, the sauerkraut can be stored in the refrigerator for up to 3 months.

3. **Make the perogy dough:** In a large bowl, combine the flour, water, vegetable oil, egg, and salt and stir together with a wooden spoon until a soft dough forms. Turn the dough out onto a lightly floured work surface and knead the dough until it is very elastic, 10 to 12 minutes. Form the dough into a smooth ball. Place the dough in an oiled medium bowl, cover with plastic wrap, and let rest for 1 hour at room temperature.

4. **Meanwhile, make the caramelized onions:** Melt the butter in a medium skillet over medium heat. Add the onions and cook, stirring often, until starting to soften, about 5 minutes. Reduce the heat to medium-low and cook, stirring often, until deep golden and a jam-like consistency, 45 to 50 minutes. Season to taste with salt and pepper. Remove from the heat and set aside.

5. **Meanwhile, make the perogy filling:** Place the potatoes in a large pot of cold salted water. Bring to a boil, then reduce the heat and simmer for about 15 minutes, until the potatoes are tender. Drain the potatoes, return to the pot, and mash with the butter and dill. Season to taste with salt and pepper.

6. **Make the perogies:** On a lightly-floured work surface, divide the dough into 2 equal portions. (Each portion is enough to make 24 perogies. At this stage, the dough can be wrapped in plastic wrap and frozen for up to 2 months. If frozen, remove from the freezer 1 hour before making the perogies.) Dust one portion of dough with flour and cover with plastic wrap to prevent it from drying out. Divide the other portion of dough into 12 pieces and roll into balls. Use a rolling pin to roll the balls out into rounds, ⅛ inch thick.

7. Place 1 tablespoon of the filling on each circle. Fold the circle in half; pinch the edges together tightly, making sure they are well sealed. Cover with plastic wrap. Repeat with the second portion of dough and the remaining filling.

8. Lightly oil a baking sheet. Bring a large pot of water to a boil. Working in batches to avoid crowding the pot, drop the perogies into the boiling water and boil for about 5 minutes until they float to the surface. Using a slotted spoon, transfer the perogies to the oiled baking sheet.

9. **Fry the perogies and finish:** Reheat the caramelized onions. Melt 1 or 2 tablespoons of butter in a large skillet over medium-high heat. Working in batches, add just enough perogies to fit into the pan in a single layer and cook until caramelized and golden brown, 1 to 2 minutes per side. Transfer to a plate and keep warm. Repeat with the remaining pierogies, adding more butter to the pan as needed. Serve with the warm caramelized onions, beet sauerkraut, and sour cream. Garnish with the dill.

NOTE: This recipe makes a lot of perogies, but uncooked perogies freeze well. Once shaped, place them on a baking sheet lined with parchment paper and freeze. Once frozen, transfer the perogies to a resealable plastic bag (remove as much air as possible) and store in the freezer for up to 4 months. When you have a craving, simply pull the frozen perogies from the freezer and drop them into a pot of boiling water, adding another minute to the boiling time.

Sweet Potato Fries with Chipotle Mayonnaise

Baked sweet potato fries are our kids' favourite after-school snack, which is just fine with us! These fries are a healthy alternative to standard french fries and they get devoured just as quickly. This is a crowd-pleasing appetizer that everyone will enjoy.

1. **Make the chipotle mayonnaise:** In a food processor, combine the yogurt, mayonnaise, chipotle pepper, lime juice, and honey and blend until smooth. Season to taste with salt and pepper. Store in an airtight container in the refrigerator for up to 2 weeks.

2. **Make the sweet potato fries:** Preheat the oven to 400°F (200°C). Line a baking sheet with parchment paper.

3. Scrub the sweet potatoes under cold running water and pat dry. Peel the potatoes and cut lengthwise into ¼-inch-thick batons.

4. Transfer the batons to a medium bowl. Add the olive oil, garlic powder, and smoked paprika. Season well with salt and pepper. Toss to coat evenly. Spread the fries in a single layer on the lined baking sheet and bake until lightly browned on the outside and soft and tender inside, 25 to 30 minutes, tossing halfway through.

5. Transfer the fries to a serving dish. Sprinkle with the Parmesan and garnish with the parsley. Serve with the chipotle mayonnaise for dipping.

SERVES 4 TO 6

**CHIPOTLE MAYONNAISE
(MAKES ABOUT ¾ CUP)**

½ cup plain full-fat Greek yogurt

½ cup mayonnaise

1 chipotle pepper in adobo sauce

1 tablespoon fresh lime juice

2 teaspoons liquid honey

Salt and cracked black pepper

SWEET POTATO FRIES

2 pounds (900 g) sweet potatoes
(about 2 medium-large potatoes)

3 tablespoons olive oil

1 teaspoon garlic powder

1 teaspoon smoked paprika

Salt and cracked black pepper

¼ cup grated Parmesan cheese

2 tablespoons chopped fresh flat-leaf
parsley, for garnish

Korean-Style Eggplant and Mushroom Lettuce Wraps

SERVES 4 TO 6

2 green onions, finely chopped

2 garlic cloves, finely chopped

2 teaspoons grated peeled fresh ginger

2 tablespoons soy sauce

1 tablespoon sesame oil

1 tablespoon brown sugar

2 teaspoons gochujang (see Note)

1 teaspoon red wine vinegar

Zest and juice of 1 orange

1 pound (450 g) Korean eggplant (3 to 4 eggplants), cut into ½-inch cubes

1 tablespoon salt, plus more for seasoning

3 tablespoons canola oil, divided, for cooking

2 shallots, finely chopped

1 cup quartered cremini mushrooms

FOR SERVING

1 large head Bibb lettuce, leaves separated

1 cup julienned peeled carrots

¼ cup thinly sliced radishes

1 jalapeño pepper, seeded if desired and thinly sliced

Leaves from 1 bunch fresh mint

Chopped fresh chives (optional)

These quick and easy to whip up lettuce wraps might be our all-time favourite summer appetizers—minimal cooking, and maximum flavour and freshness. Our vegetarian take on the popular Korean savoury dish bulgogi uses mushrooms and eggplant instead of meat. Crisp Bibb lettuce leaves are the perfect vessel to hold the veggies that have been cooked down with that traditional and familiar Korean BBQ sauce.

1. In a medium bowl, stir together the green onions, garlic, ginger, soy sauce, sesame oil, brown sugar, gochujang, red wine vinegar, and orange zest and juice. Set aside the sauce.

2. Put the eggplant in a large bowl. Sprinkle with the salt and toss well to coat. Let sit for 15 minutes, tossing every 5 minutes. Drain the eggplant in a colander. Squeeze out excess liquid from the eggplant and return it to the bowl.

3. Heat 2 tablespoons of the canola oil in a large, heavy skillet over medium-high heat, swirling the pan to evenly coat the bottom. Add the shallots and mushrooms and sauté until the shallots have softened and the mushrooms start to caramelize, 4 to 5 minutes. Add the eggplant and the remaining 1 tablespoon canola oil and sauté until the eggplant is lightly browned, 2 to 3 minutes.

4. Reduce the heat to medium. Pour in the reserved sauce, stir well, and continue to sauté until the eggplant and mushrooms are cooked through and glazed and any excess sauce has evaporated, 5 to 6 minutes. Transfer the eggplant mixture to a serving bowl.

5. Serve the eggplant with the lettuce leaves, carrots, radishes, jalapeños, mint, and chives (if using) for making lettuce wraps.

NOTE: Gochujang, a staple of Korean cooking, is a fermented red chili paste made from spicy Korean chili peppers and glutinous rice. It is one of the key ingredients in this sauce and adds a slightly salty, spicy, and umami-rich layer of flavour. The sauce is equally delicious on squash, cauliflower, or broccoli if you want to mix things up a bit.

Soups

Soba Noodle Soup with Snow Peas, Bok Choy, and Ginger Miso Broth

This umami-bursting aromatic soup is extremely satisfying and so easy to make. The ginger, miso, and soy create a surprisingly complex and layered broth that reminds us of the look and taste of a well-prepared rich consommé. Protein-rich buckwheat soba noodles add a sweet nuttiness and chewy texture to the soup. We love packing lots of green veg into this soup, and tiny snow peas add a nice little crunch.

1. In a large pot, combine the vegetable stock, miso, and soy sauce and bring to a boil over high heat. Add the ginger, garlic, and onion, then reduce the heat to medium-low and gently simmer for 15 minutes.

2. Meanwhile, bring a medium pot of water to a boil. Add the soba noodles and cook until al dente, about 5 minutes. Drain the noodles and divide among bowls.

3. Increase the heat of the broth to high. Add the bok choy and cook until bright green and tender, about 2 minutes. Add the snow peas, spinach, and green onions and stir together. Remove from the heat. Adjust the seasoning by adding more soy sauce if needed.

4. Using tongs, evenly divide the bok choy over the noodles. Ladle the hot broth over the noodles and garnish with nori, shichimi togarashi, and pea shoots, if using.

SERVES 4 TO 6

6 cups Vegetable Stock (page 162 or store-bought)
¼ cup white miso
¼ cup soy sauce, plus more to taste
1 (1-inch) piece fresh ginger, peeled and julienned
1 garlic clove, minced
½ white onion, thinly sliced
4 ounces (115 g) dried soba noodles
4 to 6 baby bok choy, halved lengthwise
2 cups snow peas, julienned
2 cups baby spinach
4 green onions, thinly sliced

GARNISHES

2 nori sheets, cut into 1-inch-wide strips
Shichimi togarashi
Pea shoots (optional)

NOTE: We enjoy this soup all year round as we swap out different veggies as the seasons change. Carrots, broccoli, green beans, kale, and mushrooms are all excellent additions.

Celery Root Soup with Brown Butter Sunflower Seed Pesto and Hickory Sticks

SERVES 8

**BROWN BUTTER
SUNFLOWER SEED PESTO
(MAKES ABOUT ¾ CUP)**

2 tablespoons unsalted butter

¼ cup sunflower seeds

¼ teaspoon red chili flakes

½ cup chopped fresh flat-leaf parsley

2 teaspoons fresh lemon juice

Salt and cracked black pepper

¼ cup olive oil

2 tablespoons grated Parmesan
cheese (optional)

CELERY ROOT SOUP

2 tablespoons unsalted butter

1 tablespoon olive oil

1 large yellow onion, finely diced

1 celery stalk, finely diced

1 medium leek (white and light green
parts only), thinly sliced

1 large celery root, peeled and diced
(about 4 cups)

8 cups Vegetable Stock (page 162 or
store-bought)

Kosher salt and cracked black pepper

GARNISHES

Hickory Sticks

Sunflower petals (optional)

Sunflowers grow all over our property and they are one of the most beautiful and happy things to see, some growing to sixteen feet tall! They certainly cheer up our garden, and inspired this cozy vegetable soup. Celery root, also known as celeriac, is often overlooked, which is a shame because its flesh has a deliciously celery-like flavour. The nutty brown butter sunflower seed pesto adds a totally different dimension to this simple but satisfying soup—a soup that will not disappoint and will make you so very happy.

1. **Make the brown butter sunflower seed pesto:** Melt the butter in a small skillet over medium heat. Add the sunflower seeds and cook, swirling the pan occasionally, until the sunflower seeds are well toasted and the butter is browned and smells nutty, 3 to 4 minutes. Remove from the heat. Sprinkle in the chili flakes and let cool for 10 minutes. Add the parsley and lemon juice, then season to taste with salt and pepper.

2. Transfer the mixture to a small blender or food processor. Add the olive oil and Parmesan (if using) and pulse until smooth. Set aside or store in an airtight container in the refrigerator for up to 1 week.

3. **Make the celery root soup:** Melt the butter with the olive oil in a large, heavy pot over medium heat. Add the onions, celery, and leeks and cook, stirring occasionally, until tender, about 5 minutes. Add the celery root and vegetable stock and bring to a boil. Season to taste with kosher salt and pepper. Once the soup reaches a boil, reduce the heat to medium-low and simmer, stirring occasionally, until the vegetables are very tender, about 20 minutes. Remove from the heat. Using an immersion blender, carefully purée until smooth. (Alternatively, allow the soup to cool until no longer steaming. Working in batches, blend the soup in a high-speed blender. See Note.)

4. Return the soup to the pot and reheat over medium heat. Taste and adjust seasoning if needed. Ladle the soup into bowls and garnish with a drizzle of brown butter sunflower seed pesto, Hickory Sticks, and sunflower petals, if using.

NOTE: Prevent a blender explosion when blending hot liquids: only fill the blender jar halfway, cover the lid firmly with a kitchen towel, start blending on the lowest speed, then gradually increase the speed.

Roasted Cauliflower Soup with Harissa, Toasted Hazelnuts, and Kale Chips

Creamy, velvety cauliflower soup just got tastier. This soup is cozy yet complex in flavour. The small extra step of roasting the cauliflower truly makes all the difference, adding such great depth of flavour and really bringing out those caramelized notes in the soup. The harissa paste adds just enough spice and heat to the soup as well as yet another layer of incredibly complementary flavour.

1. **Make the kale chips:** Preheat the oven to 325°F (160°C). Line a baking sheet with parchment paper.

2. Cut out the centre rib and stems from each kale leaf and discard. Tear or cut the leaves into bite-size pieces. Put the kale on the lined baking sheet.

3. In a small bowl, stir together the olive oil, chili powder, garlic powder, and salt. Pour the mixture over the kale and, using your hands, massage the kale until evenly coated. Spread the kale in a single layer (not overlapping) on the baking sheet. Bake until the kale is crisp and the edges are slightly browned, 12 to 20 minutes; be careful that they don't burn. Remove from the oven; increase the oven temperature to 425°F (220°C). Let the kale chips cool to room temperature. Sprinkle with salt to taste.

4. **Make the roasted cauliflower soup:** Line a baking sheet with parchment paper. In a large bowl, toss the cauliflower with 3 tablespoons of the olive oil until evenly coated. Spread the cauliflower in a single layer on the lined baking sheet. Season lightly with salt and pepper. Roast until the cauliflower is tender and caramelized around the edges, 25 to 35 minutes, tossing halfway through. Remove from the oven and reserve 6 or 8 of the best florets for garnish.

5. Meanwhile, halfway through roasting the cauliflower, melt the butter with the remaining 1 tablespoon olive oil in a large pot over medium heat. Add the onions and cook, stirring occasionally, until softened and starting to caramelize, 8 to 10 minutes. Add the garlic, harissa paste, tomato paste, chili flakes, and cumin and cook, stirring constantly, until fragrant, about 1 minute. Add the vegetable stock and thyme.

6. Add the roasted cauliflower to the pot. Increase the heat to medium-high and bring to a simmer, then reduce the heat to maintain a gentle simmer. Cook, uncovered, stirring occasionally, for 20 minutes to give the flavours time to meld. Remove from the heat and let cool for a few minutes. Discard the thyme sprigs.

7. Working in batches, carefully transfer the hot soup to a high-speed blender. Blend until smooth. Add the lemon juice and season with salt and pepper to taste. Blend again.

8. Ladle the soup into warm bowls. Garnish with the reserved roasted cauliflower florets, hazelnuts, and kale chips.

SERVES 6 TO 8

**KALE CHIPS
(MAKES ABOUT 8 CUPS)**

1 bunch lacinato kale, washed and patted dry

2 tablespoons olive oil

½ teaspoon chili powder

½ teaspoon garlic powder

½ teaspoon salt

ROASTED CAULIFLOWER SOUP

1 large head cauliflower (about 2 pounds/900 g), cut into bite-size florets

4 tablespoons olive oil, divided

Salt and cracked black pepper

2 tablespoons unsalted butter

2 yellow onions, thinly sliced

4 garlic cloves, finely chopped

2 tablespoons Harissa Paste (page 163 or store-bought)

1 tablespoon tomato paste

½ teaspoon red chili flakes

½ teaspoon ground cumin

6 cups Vegetable Stock (page 162 or store-bought)

2 sprigs fresh thyme

1 tablespoon fresh lemon juice, more if needed

Toasted hazelnuts, roughly chopped, for garnish

Vegetable Stock

Makes about 8 cups

Every time we make vegetable stock, we wonder why people ever bother buying it in the store. It is so easy! Chop up some vegetables, cover with water, and simmer. You will have enough stock to make soups, casseroles, and pilafs for weeks to come, and all in just a little over an hour.

 6 carrots, cut into 1-inch pieces
 4 celery stalks, thinly sliced
 2 leeks (white part only), thinly sliced
 3 white onions, thinly sliced
 2 cups mushrooms or mushroom stems
 6 sprigs fresh flat-leaf parsley
 4 sprigs fresh thyme
 1 star anise
 5 white peppercorns
 1 teaspoon fennel seeds
 ½ lemon, sliced

1. Combine the carrots, celery, leeks, onions, and mushrooms in a stock pot. Add enough water to cover the vegetables. Bring to a boil over medium-high heat.

2. Once boiling, reduce the heat to low and simmer for 50 minutes. Add the parsley, thyme, star anise, peppercorns, and fennel seeds and simmer for another 10 minutes. Remove from the heat and stir in the lemon slices.

3. Strain the stock through a fine-mesh sieve into a large container. Discard the solids. Set the container in a sink of ice water to cool as quickly as possible. Store the cooled stock in airtight containers in the refrigerator for up to 1 week or in the freezer for up to 3 months.

Harissa Paste

Makes about 1 cup

Harissa is a hot chili paste found in many North African cuisines. Unlike other spicy pastes, ours is not too fiery and delivers a decadent smokiness that you will come to love and rely on.

4 red bell peppers, roasted, seeded, and chopped
3 tablespoons extra-virgin olive oil
4 teaspoons sriracha sauce
1 tablespoon minced garlic
2 teaspoons ground cumin
1 teaspoon ground cardamom
1 teaspoon ground coriander
Kosher salt and cracked black pepper

1. In a food processor or blender, combine the bell peppers, olive oil, sriracha, garlic, cumin, cardamom, and coriander. Blend until smooth. Season with salt and pepper. Store in an airtight container in the refrigerator for up to 1 month.

Ribollita

Tuscany is a magical place. It is stunningly breathtaking. When Lynn arrived on a sunny fall afternoon several years ago to visit her incredibly talented, generous, inspiring, and creative friend Debbie Travis, it was lunchtime and a chance to catch up. Words cannot express what an impact Tuscany and Debbie have had on Lynn's life, bringing her so much joy. That day, Lynn and Debbie shared lots of conversation, laughs, and wine with Debbie's husband Hans and her bestie Jacky Brown. Ribollita, a traditional Tuscan soup, was served, prepared with vegetables from Debbie's garden and topped with her delicious rich peppery olive oil. It was superb!

1. **Make the basil pesto:** Combine the basil, pine nuts, and garlic in a food processor and process until very finely minced. With the processor running, slowly add the olive oil and process until the mixture is smooth. Add the Parmesan and process very briefly, just long enough to combine. Season to taste with salt and pepper. Set aside or store in an airtight container in the refrigerator for 2 weeks or in the freezer for up to 3 months.

2. **Make the ribollita:** Heat the olive oil in a large pot over medium heat. Add the onions and garlic and cook, stirring occasionally, until softened, 6 to 8 minutes. Add the carrots, celery, and chili flakes and cook until the carrots are tender, about 5 minutes.

3. Add the tomatoes with their juices, kale, green beans, cannellini beans, vegetable stock, thyme, and rosemary. Bring to a boil over medium-high heat, then reduce the heat to low and simmer, uncovered, for 20 minutes. Discard the thyme and rosemary sprigs. Stir in the parsley and season with salt and pepper to taste.

4. Ladle the soup into bowls. Drizzle with the basil pesto or olive oil. Generously sprinkle with the cheese. Serve with olive rosemary focaccia.

SERVES 8

BASIL PESTO (MAKES 2 CUPS)

2 cups tightly packed fresh basil leaves

¼ cup pine nuts, toasted

2 garlic cloves

½ cup olive oil

½ cup grated Parmesan cheese

Salt and cracked black pepper

RIBOLLITA

¼ cup extra-virgin olive oil

1 yellow onion, chopped

3 garlic cloves, chopped

1 carrot, peeled and chopped

2 celery stalks, chopped

¼ teaspoon red chili flakes

4 cups chopped fresh Roma tomatoes, juices reserved

4 cups finely chopped lacinato kale

1 cup green beans cut into ½-inch pieces

2 cups cooked cannellini beans (or two 19-ounce/540 mL cans, rinsed and drained)

6 cups Vegetable Stock (page 162 or store-bought)

2 sprigs fresh thyme

1 sprig fresh rosemary

½ cup chopped fresh flat-leaf parsley

Salt and cracked black pepper

Basil Pesto (recipe above) or extra-virgin olive oil, for garnish

Pecorino Romano or Parmesan cheese, grated, for garnish

Olive Rosemary Focaccia (page 90) or crusty bread, toasted, for serving

NOTE: Ribollita means "reboiled." Traditionally, it's a big pot of soup made from seasonal garden vegetables, including kale and cannellini beans, in a flavourful vegetable stock, thickened with leftover bread, then reheated and eaten for a few days, getting better and better each day. Feel free to swap out whatever vegetables you have on hand.

Butternut Squash Mulligatawny Soup

SERVES 8

3 tablespoons olive oil

1 yellow onion, finely chopped

3 garlic cloves, minced

2 tablespoons minced peeled
fresh ginger (about a 2-inch piece
of ginger)

2 tablespoons curry powder

1 teaspoon ground turmeric

1 teaspoon black or brown
mustard seeds

½ teaspoon cumin seeds

½ teaspoon cayenne pepper, plus
more to taste

1 apple (any variety), peeled and
finely chopped

1 carrot, peeled and finely chopped

2 celery stalks, finely chopped

1 fennel bulb, finely chopped (chop
and reserve fronds for garnish)

1 butternut squash, peeled, seeded,
and chopped (about 6 cups)

6 cups Vegetable Stock (page 162 or
store-bought)

1 can (14 ounces/400 mL) full-fat
coconut milk

Salt and cracked black pepper

GARNISH

1 large apple (any variety), peeled
and cut into ¼-inch dice

1 cup cooked rice (basmati, jasmine,
or other long-grain rice)

Zest and juice of 1 lime

Garlic Herb Naan (page 86) or
8 store-bought naan, warmed,
for serving

Our vegetarian twist on this traditional curry soup is comforting and easy to fire up on the stove. Mulligatawny soup is the perfect combination of Sri Lankan, Indian, and British food cultures. It has a good amount of spice but it's not spicy. It's creamy, but there is no cream. It's loaded with apples, rice, and bright fennel notes, and it's simply incredible.

1. **Make the soup:** Heat the olive oil in a large pot over medium heat. Add the onions and cook, stirring occasionally, until softened, about 8 minutes. Add the garlic, ginger, curry powder, turmeric, mustard seeds, cumin seeds, and cayenne pepper. Stir together and cook for another 2 minutes, until fragrant.

2. Add the apple, carrots, celery, fennel, and squash. Pour in the vegetable stock. Bring to a boil over high heat, then reduce the heat to medium-low and simmer gently, uncovered, until the vegetables are tender, 20 to 25 minutes. Remove from the heat.

3. Using a slotted spoon, scoop out the cooked vegetables and transfer to a food processor or high-speed blender (work in batches if needed). Blend to a smooth purée. Return the purée to the pot and stir. (Alternatively, use an immersion blender to purée the soup in the pot.)

4. Stir in the coconut milk. Return the soup to a gentle simmer over low heat and simmer for 5 to 10 minutes, until heated through. Season to taste with salt and pepper.

5. **Prepare the garnish and finish:** In a small bowl, combine the apple and cooked rice. Season with the lime zest and juice. Stir in the reserved chopped fennel fronds. Season to taste with salt and pepper.

6. Ladle the soup into bowls. Place a small scoop of the apple and rice mixture in the centre of the soup. Serve with garlic herb naan.

NOTE: You can replace the butternut squash with acorn squash, Hubbard squash, or sweet potatoes. They are all great alternatives.

Coconut Carrot Rice Noodle Soup

This Thai coconut soup starts with a seriously aromatic coconut carrot broth bursting with hot, sour, salty, and sweet flavours—everything you'd expect in tom kha gai (coconut soup with chicken), except there is no chicken. Instead, chickpeas add a surprisingly hearty bite. It's all about flavour balance in this soup, so if you'd like a touch more spice, add a bit more curry paste. If you want a bit more zip in the broth, simply add a little more lime juice or a dash more fish sauce.

1. Heat the olive oil in a large, heavy pot over medium heat. Add the shallots, garlic, ginger, lemongrass, celery, chili, and red curry paste and cook, stirring frequently, until the shallots have softened, 5 minutes. Add the carrots, bell peppers, lime leaves, and vegetable stock. Bring to a boil over high heat, then reduce the heat to low and simmer, uncovered, for 20 minutes or until the carrots are just tender.

2. Meanwhile, put the rice noodles in a deep soup bowl. Bring a small pot of salted water to a boil. Pour the boiling water over the rice noodles until they are completely submerged and let sit until tender, 6 to 8 minutes, giving the noodles a stir to loosen them every 1 to 2 minutes. Once the noodles are tender, drain and rinse under cool running water to stop the cooking process. Toss the noodles with a bit of olive oil to prevent them from sticking together. Set aside until ready to serve.

3. Once the carrots are tender, add the coconut milk, carrot juice, and chickpeas to the soup. Bring to a boil over medium-high heat and cook for another 5 minutes. Stir in the lime juice, fish sauce to taste, and brown sugar. Season to taste with salt and pepper.

4. Divide the noodles between bowls. Ladle the hot soup over the noodles. Garnish with the green onions and cilantro.

SERVES 8

2 tablespoons olive oil

2 shallots, finely chopped

2 garlic cloves, minced

1 tablespoon finely chopped peeled fresh ginger

3 tablespoons finely chopped lemongrass

1 celery stalk, finely diced

1 fresh red bird's-eye chili, thinly sliced

1 teaspoon Thai red curry paste

2 carrots, peeled and sliced crosswise ¼ inch thick

1 red bell pepper, finely diced

6 makrut lime leaves

4 cups Vegetable Stock (page 162 or store-bought)

4 ounces (115 g) ¼-inch-wide rice vermicelli noodles

1 can (14 ounces/400 mL) full-fat coconut milk

1 cup carrot juice

1 cup canned chickpeas, rinsed and drained

2 tablespoons fresh lime juice

1 to 2 tablespoons vegan fish sauce

1 tablespoon brown sugar

Salt and cracked black pepper

GARNISHES

2 green onions, sliced diagonally

Chopped fresh cilantro

Tomato Soup with Cheese Toasts

SERVES 8

TOMATO SOUP

3 pounds (1.35 kg) ripe Roma tomatoes, cored and cut into wedges

¼ cup + 2 tablespoons olive oil

Salt and cracked black pepper

2 tablespoons unsalted butter

1 yellow onion, finely chopped

2 celery stalks, finely chopped

1 carrot, peeled and finely chopped

4 garlic cloves, finely chopped

2 tablespoons liquid honey or granulated sugar

½ teaspoon red chili flakes

4 cups Vegetable Stock (page 162 or store-bought)

2 sprigs fresh thyme

2 sprigs fresh basil, plus more leaves for garnish

½ cup cherry tomatoes, halved, for garnish

Extra-virgin olive oil, for drizzling

CHEESE TOASTS

¼ cup mayonnaise

¼ cup grated aged cheddar cheese

¼ cup grated Parmesan cheese

1 teaspoon sriracha sauce

2 teaspoons fresh lemon juice

Salt and cracked black pepper

1 baguette, cut diagonally into 4-inch-thick slices

That childhood pleasure of seeing your mom make your favourite hot soup for lunch is one of Lora's fondest memories. Tomato soup and grilled cheese sandwiches . . . Lora swears she could eat that iconic combo every day of the week as a kid, so she was keen to recreate her mom's memorable tomato soup using ripe, juicy, sun-kissed tomatoes—of course, just picked from our garden—and serve it with cheese toasts. This winner of a soup is rich, full of tomato flavour, and almost as good as Mom's!

1. **Start the soup:** Preheat the oven to 375°F (190°C). Line 2 baking sheets with parchment paper.

2. Put the tomatoes in a large bowl. Toss with ¼ cup of the olive oil and salt and pepper to taste. Spread the tomatoes in a single layer on one of the lined baking sheets and roast for 45 minutes or until they are very soft and starting to brown around the edges. Remove from the oven; leave the oven on.

3. Melt the butter with the remaining 2 tablespoons olive oil in a large pot over medium heat. Add the onions, celery, carrots, and garlic and cook, stirring occasionally, for 8 minutes or until softened.

4. Stir in the honey and chili flakes. Add the roasted tomatoes, vegetable stock, thyme, and basil. Season with salt and pepper. Simmer, uncovered and stirring occasionally, until the vegetables are tender, 20 to 25 minutes.

5. **Meanwhile, make the cheese toasts:** In a small bowl, whisk together the mayonnaise, cheddar, Parmesan, sriracha, and lemon juice. Season to taste with salt and pepper. Smear the cheese mixture evenly on the baguette slices. Arrange the slices on the second baking sheet and bake until golden brown, 6 to 8 minutes.

6. **Finish the soup:** Once the vegetables are tender, remove the pot from the heat. Discard the thyme and basil sprigs. Working in batches, transfer the soup to a high-speed blender, filling the blender jar halfway. Cover the lid firmly with a kitchen towel. Start on the slowest speed, then gradually increase the speed and purée until smooth. (Be careful; the soup is hot.)

7. Return the puréed soup to the pot. Reheat and season well with salt and pepper.

8. Ladle the soup into bowls. Top with the cherry tomatoes, a drizzle of extra-virgin olive oil, and basil leaves. Serve with the cheese toasts.

Sweet Corn, Potato, and Leek Chowder

Driving along local back roads in late July and early August, we can see fields and fields of corn. That's our cue to pull over because, finally, the first corn of the season is available at the farmers' markets and farm stands. We love going to Dorisdale Farm, where Lora's family has been visiting since she was a kid and where we now take our own kids. They grow the sweetest corn you ever tasted! This quick and easy chowder highlights the taste of long-awaited sweet summer corn.

1. Cut the corn kernels off the cobs in a large bowl. Holding each cob over the kernels, use the back of the knife to scrape the cob to release the milky liquid. Snap or cut the cobs in half and set aside separately.

2. Melt the butter in a large pot over medium heat. Add the onions, leeks, celery, and garlic and cook, stirring occasionally, for 8 minutes or until softened. Add the potatoes, thyme, bay leaf, Old Bay seasoning, several grinds of pepper, the reserved corn cobs, vegetable stock, milk and cream. Simmer, uncovered, for 20 minutes.

3. Discard the corn cobs, thyme sprigs, and bay leaf. Add the corn kernels and corn liquid and simmer until the potatoes are tender, 10 to 15 minutes.

4. Transfer 3 cups of the soup to a high-speed blender. Blend until smooth. (Be careful; the soup is hot.) Pour the mixture back into the pot. Stir in the lemon juice and season with salt and pepper to taste.

5. Ladle the soup into bowls. Garnish with green onions and serve with dollops of sour cream, if using.

SERVES 6 TO 8

6 sweet corn cobs (you'll need 4 cups corn kernels)

3 tablespoons unsalted butter

1 white onion, finely diced

1 leek, finely diced

2 celery stalks, finely diced

2 garlic cloves, minced

2 cups peeled Yukon Gold potatoes cut into ½-inch cubes

2 sprigs fresh thyme

1 fresh bay leaf

2 teaspoons Old Bay seasoning

4 cups Vegetable Stock (page 162 or store-bought)

1 cup whole milk

1 cup heavy (35%) cream

1 tablespoon fresh lemon juice

Salt and cracked black pepper

2 green onions, thinly sliced, for garnish

Sour cream, for serving (optional)

NOTE: Freeze corn at the end of summer so you have it available for this recipe in the winter. Remove the kernels and milk from the cobs and freeze the kernels and cobs separately.

Salads

Simple Salad

What greens make the best salad? There is no easy answer. It's all about your tastes and of course the best leaves of the season. In the summer, we love arugula, basil leaves, watercress, Boston and Bibb lettuce, and nasturtium flowers, which make for a stunning salad tossed in a bright lemon herb vinaigrette. In the cooler months, there is endive, Treviso, romaine, and frisée, which love to be dressed in a creamy ranch or green goddess dressing. There are endless variations to be made—just pick your "star," the lettuce you would like to showcase, then add supporting greens that add various flavours, textures, and beauty to your salad. Choose the dressing that will best dress up that winning combination for a gorgeous, simple, delicious salad.

    1 to 2 large handfuls salad greens per person
    Your favourite vinaigrette or dressing (pages 178 to 179)

1. In a large bowl, toss the greens with your favourite vinaigrette or dressing.

Our House Vinaigrette

MAKES ABOUT 2 CUPS

½ cup red wine vinegar
2 teaspoons balsamic vinegar
2 tablespoons liquid honey
2 tablespoons Dijon mustard
1 tablespoon Worcestershire sauce
Juice of 1 lemon
1⅓ cups canola oil
Salt and cracked black pepper

1. In a medium bowl, whisk together the red wine vinegar, balsamic vinegar, honey, mustard, Worcestershire sauce, and lemon juice until well combined. While whisking, slowly drizzle in the canola oil until emulsified. Season to taste with salt and pepper. Store in an airtight container in the refrigerator for up to 2 weeks.

Lemon Dill Vinaigrette

MAKES ABOUT 1½ CUPS

¼ cup fresh lemon juice
2 teaspoons Dijon mustard
1 shallot, finely chopped
1 small garlic clove, minced
¼ cup chopped fresh dill
1 cup olive oil
Salt and cracked black pepper

1. In a small blender, combine the lemon juice, mustard, shallot, garlic, and dill. Process until blended. With the blender running, slowly add the olive oil in a steady stream and blend until emulsified. Season to taste with salt and pepper. Store in an airtight container in the refrigerator for up to 2 weeks.

Green Goddess Dressing

MAKES 1½ CUPS

1 avocado, pitted and peeled
1 cup mayonnaise
½ cup sour cream
1 shallot, chopped
1 garlic clove
½ cup loosely packed fresh flat-leaf parsley leaves
2 tablespoons chopped fresh chives
2 tablespoons fresh lemon juice
Salt and cracked black pepper

1. In a small blender, combine the avocado, mayonnaise, sour cream, shallot, garlic, parsley, chives, and lemon juice and process until blended. Season to taste with salt and pepper. Store in an airtight container in the refrigerator for up to 1 week.

Buttermilk Basil Ranch Dressing

MAKES ABOUT 1¼ CUPS

1. In a medium bowl, whisk together the buttermilk, mayonnaise, sour cream, and white wine vinegar until well combined. Stir in the basil, chives, and garlic. Season to taste with salt and pepper. Store in an airtight container in the refrigerator for up to 3 days.

1 cup buttermilk
¼ cup mayonnaise
¼ cup sour cream
1 tablespoon white wine vinegar
3 tablespoons finely chopped fresh basil
2 tablespoons finely chopped fresh chives
1 garlic clove, minced
Salt and cracked black pepper

Honey Mustard Vinaigrette

MAKES 1¼ CUPS

1. In a medium bowl, whisk together the white wine vinegar, mustard, and honey until well combined. While whisking, slowing drizzle in the vegetable oil and the olive oil until emulsified. Season to taste with salt and pepper. Store in an airtight container in the refrigerator for up to 2 weeks.

¼ cup white wine vinegar
2 tablespoons Dijon mustard
2 tablespoons liquid honey
½ cup vegetable oil or canola oil
¼ cup extra-virgin olive oil
Salt and cracked black pepper

Celery Root Waldorf Salad with Celery Leaf Horseradish Dressing

This is our riff on the classic Waldorf salad said to have been invented at the famous Waldorf Hotel in New York City in the 1890s. The salad was originally composed of three ingredients: apples, celery, and a rich mayonnaise. Our version features roasted celery root, earthy lentils, juicy grapes, and crunchy pomegranate seeds tossed in a creamy celery leaf horseradish dressing with a good bite to it. The dressing really makes it!

1. **Make the celery leaf horseradish dressing:** In a medium bowl, whisk together the mayonnaise, sour cream, lemon zest, lemon juice, honey, horseradish, mustard, celery leaves, parsley, and chives. Season to taste with salt and pepper. Set aside or store in an airtight container in the refrigerator for up to 1 week.

2. **Make the celery root Waldorf salad:** Preheat the oven to 400°F (200°C). Line a baking sheet with parchment paper.

3. In a medium bowl, toss the celery root with the olive oil and salt and pepper to taste. Spread the celery root in a single layer on the lined baking sheet and roast until golden brown and fork-tender, 15 to 20 minutes. Remove from the oven and let cool.

4. In a large bowl, combine the roasted celery root, lentils, apples, grapes, celery, celery leaves, pomegranate seeds, dill, and parsley. Mix thoroughly, then season to taste with salt and pepper.

5. Add about ¼ cup of the celery leaf horseradish dressing or more to taste and toss well. Sprinkle microgreens (if using) on top of the salad and serve.

SERVES 4 TO 6

**CELERY LEAF HORSERADISH DRESSING
(MAKES ABOUT 1 CUP)**

½ cup mayonnaise

¼ cup sour cream

Zest of 1 lemon

1 tablespoon fresh lemon juice

1 tablespoon liquid honey

2 teaspoons prepared horseradish

1 teaspoon sweet and smoky mustard

1 tablespoon finely chopped celery leaves

1 tablespoon finely chopped fresh flat-leaf parsley

1 tablespoon finely chopped fresh chives

Salt and cracked black pepper

CELERY ROOT WALDORF SALAD

1 cup peeled celery root cut into ½-inch cubes

2 tablespoons olive oil

Salt and cracked black pepper

1 can (19 ounces/540 mL) lentils, rinsed and drained

1 cup Gala apple cut into ½-inch cubes

1 cup halved red grapes

½ cup thinly sliced celery stalk

½ cup celery leaves

¼ cup fresh pomegranate seeds

2 tablespoons chopped fresh dill

2 tablespoons chopped fresh flat-leaf parsley

Microgreens, for garnish (optional)

NOTE: You could replace the celery root with any vegetable that is great roasted—try sweet potatoes, squash, or carrots. Also, feel free to swap the lentils for any other protein-packed legumes, like chickpeas, lima beans, or kidney beans.

Five-Spice Beet and Burrata Salad

Beets and burrata are a match made in heaven. Five-spice powder adds many distinct flavours to the earthy beets: licorice from the star anise; sweetness and warmth from the cinnamon, fennel, and cloves; and aromatic spice from the Szechuan peppercorns. Once the beets have been roasted with these incredible spices, they are all dressed up in the luscious blackberry vinaigrette and served alongside creamy burrata cheese and fresh greens topped with crunchy candied walnuts. The whole is so incredibly satisfying.

SERVES 4 TO 6

CANDIED WALNUTS
(MAKES 2 CUPS)
½ cup granulated sugar
2 tablespoons liquid honey
1 teaspoon sea salt
1 teaspoon orange zest
1 teaspoon cinnamon
½ teaspoon red chili flakes
½ cup cold water
2 cups walnut halves

BLACKBERRY VINAIGRETTE
(MAKES ABOUT ¾ CUP)
1 cup fresh blackberries
1 tablespoon grated peeled ginger
1 tablespoon liquid honey
1 teaspoon Dijon mustard
3 tablespoons olive oil
2 tablespoons balsamic vinegar
Zest and juice of 1 orange
Salt and cracked black pepper

FIVE-SPICE BEET AND BURRATA SALAD
6 medium red beets (reserve the
    leaves for the salad)
3 tablespoons olive oil
1 tablespoon five-spice powder
Salt and cracked black pepper
4 cups torn greens (one type such as
    radicchio or a mixture)
1 ball (12 ounces/340 g) burrata
    cheese, drained
Flaky sea salt, for sprinkling

Country Morning Loaf (page 77),
    toasted or grilled, for serving

1. **Make the candied walnuts:** Preheat the oven to 350°F (180°C). Line a baking sheet with parchment paper.

2. In a medium saucepan, combine the sugar, honey, sea salt, orange zest, cinnamon, chili flakes, and cold water. Cook over low heat, stirring occasionally, for 5 minutes or until the sugar has dissolved. Increase the heat to high and boil, without stirring, until the mixture turns light golden, 5 to 7 minutes. Remove from the heat.

3. Immediately add the walnuts to the hot syrup and stir to completely coat the walnuts. Pour onto the lined baking sheet and spread out in a single layer. Bake until the walnuts are golden, 5 to 7 minutes. Remove from the oven and let cool. Set aside or store in an airtight container at room temperature for up to 1 week.

4. **Make the blackberry vinaigrette:** In a food processor or blender, combine the blackberries, ginger, honey, mustard, olive oil, balsamic vinegar, and orange zest and juice. Process until blended. Strain the mixture through a fine-mesh sieve into a bowl or container to remove the seeds. Season to taste with salt and pepper. Set aside or store in an airtight container in the refrigerator for up to 1 week.

5. **Roast and marinate the beets:** Preheat the oven to 375°F (190°C). Line a baking sheet with parchment paper. Cut 6 pieces of foil large enough to wrap a beet.

6. Rinse the beets and pat dry. Place a beet on each sheet of foil. Drizzle the beets with olive oil and sprinkle with the five-spice powder and salt and pepper to taste. Tightly wrap the beets in the foil, place on the lined baking sheet, and roast for 60 to 75 minutes, until fork-tender. Open the foil pouches and let the beets sit until cool enough to handle.

7. While the beets are still warm, wearing gloves, peel the beets and cut them into wedges. Place the beet wedges in a large bowl and toss with about half of the blackberry vinaigrette. Marinate for at least 20 minutes while the beets cool.

8. **Assemble the salad:** Arrange the reserved beet leaves and greens of choice on a large serving platter. Place the whole burrata in the centre. Arrange the beets on top of the greens. Garnish with the candied walnuts and sprinkle with flaky sea salt. Serve with the remaining blackberry vinaigrette on the side and toasted or grilled bread.

NOTE: Beets and cheese make the ultimate pairing in a salad. Beets love creamy cheeses like goat cheese and ricotta, anything blue, salty briny cheeses like feta and pecorino, and well-aged ones like Gouda or Canadian cheddar. These are all great alternatives to burrata, which means you'll be making this salad a lot!

The blackberry vinaigrette is sweet and tart with a nice hint of ginger. It also makes a fantastic marinade for other vegetables such as zucchini, eggplant, and mushrooms.

The candied walnuts, with their hint of red chili, are delicious as part of an entertaining platter or as an anytime snack.

New Potato Salad with Green Beans, Candied Olives, and Mustard Herb Vinaigrette

This simple, stunning potato salad is what every summer table or picnic deserves. The sweet first new potatoes of summer are tossed with two types of tangy mustard and lots of fresh herbs, resulting in a light, fresh salad that's easy to devour.

1. **Make the candied olives:** Preheat the oven to 250°F (120°C). Line a baking sheet with parchment paper.

2. In a small bowl, toss the olives with the maple syrup. Spread out evenly on the lined baking sheet and bake, stirring occasionally, until dry and crispy, 1 to 1½ hours. Remove from the oven and let the olives cool completely on the baking sheet. Set aside or store in an airtight container at room temperature for up to 2 weeks.

3. **Make the new potato salad with green beans:** Fill a medium bowl with ice water. Bring a large pot of salted water to a boil. Add the green and yellow beans and blanch until just barely cooked through (the green beans should be bright green), 1 to 2 minutes. Using a slotted spoon, remove the beans from the boiling water and plunge them into the ice bath. (Keep the water at a boil.) When the beans are cooled, drain them and pat dry.

4. Add the potatoes to the boiling water and cook until fork-tender, 15 to 20 minutes. Drain and let cool slightly for a few minutes.

5. **Make the Mustard Herb Vinaigrette:** In a large bowl, whisk together the balsamic vinegar, lemon juice, grainy mustard, Dijon mustard, honey, garlic, shallot, tarragon, parsley, and chives. While whisking, slowly drizzle in the olive oil until thickened and emulsified. Season to taste with salt and pepper.

6. **Assemble:** Add the potatoes and green beans to the dressing and toss until well coated.

7. Line a serving bowl or platter with the lettuce leaves. Spoon the potato salad mixture on top and garnish with the candied olives.

SERVES 4 TO 6

**CANDIED OLIVES
(MAKES ¼ CUP)**
¼ cup pitted Kalamata olives, rinsed and patted dry
1 teaspoon pure maple syrup

NEW POTATO SALAD WITH GREEN BEANS
3 cups mixed fresh green and yellow beans, trimmed and cut in half
1 pound (450 g) small new potatoes (white and purple), washed and halved

MUSTARD HERB VINAIGRETTE
2 tablespoons balsamic vinegar
1 tablespoon fresh lemon juice
2 teaspoons grainy mustard
1 teaspoon Dijon mustard
½ teaspoon liquid honey
1 garlic clove, minced
1 tablespoon finely chopped shallot
1 tablespoon finely chopped fresh tarragon
1½ teaspoons finely chopped fresh flat-leaf parsley
1½ teaspoons finely chopped fresh chives
½ cup olive oil
Salt and cracked black pepper

1 head Bibb lettuce, leaves separated

NOTE: Candied olives are a wicked combination of sweet and savoury. We like to make a big batch and use them to garnish salads or just have them out in small bowls as an addictive bar snack when Aperol spritzes are on the happy hour menu making us very happy. In this recipe, you can easily replace the candied olives with pitted olives.

Thai Noodle Salad with Cashew Coconut Dressing

SERVES 4 TO 6

THAI NOODLE SALAD

4 cups broccoli florets (from 1 large
    bunch broccoli)

1 garlic clove, minced

2 tablespoons olive oil

Salt and cracked black pepper

12 ounces (340 g) wide rice noodles
    or udon noodles

1 cup finely shredded red cabbage

1 carrot, peeled and julienned

1 red bell pepper, julienned

3 green onions (green part only),
    thinly sliced

¼ cup thinly sliced radishes

¼ cup cashews, toasted and
    chopped, for garnish

Fresh cilantro sprigs, for garnish

**CASHEW COCONUT DRESSING
(MAKES ABOUT 1½ CUPS)**

1 cup full-fat coconut milk

½ cup cashew butter

2 teaspoons grated peeled fresh
    ginger

2 tablespoons soy sauce, more if
    needed

1 tablespoon rice vinegar

1 tablespoon yellow miso

1 tablespoon fresh lime juice

1 teaspoon sesame oil

1 to 2 teaspoons sambal oelek or
    sriracha sauce

When the weather is hot, we find ourselves craving cooling, satisfying meals that come together fast. Garlic-roasted broccoli tossed with a nutty cashew coconut dressing makes this cool noodle salad very cool. It hits all the spots—it's fresh, saucy, filling, flavourful, and delicious served warm or cold.

1. **Start the salad—roast the broccoli:** Preheat the oven to 450°F (230°C). Line a baking sheet with parchment paper.

2. In a large bowl, toss the broccoli with the garlic, olive oil, and salt and pepper to taste. Spread out evenly on the lined baking sheet and roast, tossing occasionally, until tender, 20 to 25 minutes.

3. **Meanwhile, make the cashew coconut dressing:** In a small saucepan, combine the coconut milk, cashew butter, ginger, soy sauce, rice vinegar, miso, lime juice, sesame oil, and sambal oelek; and whisk together. Heat the sauce over medium heat, stirring until smooth, about 1 minute. Remove from the heat.

4. **Cook the noodles and assemble the salad:** Bring a large pot of salted water to a boil. Add the noodles and cook until tender , about 4 minutes. Drain, then rinse with cold running water.

5. In a large bowl, combine the noodles, cabbage, carrots, bell peppers, green onions, radishes, and roasted broccoli. Toss until combined. Pour over enough cashew coconut dressing to coat the noodles and the vegetables. Taste and add more soy sauce if desired. Garnish with the cashews and cilantro. (Any remaining sauce can be stored in an airtight container in the refrigerator for up to 1 week.)

NOTE: You can use any kind of noodle you like, even good old spaghetti!
    Peanut butter works just as well in this sauce if you have run out of cashew butter.

Grilled Corn and Avocado Salad with Honey Lime Vinaigrette

This corn salad is the ultimate summer salad or side dish that's brimming with peak-of-the-season ingredients. It's packed with fresh great-tasting charred grilled corn, juicy tomatoes, and creamy avocado, all tossed with a crazy good honey lime vinaigrette that's spiced up with a hint of ancho chili powder.

1. Preheat the grill to medium-high heat.

2. Brush the corn and poblano pepper with 2 tablespoons of the avocado oil. Place the corn and the poblano on the grill, close the lid, and grill, turning often, until nicely charred on all sides, 8 to 10 minutes. Transfer to a plate and let sit until cool enough to handle.

3. In a small bowl, whisk together the lime juice, honey, and ancho chili powder. While whisking, slowly drizzle in the remaining ⅓ cup avocado oil until emulsified. Season well with salt and pepper.

4. Cut the corn kernels off the cobs in a large bowl. Peel the poblano, discard the seeds, and roughly chop. Add the poblano to the corn.

5. Add the tomato, cheddar, radishes, cilantro, green onions, and avocado and toss.

6. In a separate large bowl, toss the lettuce with half of the honey lime vinaigrette. Transfer the lettuce to a serving platter. Top with the corn mixture and drizzle with the remaining vinaigrette. Garnish with cilantro leaves.

SERVES 4 TO 6

4 sweet corn cobs, shucked

1 poblano pepper

⅓ cup + 2 tablespoons avocado oil or olive oil, divided

3 tablespoons fresh lime juice

1 tablespoon liquid honey

½ teaspoon ancho chili powder

Salt and cracked black pepper

1 medium tomato, chopped

½ cup grated aged white cheddar cheese

¼ cup thinly sliced radishes

¼ cup chopped fresh cilantro, plus more leaves for garnish

3 green onions (green part only), thinly sliced

1 avocado, pitted, peeled, and chopped

1 head romaine lettuce, chopped

NOTE: If you don't have the grill going, it is perfectly fine to use just-boiled corn kernels and poblano pepper, or sauté the corn kernels with some butter and salt.

Summer Melon and Cucumber Salad with Feta, Mint, and Tajín

SERVES 4 TO 6

TAJÍN
(MAKES ABOUT ½ CUP)
3 tablespoons dried lime zest
2 tablespoons sea salt
1 tablespoon smoked paprika
1 tablespoon guajillo chili powder
1 tablespoon granulated sugar

SALAD
3 tablespoons olive oil
2 tablespoons rice vinegar
1 teaspoon lime zest
2 tablespoons fresh lime juice
1 tablespoon liquid honey
1 jalapeño pepper, seeded and thinly
    sliced
Salt and cracked black pepper
4 cups diced melon (mix of
    watermelon, honeydew, and
    cantaloupe)
2 cups diced cucumber
2 heirloom tomatoes, diced
½ cup crumbled feta cheese
¼ cup fresh mint leaves
6 to 8 fresh basil leaves, torn

The saltiness of feta in this wonderful salad brings out the sweetness of the melon, making it super refreshing. We love the dash of Tajín Clásico, a popular Mexican seasoning blend of chili peppers, lime, and sea salt, for finishing the salad—it brings the right combination of tangy and spicy to satisfy your taste buds. We've created our own version of Tajín, but you can used store-bought if desired.

1. **Make the Tajín:** In a small bowl, whisk together the dried lime zest, sea salt, smoked paprika, chili powder, and sugar. Set aside or store in an airtight container at room temperature for up to 3 months.

2. **Make the salad:** In a large bowl, whisk together the olive oil, rice vinegar, lime zest, lime juice, honey, and jalapeño. Season generously with salt and pepper.

3. In a large bowl, toss together the melon, cucumber, and tomatoes with the vinaigrette. Add the feta, mint, and basil and toss again. Sprinkle with Tajín to taste.

Roasted Fennel, Pear, and Radicchio Salad with Maple Walnut Vinaigrette

We love fennel for its distinctive mild anise or licorice flavour, which in this salad is enhanced and sweetened by roasting. Bartlett pears are the juiciest pear to use and they work so well with the crimson, slightly bitter radicchio leaves.

SERVES 4 TO 6

MAPLE WALNUT VINAIGRETTE

1 tablespoon orange zest
¼ cup fresh orange juice
1 teaspoon lemon zest
2 tablespoons fresh lemon juice
2 tablespoons red wine vinegar
2 tablespoons pure maple syrup
2 teaspoons Dijon mustard
½ cup olive oil
3 tablespoons walnut oil
¼ cup walnuts, toasted
Salt and cracked black pepper

ROASTED FENNEL, PEAR, AND RADICCHIO SALAD

2 fennel bulbs, cored and sliced crosswise ½ inch thick (chop and reserve fronds for garnish)
2 teaspoons finely chopped jarred red peperoncini piccanti (see Note)
2 tablespoons olive oil
Salt and cracked black pepper
2 Bartlett pears, quartered, cored, and thinly sliced
1 small head radicchio, leaves separated

GARNISHES

½ cup walnuts, toasted and chopped
2 tablespoons grated aged Gouda cheese or Parmesan cheese

1. **Make the maple walnut vinaigrette:** In a blender, combine the orange zest, orange juice, lemon zest, lemon juice, red wine vinegar, maple syrup, and mustard and blend until smooth. With the blender running, slowly drizzle in the olive oil and walnut oil and blend until emulsified. Add the walnuts and pulse until finely chopped. Season to taste with salt and pepper. Set aside or store in an airtight container in the refrigerator for up to 5 days.

2. **Make the roasted fennel, pear, and radicchio salad:** Preheat the oven to 400°F (200°C). Line a baking sheet with parchment paper.

3. In a large bowl, toss together the fennel, peperoncini, olive oil, and salt and pepper to taste. Spread out evenly on the lined baking sheet and roast until the fennel is fork-tender, 15 to 20 minutes. (Wipe the bowl and set it aside.) Remove from the oven and let cool slightly.

4. In the same large bowl, combine the pears, radicchio, and reserved fennel fronds. Toss with the maple walnut vinaigrette to coat.

5. Arrange the dressed radicchio leaves on a serving platter, then top with the roasted fennel and the pears. Garnish with the toasted walnuts and cheese.

NOTE: Peperoncini piccanti is colourful and spicy chopped red chili peppers that are drenched in sunflower oil. Add a spoonful to pizzas, sandwiches, pastas, or salads. You can find them at your local grocer—a great addition to your pantry staples.

Garden Ratatouille Pasta Salad

SERVES 6 TO 8

12 ounces (340 g) radiatore

6 tablespoons olive oil, divided, plus
more for drizzling

1 large globe or graffiti eggplant, cut
into ½-inch dice

Kosher salt

2 medium zucchini, cut into ½-inch
dice

1 medium yellow onion, finely diced

1 red bell pepper, cut into ½-inch dice

4 garlic cloves, minced

2 cups cherry tomatoes, halved

2 cups tomato juice

¼ cup drained capers

½ teaspoon red chili flakes, plus more
for serving

1 sprig fresh thyme

¼ cup fresh basil leaves, torn, for
garnish

1 ball (about 5 ounces/140 g) buffalo
mozzarella, torn into pieces

Everyone needs a great pasta salad recipe. Eggplant, zucchini, bell peppers, and tomatoes are the star summer vegetables in that classic Provençal dish we all know and love—ratatouille. This summer dish turns into the best pasta salad with the addition of capers and their briny punch, buffalo mozzarella that brings a creaminess to the dish, and lots of fresh basil that adds sweet flavour and aroma.

1. Bring a large pot of salted water to a boil. Add the pasta to the boiling water and cook until al dente, 6 to 7 minutes. Drain and let cool briefly; do not rinse. Toss the pasta with 1 tablespoon of the olive oil. Spread out evenly on a baking sheet to cool while preparing the ratatouille.

2. Heat 2 tablespoons of the olive oil in a large nonstick skillet over medium heat. Add the eggplant, season with salt, and cook, stirring frequently, until soft and starting to brown, 10 to 12 minutes. Transfer to a large plate.

3. In the same skillet (no need to wipe it), heat 1 tablespoon of the olive oil over medium-high heat. Add the zucchini and cook, stirring frequently, until tender-crisp, 3 to 4 minutes. Transfer to the plate with the eggplant.

4. Heat the remaining 2 tablespoons olive oil in the same pan. Add the onions, bell peppers, and garlic and cook, stirring frequently, until softened, 4 to 5 minutes. Add the tomatoes, tomato juice, capers, chili flakes, and thyme and cook, stirring occasionally, until the tomatoes have broken down into a sauce, 8 to 10 minutes. Add the cooked eggplant and zucchini. Bring to a gentle boil, then reduce the heat to low and simmer until the eggplant is soft, about 5 minutes. Remove from the heat. Taste and adjust seasoning as needed. Discard the thyme sprig.

5. Add the cooked pasta to the ratatouille mixture and toss to evenly coat the noodles. Transfer to a serving bowl. (The salad can be served warm or at room temperature.) Before serving, sprinkle with the basil and garnish with the mozzarella. Drizzle with some olive oil. Leftovers can be stored in an airtight container the refrigerator for up to 2 days.

NOTE: The ratatouille tastes even better the next day, so if you have the time, make it the day before you plan to prepare the pasta salad. Store the cooled ratatouille in an airtight container in the refrigerator.

Roasted Sweet Potato, Spinach, and Quinoa Salad with Orange Vinaigrette

SERVES 4 TO 6

**JERK SPICE BLEND
(MAKES ABOUT ¾ CUP)**

2 tablespoons brown sugar

2 tablespoons garlic powder

2 tablespoons dried parsley

2 tablespoons salt

1 tablespoon cracked black pepper

1 tablespoon onion powder

2 teaspoons dried thyme

2 teaspoons smoked paprika

1 teaspoon cayenne pepper

1 teaspoon red chili flakes

1 teaspoon ground allspice

½ teaspoon cinnamon

½ teaspoon ground nutmeg

ORANGE VINAIGRETTE

2 tablespoons minced shallot

2 teaspoons orange zest

⅓ cup fresh orange juice

⅓ cup extra-virgin olive oil

2 tablespoons rice vinegar

1 tablespoon Dijon mustard

2 teaspoons liquid honey

Salt and cracked black pepper

Our jerk spice blend is a mixture of warm spices with just enough heat, and it's a perfect way to infuse the Jamaican jerk flavour into these roasted sweet potatoes. It is wonderfully spicy, smoky, and fragrant—everything you want jerk spice to be. The bright, sweet burst of orange in the dressing helps cool off the warm spices.

1. **Make the jerk spice blend:** In a small bowl, whisk together the brown sugar, garlic powder, parsley, salt, black pepper, onion powder, thyme, smoked paprika, cayenne pepper, chili flakes, allspice, cinnamon, and nutmeg. Set aside or store in an airtight container for up to 3 months.

2. **Make the orange vinaigrette:** In a small bowl, whisk together the shallot, orange zest, orange juice, olive oil, rice vinegar, mustard, and honey until emulsified. Season to taste with salt and pepper. Set aside or store in an airtight container in the refrigerator for up to 1 week.

3. **Make the salad:** Preheat the oven to 400°F (200°C). Line a baking sheet with parchment paper.

4. In a large bowl, toss together the sweet potatoes and red onions with the olive oil. Spread out evenly on the lined baking sheet. Roast for 15 minutes. Turn the vegetables, sprinkle the jerk spice blend over them, and roast for another 10 to 15 minutes or until the potatoes are fork-tender. Remove from the oven and let cool.

5. In a medium saucepan, combine the quinoa with the water and salt. Bring to a boil, then reduce the heat to low, cover, and cook for 15 minutes or until the water is completely absorbed. Remove from the heat and let stand, covered, for 5 to 10 minutes. Remove the lid and fluff the quinoa with a fork. Set aside to cool to room temperature.

6. In a large bowl, combine the roasted vegetables, cooked quinoa, spinach, and orange segments. Toss with the orange vinaigrette. Season to taste with salt and pepper. Transfer to a serving platter and top with the toasted pumpkin seeds and cranberries.

NOTE: We love quinoa. It's a protein-packed superfood that we are always including in our salads. You can swap out the quinoa for brown rice or couscous. You could also use cooked chickpeas (in which case, skip step 5).

To get more citrus flavour into the dish, replace half of the water with orange juice to cook the quinoa.

SALAD

2 medium sweet potatoes, peeled
    and cut into wedges
2 medium red onions, cut into
    16 wedges
2 tablespoons olive oil
2 tablespoons Jerk Spice Blend
    (recipe at left)
1 cup white quinoa, rinsed and
    drained
2 cups water
2 teaspoons salt, plus more for
    seasoning
2 cups baby spinach
2 oranges, peeled and separated
    into segments
Cracked black pepper
¼ cup pumpkin seeds, toasted
½ cup sun-dried cranberries

Eggplant Banh Mi Salad

SERVES 4 TO 6

BROWN BUTTER PARMESAN CROUTONS
(MAKES ABOUT 2 CUPS)

2 cups cubed sourdough or
　　multigrain bread
8 tablespoons unsalted butter
4 garlic cloves, smashed
¼ cup grated Parmesan cheese
Salt and cracked black pepper

BANH MI MAYO
(MAKES ½ CUP)

½ cup mayonnaise
1 tablespoon sriracha sauce
1 tablespoon hoisin sauce
1 teaspoon soy sauce
½ teaspoon fresh lime juice

EGGPLANT BANH MI SALAD

3 cups globe eggplant cut into 1-inch
　　cubes
4 tablespoons extra-virgin olive oil,
　　divided
2 tablespoons soy sauce
2 tablespoons fresh lime juice
5 tablespoons seasoned rice vinegar,
　　divided
1 tablespoon + 1 teaspoon granulated
　　sugar, divided
1 garlic clove, minced
2 teaspoons white and black sesame
　　seeds, toasted
1 cup thinly sliced red cabbage
2 radishes, julienned
1 carrot, peeled and julienned
1 mini cucumber, thinly sliced
2 cups thinly sliced iceberg lettuce

GARNISHES

1 tablespoon sliced Pickled Jalapeños
　　(page 202)
½ cup packed fresh cilantro leaves

This salad, inspired by the Vietnamese banh mi sandwich, highlights eggplant tossed with a sweet-and-briny glaze of soy sauce, lime juice, rice vinegar, and garlic, then roasted to perfection. Iceberg lettuce adds crunch, as do the carrots, cucumbers, and toasty garlic Parmesan croutons. A creamy banh mi special sauce tops everything off.

1.　**Make the brown butter Parmesan croutons:** Preheat the oven to 375°F (190°C). Line a baking sheet with parchment paper.

2.　Put the cubed bread in a large bowl. Combine the butter and garlic in a medium saucepan and cook over medium-low heat, swirling the pan often, until the foaming subsides, the butter turns golden brown, and the garlic is fragrant, 6 to 8 minutes. Drizzle the garlic butter over the bread, add the Parmesan, and toss to evenly coat. Season to taste with salt and pepper.

3.　Spread out the bread on the lined baking sheet. Bake until deep golden brown and crisp, 20 to 25 minutes, stirring halfway through. Remove from the oven and let the croutons cool on the baking sheet. Discard the garlic. The croutons can be stored in an airtight container at room temperature for up to 1 week.

4.　**Make the banh mi mayo:** In a small bowl, whisk together the mayonnaise, sriracha, hoisin sauce, soy sauce, and lime juice until well blended. Store in the refrigerator until ready to use or in an airtight container for up to 1 week.

5.　**Make the eggplant banh mi salad:** Increase the oven temperature to 425°F (220°C). Line a baking sheet with parchment paper. Arrange the eggplant in a single layer on the baking sheet and drizzle with 1 tablespoon of the olive oil. Roast, flipping halfway through, until golden brown and very tender, about 10 minutes.

6.　While the eggplant is roasting, in a small bowl, stir together the soy sauce, lime juice, 1 tablespoon of the rice vinegar, 1 tablespoon of the sugar, garlic, and the remaining 3 tablespoons olive oil. Once the eggplant has roasted for 10 minutes, pour the soy mixture over it, stir well with a spatula, and continue roasting until the eggplant is caramelized, another 7 to 10 minutes. Remove from the oven and sprinkle with the toasted sesame seeds.

7.　Meanwhile, in a large bowl, toss together the cabbage, radishes, carrot, cucumber, the remaining 4 tablespoons rice vinegar, and the remaining 1 teaspoon sugar. Let marinate until the cabbage wilts slightly, 15 to 20 minutes. Drain.

8.　**Assemble the eggplant banh mi salad:** Put the lettuce in a serving bowl. Top with the pickled cabbage mixture, then the roasted eggplant. Scatter the brown butter Parmesan croutons over the top and garnish with the pickled jalapeños and cilantro. Serve the bahn mi mayo on the side.

NOTE: Eggplant roasts up beautifully in this recipe and really soaks up the soy mixture. Zucchini, mushrooms, and tofu also work well.

Picked Jalapeños

Makes 2 cups

These fiery little peppers are tamed down a bit in this vibrant pickling liquid. We use them in salads, dressings, sandwiches, and tacos.

   5 jalapeño peppers, thinly sliced
   2 garlic cloves, peeled
   ½ cup water
   ½ cup apple cider vinegar
   1 tablespoon yellow mustard seeds
   1 tablespoon granulated sugar
   2 teaspoons kosher salt
   1 bay leaf

1.   Put the sliced jalapeños in a 2-cup mason jar.

2.   In a small saucepan, combine the garlic, water, apple cider vinegar, mustard seeds, sugar, salt, and bay leaf. Bring to a boil, stirring occasionally to dissolve the sugar and salt. Once the liquid comes to a boil, pour over the jalapeños. Let cool, then seal the jar with a lid and store in the refrigerator for up to 2 months.

Pickled Shallots

Makes about 1 cup

These pretty pink refrigerator pickles are almost instant in terms of gratification and undeniably complex in terms of satisfaction. It's the best way to extend shallot season.

    1 cup thinly sliced shallots (about 6 shallots)
    ½ cup apple cider vinegar
    ½ cup water
    1 tablespoon granulated sugar
    1 teaspoon kosher salt

1. Put the sliced shallots in a 2-cup mason jar.

2. In a small saucepan, combine the apple cider vinegar, water, sugar, and salt. Bring to a boil over high heat, stirring frequently until the sugar has dissolved. Remove from the heat and pour over the shallots. Let cool, then seal the jar with a lid and store in the refrigerator for up to 2 months.

Snap Pea and Strawberry Salad with Poppy Seed Vinaigrette

SERVES 4

**POPPY SEED VINAIGRETTE
(MAKES ABOUT 1½ CUPS)**

1 cup quartered hulled fresh
    strawberries

2 tablespoons granulated sugar

⅓ cup white wine vinegar

½ teaspoon Dijon mustard

⅓ cup olive oil

1 tablespoon poppy seeds

Salt and cracked black pepper

SNAP PEA AND STRAWBERRY SALAD

2 cups pea tendrils, baby spinach, or
    greens of your choice

1 cup snow peas, trimmed

1 cup snap peas, trimmed

1 cup fresh strawberries, hulled and
    quartered

¼ cup Pickled Shallots (page 203)

¼ cup crumbled feta cheese

½ cup sunflower seeds, toasted

GARNISHES

Fresh basil leaves

Fresh mint leaves

¼ cup sunflower petals (optional)

Strawberry season is one of our favourite times of year. When we first moved into our new home in the country, we went to visit Erin, the owner of McLean Berry Farm, where they grow a wide variety of fruits and vegetables just outside Lakefield, Ontario. They are known in the community for growing the sweetest, juiciest strawberries that you will ever taste. We asked Erin to purchase for us over a hundred young strawberry plants for us to grow in our garden, and she made it happen! We had our very own strawberry patch bearing baskets filled with perfect strawberries. This salad was inspired by the hard work and passion that Erin and her family put into their farm every year to produce the tastiest produce for all of us to cook with, and we thank them so much for all the delicious gifts! This salad really captures the sweet taste of peak-season strawberries served with a classic and delicious poppy seed vinaigrette.

1. **Make the poppy seed vinaigrette:** In a large bowl, toss together the strawberries, sugar, white wine vinegar, and mustard. Let sit for 15 minutes. Transfer the strawberry mixture to a blender and blend until smooth, about 30 seconds. (Wipe the bowl and set it aside.) With the blender on low speed, slowly drizzle in the olive oil and blend until emulsified. Pour the vinaigrette into the bowl. Whisk in the poppy seeds and season to taste with salt and pepper. Set aside or store in an airtight container in the refrigerator for up to 1 week.

2. **Assemble the snap pea and strawberry salad:** In a large bowl, combine the pea tendrils, snow peas, snap peas, strawberries, and pickled shallots. Sprinkle the feta and sunflower seeds over top. Drizzle with some of poppy seed vinaigrette. Toss lightly to combine, then season to taste with salt and pepper. Garnish with the basil, mint, and sunflower petals, if using.

Zucchini Salad with Parmesan and Pine Nuts with Lemon Tahini Vinaigrette

This zucchini salad is a feast for the eyes as well as the taste buds! The way the raw zucchini ribbons curl around the crunchy pine nuts and fresh herbs makes for a beautiful presentation. Parmesan cheese adds a salty bite, and the lemon tahini vinaigrette fills the salad with bright flavour. It's the perfect way to use summer zucchini when they are abundant.

1. Using a sharp knife, vegetable peeler, or mandoline, shave the zucchini lengthwise into thin ribbons. Put the zucchini in a colander and sprinkle evenly with the salt. Let stand until the zucchini is limp but still has some bite, 10 to 20 minutes.

2. In a small bowl, whisk together the shallot, garlic, lemon juice, and tahini. Season to taste with salt and pepper.

3. Shake the moisture off the zucchini. In a medium bowl, toss the zucchini with the olive oil, then add the pine nuts. Spoon some of the lemon tahini vinaigrette over top and toss again. Season with more salt, pepper, and lemon juice if needed.

4. Place the lettuce in the centre of a serving platter. Arrange the dressed zucchini ribbons over the lettuce. Drizzle with the remaining dressing. Garnish with the Parmesan, zucchini blossoms (if using), and fresh herbs.

SERVES 4

2 zucchini
1 teaspoon salt, plus more for seasoning
1 tablespoon minced shallot
1 garlic clove, minced
2 tablespoons fresh lemon juice, more if needed
2 tablespoons tahini
Cracked black pepper
¼ cup olive oil
¼ cup pine nuts, toasted and roughly chopped
2 cups baby lettuce leaves
¼ cup shaved Parmesan cheese
4 zucchini blossoms, for garnish (optional)
¼ cup fresh soft herbs (such as parsley, basil, mint, or chives)

NOTE: You will never run out of zucchini from your summer vegetable patch, so it's good that this versatile veggie tastes so good! Eat them raw or cooked—turn them into Sweet Corn Fritters (page 127), make a big batch of Garden Ratatouille Pasta Salad (page 196), or grate them to make sweet decadent treats like our Chocolate Zucchini Bread (page 19). There are an endless number of ways to enjoy them.

Cauliflower Tabbouleh with Pistachio Lemon Dressing

SERVES 4 TO 6

**PISTACHIO LEMON DRESSING
(MAKES ABOUT 1 CUP)**

1 tablespoon lemon zest

¼ cup fresh lemon juice

1 garlic clove

2 teaspoons liquid honey

2 teaspoons Dijon mustard

2 teaspoons sumac

¾ cup olive oil

¼ cup pistachios, toasted

Salt and cracked black pepper

CAULIFLOWER TABBOULEH

1 medium head cauliflower

2 tablespoons olive oil

1 cup finely chopped fresh flat-leaf
    parsley

½ cup fresh dill, finely chopped

¼ cup fresh mint leaves, finely
    chopped

1 cup halved cherry tomatoes

1 cup sliced mini cucumbers

2 green onions, thinly sliced

Salt and cracked black pepper

Cauliflower tabbouleh is our grain-free spin on the traditional Middle Eastern bulgur salad. It's so fresh and light and packed with chopped parsley, tomatoes, cucumber, green onions, dill, mint, and of course very finely grated cauliflower. The pistachio lemon dressing is bright green and tangy, adding a wonderful creaminess to this salad.

1. **Make the pistachio lemon dressing:** In a blender, combine the lemon zest, lemon juice, garlic, honey, mustard, and sumac and blend until combined. With the blender running, slowly drizzle in the olive oil and blend until smooth. Add the pistachios and pulse until finely chopped. Season to taste with salt and pepper. Set aside or store in an airtight container in the refrigerator for up to 5 days.

2. **Make the cauliflower tabbouleh:** Grate the cauliflower on the large holes of a box grater.

3. Heat the olive oil in a large skillet over medium-low heat. Add the cauliflower and cook, stirring occasionally, until just softened slightly, about 5 minutes. Transfer to a large serving bowl and let cool completely.

4. When the cauliflower is cool, add the parsley, dill, mint, tomatoes, cucumbers, and green onions. Add some of the pistachio lemon dressing and stir together so that everything is well dressed, then season to taste with salt and pepper.

NOTE: For a full-on lunch or dinner feast, serve with Pastrami-Spiced Roasted Carrot Hummus (page 105), Baked Caprese Feta (page 119), and warm Pita Bread (page 82).

Heirloom Tomato and Peach Salad with Whipped Goat Cheese and Pecan Pesto

Our first year growing heirloom tomatoes, we went a little crazy and planted as many varieties as we could find. The reasoning was we wanted to show our girls just how many different varieties of tomatoes there are in the world. Like most kids, they thought there was only one type of tomato—their favourite, tiny cherry tomatoes! They have now become our little Tomato Explorers and are absolutely fascinated with the wide range of colours, patterns, shapes, and sizes of tomatoes in our garden. This is our favourite tomato salad to date, and it tastes as fantastic as it looks.

1. **Make the pecan pesto:** In a food processor, combine the basil and garlic. With the processor running, slowly add the olive oil, lemon juice, and Parmesan and blend until the mixture is mostly smooth. Season to taste with salt and pepper. Stir in the pecans. Set aside or store in an airtight container in the refrigerator for up to 1 week. Wipe out the food processor bowl.

2. **Make the vinaigrette:** In a blender, combine the peach, olive oil, sherry vinegar, maple syrup, and lemon juice and blend until smooth. Pour into a small bowl. Whisk in the mustard, then season to taste with salt and pepper. Set aside.

3. **Make the whipped goat cheese:** Crumble the goat cheese into the food processor. Process until creamy, scraping down the sides of the bowl as needed, 1 to 2 minutes. Add the cream and process just until fluffy, about 1 minute. Transfer to a small bowl and season to taste with salt and pepper.

4. **Assemble the heirloom tomato and peach salad:** Using the back of a spoon, spread the whipped goat cheese on a large serving platter.

5. In a large bowl, combine the tomatoes, peaches, and arugula and toss with the vinaigrette. Season to taste with salt and pepper. Arrange the tomato and peach mixture on top of the goat cheese. Drizzle with the pecan pesto and sprinkle with the sea salt and basil.

SERVES 4 TO 6

PECAN PESTO

3 cups fresh basil leaves

1 garlic clove

⅓ cup extra-virgin olive oil

Juice of ½ lemon

¼ cup grated Parmesan cheese

Salt and cracked black pepper

⅓ cup pecans, toasted and roughly chopped

VINAIGRETTE

1 ripe peach, pitted and roughly chopped

½ cup olive oil

3 tablespoons sherry vinegar

2 tablespoons pure maple syrup

1 tablespoon fresh lemon juice

1 tablespoon grainy mustard

Salt and cracked black pepper

WHIPPED GOAT CHEESE

4 ounces (115 g) soft goat cheese

6 tablespoons heavy (35%) cream

Salt and cracked black pepper

HEIRLOOM TOMATO AND PEACH SALAD

2 large heirloom tomatoes, cored and cut into 1-inch wedges

2 ripe medium peaches, pitted and cut into ½-inch wedges

2 cups baby arugula

Salt and cracked black pepper

Sea salt, for finishing

6 to 8 fresh basil leaves, for garnish

Pasta

Bucatini al Limone with Green Beans, Olives, and Pine Nuts

One thing about growing beans in your garden is that you'll never run out of them. They magically appear almost overnight—the more you pick, the more you get! Beans are one of our girls' favourite vegetables in our garden and one we love to grow and eat.

There are so many things to love about this super quick and easy summer pasta dish. It has a bright, fresh lemony sauce that is studded with nutty toasted pine nuts, briny olives, and sweet golden raisins, but the real star is the fresh, crisp green beans that add a delectable summer flavour and delightful texture. Parmesan is a staple in everyone's kitchen, but feel free to swap it for Pecorino Toscano for a more dense and nutty rustic finish.

1. **Make the crispy panko breadcrumbs:** Melt the butter in a medium skillet over medium-low heat. When the butter is melted and frothy, stir in the panko. Continue stirring until the crumbs are evenly crisp and golden brown. Season with salt and pepper. Remove from the heat and let cool. Store in an airtight container at room temperature for up to 2 weeks.

2. **Make the bucatini al limone:** Fill a large bowl with ice water. Bring a large pot of salted water to a boil. Add the green beans and blanch until bright green and just barely cooked through, 1 to 2 minutes. Using a slotted spoon, remove the green beans from the boiling water and plunge them into the ice bath. (Keep the water at a boil.) When the beans are cooled, drain.

3. While the beans are cooling, add the pasta to the boiling water and cook until al dente, about 8 minutes. Drain the pasta, reserving ½ cup of the cooking liquid.

4. When the pasta is almost done, heat the olive oil in a large saucepan over medium-high heat. Add the garlic, chili flakes, and olives and cook until fragrant, about 1 minute. Add the lemon zest and juice, butter, and reserved cooking liquid. Stir until the butter has melted and the sauce begins to thicken, about 1 minute.

5. Add the pasta, raisins, pine nuts, green beans, and parsley. Add the Parmesan and toss together until well combined. Season to taste with salt and pepper.

6. Divide the pasta between warm pasta bowls. Sprinkle with more Parmesan and crispy panko breadcrumbs.

SERVES 4 TO 6

CRISPY PANKO BREADCRUMBS (MAKES 1 CUP)
3 tablespoons unsalted butter
1 cup panko breadcrumbs
Kosher salt and freshly ground black pepper

BUCATINI AL LIMONE
12 ounces (340 g) green beans and/or yellow beans, trimmed and thinly sliced lengthwise
1 pound (450 g) bucatini
¼ cup olive oil
1 tablespoon finely chopped garlic
½ teaspoon red chili flakes
¼ cup slivered pitted olives (any type)
Zest and juice of 2 lemons
2 tablespoons unsalted butter
2 tablespoons golden raisins
2 tablespoons pine nuts, toasted
⅓ cup fresh flat-leaf parsley leaves, roughly chopped
⅔ cup grated Parmesan cheese, plus more for serving
Salt and cracked black pepper

Pumpkin Mac and Cheese

SERVES 6 TO 8

PUMPKIN PURÉE

1 Sugar Pie pumpkin or large squash
    such as butternut or kabocha
    (1½ pounds/675 g)
4 tablespoons unsalted butter,
    divided
½ teaspoon chopped fresh rosemary,
    divided
2 tablespoons pure maple syrup,
    divided
2 teaspoons chili powder
Salt and cracked black pepper

MAC AND CHEESE

1 pound (450 g) elbow macaroni
⅓ cup unsalted butter
⅓ cup all-purpose flour
2½ cups whole milk
2 teaspoons Dijon mustard
¼ teaspoon ground nutmeg
1 tablespoon chopped Pickled
    Jalapeños (page 202; optional)
2 cups grated cheddar cheese
¼ cup grated Parmesan cheese
Salt and cracked black pepper

TOPPING

2 tablespoons unsalted butter
¼ cup finely chopped pecans
2 tablespoons panko breadcrumbs
2 teaspoons chopped fresh sage
Salt and cracked black pepper

Slipping veggies into one of the ultimate comfort dishes is pretty awesome! This cheesy, creamy version of a classic macaroni casserole is a family favourite. The secret ingredient is the pumpkin purée, but you can swap that for other seasonal vegetables like cauliflower or broccoli florets, diced sweet potato, or kale. We love making our own pumpkin purée, but to save time you can use 2 cups of canned pure pumpkin purée and season it with the rosemary, maple syrup, and chili powder.

1. **Make the pumpkin purée:** Preheat the oven to 425°F (220°C).

2. Slice the pumpkin in half crosswise and scoop out the seeds. (Save the seeds for roasting.) Place the halves cut side up in a shallow baking pan or on a baking sheet. Place 2 tablespoons of the butter and ¼ teaspoon of the rosemary in each pumpkin cavity, then drizzle each with 1 tablespoon of the maple syrup. Sprinkle both halves with the chili powder and season to taste with salt and pepper. Roast until the pumpkin flesh is fork-tender, 45 to 50 minutes. Remove from the oven and let sit until cool enough to handle. Lower the oven temperature to 375°F (190°C).

3. Scoop out the cooked pumpkin flesh and transfer to a food processor. (Discard the pumpkin skin.) Purée until smooth, scraping down the sides of the bowl as needed. You should have 2 cups of pumpkin purée. Set aside or let cool, then store in an airtight container in the refrigerator for up to 4 days or in the freezer for up to 4 months.

4. **Prepare the mac and cheese:** Butter a 13 × 9-inch (3-quart) baking dish. Bring a large pot of salted water to a boil. When the water is boiling, add the pasta and cook until al dente, about 8 minutes. Drain and set aside.

5. Meanwhile, melt the butter in a large pot over medium heat. Gradually whisk in the flour and cook, whisking, until the mixture is foamy and just starting to turn a light golden brown, about 3 minutes. While whisking, slowly add the milk and whisk until smooth. Add the mustard, nutmeg, pickled jalapeños (if using), and pumpkin purée and continue whisking until the sauce has thickened, about 5 minutes. Remove from the heat, add the cheddar and Parmesan, and stir until melted. Season well with salt and pepper.

6. **Make the topping:** Melt the butter in a small saucepan over medium heat. Add the pecans, panko, and sage and season to taste with salt and pepper. Toss together and cook, stirring, for a couple of minutes, then remove from the heat.

7. Add the drained pasta to the pumpkin cheese sauce and stir well to coat. Transfer the macaroni mixture to the prepared baking dish. Sprinkle the topping mixture evenly over the macaroni. Bake until golden brown and bubbling, 20 to 25 minutes. Let cool for 5 minutes before serving. To store, let the mac and cheese cool completely. Cover tightly with plastic wrap and store in the refrigerator for up to 3 days or in the freezer for up to 2 months. If frozen, thaw in the refrigerator overnight before reheating.

Penne Peperonata

Peperonata is a rustic southern Italian vegetable stew made with two of summer's greatest ingredients—tomatoes and sweet bell peppers—cooked down in olive oil with onions and garlic. Stir it into pasta for the perfect summertime dish.

1. Heat the olive oil in a large skillet over medium heat. Add the onions and garlic and cook, stirring often, until softened, about 8 minutes. Add the bell peppers and tomatoes and stir together. Add the basil and thyme. Cover and simmer over low heat, stirring occasionally, until the peppers are very soft, 30 to 40 minutes. Discard the basil and thyme sprigs. Stir in the red wine vinegar.

2. When the peperonata is nearly done, bring a large pot of salted water to a boil. When the water is boiling, add the pasta and cook until al dente, about 8 minutes. Drain the pasta, reserving 1 cup of the cooking liquid.

3. Add the pasta to the peperonata. Toss, adding a little of the cooking liquid, until the pasta is evenly coated with the creamy sauce. Season to taste with salt and pepper.

4. Divide the pasta between warm pasta bowls. Sprinkle with Parmesan.

SERVES 4 TO 6

½ cup extra-virgin olive oil

1 medium yellow onion, thinly sliced

3 garlic cloves, finely chopped

3 pounds (1.35 kg) red, yellow, and/or orange bell peppers (about 4 large peppers), thinly sliced

2 cups fresh or canned diced tomatoes

2 sprigs fresh basil

2 sprigs fresh thyme

1 tablespoon red or white wine vinegar

12 ounces (340 g) penne

Salt and cracked black pepper

Grated Parmesan cheese, for serving

NOTE: This savoury and sweet stew is also delicious on toasted bread as an appetizer or is a perfect garnish for grilled chicken or fish.

Pici Pasta with Broccoli Almond Pesto

Pici pasta, an ancient pasta from Tuscany, swimming in a creamy pesto sauce is one of our all-time favourites. We love introducing our friends and family to this recipe for quick and easy homemade pasta. We are always in stitches of laughter as we watch the shenanigans of everyone gathered around the kitchen island, dressed in aprons, dusted in flour, excited to roll and shape these long, thick spaghetti-like noodles. This easy Tuscan classic is rich in history, delicious in taste, and super fun to make.

SERVES 6

BROCCOLI ALMOND PESTO
4 cups broccoli florets
1 cup tightly packed fresh basil leaves
2 garlic cloves
½ cup almonds, toasted
1 teaspoon lemon zest
1 tablespoon fresh lemon juice
¾ cup extra-virgin olive oil, plus more for drizzling
½ cup grated Parmesan cheese, plus more for serving
Salt and cracked black pepper, plus more for garnish

PICI DOUGH
1 cup all-purpose flour, plus more for dusting
1 cup semolina flour, plus more for dusting
1 teaspoon salt
1 large egg
⅔ cup warm water
2 tablespoons olive oil

1. **Make the broccoli almond pesto:** Fill a large bowl with ice water. Bring a large pot of salted water to a boil over high heat. Add the broccoli and blanch until just slightly tender, about 2 minutes. Using a slotted spoon, remove the broccoli from the boiling water and plunge it into the ice bath. (Set aside the pot of water.) When the broccoli is cooled, drain and pat dry with paper towel.

2. In a food processor, combine 3 cups of the broccoli, the basil, garlic, almonds, lemon zest, and lemon juice. Pulse until roughly chopped. Add the olive oil and Parmesan and purée until smooth. Season to taste with salt and pepper. Set aside or store in an airtight container in the refrigerator for up to 1 week or in the freezer for up to 6 months.

3. **Make the pici dough and shape the pasta:** In a large bowl, stir together the all-purpose flour, semolina flour, and salt. Make a well in the centre of the flour.

4. In a measuring cup, combine the egg, warm water, and olive oil and mix well with a fork. Slowly pour the egg mixture into the well, mixing with a fork until a rough dough forms.

5. Turn the dough out onto a lightly floured work surface and knead the dough until it forms a smooth ball, 8 to 10 minutes. Wrap the dough in plastic wrap and let it rest at room temperature for 20 minutes.

6. Dust a baking sheet with semolina flour. Turn the dough out onto a lightly floured work surface. Divide the dough into 2 equal portions; rewrap one portion to prevent it from drying out. Use a rolling pin to roll out the first portion of dough into a 6 × 8-inch rectangle, about ⅛ inch thick. Using a sharp knife, cut the dough into 6-inch-long strips, about ⅛ inch wide. Repeat with the other portion of dough.

7. On a clean work surface, roll each strip of dough under your fingers to make a slightly rounded strand. Place the pasta on the dusted baking sheet.

8. **Cook the pasta and finish:** Return the pot of salted water to a boil. When the water is boiling, add the pasta and cook until al dente, 4 to 5 minutes. Add the remaining 1 cup broccoli and cook for another 30 seconds. Drain the pasta and broccoli, reserving ½ cup of the cooking liquid.

9. In a large skillet over medium heat, combine the broccoli almond pesto and ¼ cup of the reserved cooking liquid; stir together. Once hot, remove from the heat, add the pasta and broccoli, and toss until the pasta is evenly coated. If needed, thin to the desired consistency with additional cooking liquid. Season to taste with salt and pepper.

10. Divide the pasta between warm pasta bowls. Drizzle with olive oil and sprinkle with grated Parmesan.

Whole Wheat Spaghetti with Roasted Cauliflower, Caramelized Onions, and Brown Butter Parmesan Croutons

Roasted cauliflower with pasta is so good, but adding a creamy, silky cauliflower purée makes it irresistible. The toasty, cheesy croutons add great texture to this dish, and we love how they are a perfect match for the tender, nutty roasted cauliflower florets. We like to layer the dish, starting with a pool of the sauce in the bottom of each pasta bowl, then take a serious moment to twirl the pasta and drape it on top of the purée, and finish with lots of Parmesan "snow" for a beautiful presentation. But once served, mix it up so all those delicious layers of flavour are tossed together!

1. Preheat the oven to 425°F (220°C). Line a baking sheet with parchment paper.

2. In a large bowl, toss half the cauliflower florets with ¼ cup of the olive oil, rosemary, lemon zest, and chili flakes. Season with salt and pepper to taste. Evenly spread the mixture in a single layer on the lined baking sheet. Roast until golden brown, about 25 minutes., stirring halfway through.

3. In a medium saucepan, combine the remaining cauliflower florets, milk, and enough water to just cover the cauliflower. Season to taste with salt and pepper. Bring to a boil over medium-high heat, then reduce the heat to a simmer and cook until fork-tender, 12 to 15 minutes.

4. Using a slotted spoon, transfer the cauliflower to a high-speed blender. Add about a third of the cooking liquid. Purée until smooth, adding more cooking liquid if necessary. (Be careful; the mixture is hot.) Stir in the butter until melted and season to taste with salt and pepper. Pour into a small saucepan and keep warm.

5. Bring a large pot of salted water to a boil. When the water is boiling, add the pasta and cook until al dente, about 8 minutes. Drain the pasta.

6. Meanwhile, heat the remaining 2 tablespoons olive oil in a large skillet over medium heat. Add the red onion and garlic and cook, stirring occasionally, until caramelized, 8 to 10 minutes. Add the red wine vinegar and sugar, stir together, and cook until the vinegar is absorbed. Add the roasted cauliflower florets, pasta, Parmesan, and brown butter Parmesan croutons and toss to combine.

7. Spoon the warm cauliflower purée into warm pasta bowls. Divide the pasta evenly between the bowls. Top with a drizzle of olive oil, a sprinkling of lemon juice, and more Parmesan, if desired.

SERVES 4 TO 6

1 head cauliflower, cut into bite-size florets (about 4 cups), divided
¼ cup + 2 tablespoons olive oil, divided, plus more for serving
1 teaspoon finely chopped fresh rosemary
½ teaspoon lemon zest
¼ teaspoon red chili flakes, more to taste
Salt and cracked black pepper
1 cup whole milk
2 tablespoons unsalted butter
1 pound (450 g) whole wheat spaghetti
1 medium red onion, cut into 8 wedges
2 garlic cloves, minced
2 tablespoons red wine vinegar
1 teaspoon granulated sugar
¼ cup grated Parmesan cheese, plus more for serving
Brown Butter Parmesan Croutons (page 200)
Fresh lemon juice, for serving

Orecchiette with Cherry Tomatoes and Rosé Sauce

SERVES 4 TO 6

¼ cup extra-virgin olive oil
1 small red onion, finely diced
2 garlic cloves, thinly sliced
1 teaspoon red chili flakes
1 can (28 ounces/796 mL) diced
    tomatoes
Salt
1 pound (450 g) orecchiette
2 cups mixed yellow and red cherry
    tomatoes, halved
1 cup heavy (35%) cream
2 tablespoons finely chopped fresh
    basil
½ cup grated Parmesan cheese,
    plus more for serving
Cracked black pepper

This combination of tomato and cream in a velvety sauce is good on any pasta, but orecchiette are like little pockets, ensuring that every bite will be filled with the creamy sauce and those ever so sweet cherry tomatoes that will burst with summertime flavour.

1. Heat the olive oil in a large skillet over medium heat. Add the red onions, garlic, and chili flakes and cook, stirring often, until the onions and garlic soften, 2 to 3 minutes.

2. Add the diced tomatoes and season with salt. Increase the heat to medium-high and bring to a boil, then reduce the heat to medium-low and simmer, uncovered, until the sauce thickens, 25 to 30 minutes.

3. While the sauce is simmering, bring a large pot of salted water to a boil. Add the pasta to the boiling water and cook until al dente, about 8 minutes. Drain the pasta.

4. When the sauce is thickened, add the cherry tomatoes and cream and continue to cook for 5 minutes. Reduce the heat to low.

5. Add the pasta, basil, and Parmesan to the sauce. Toss until the pasta is evenly coated. Season with salt and pepper. Divide the pasta between warm pasta bowls and sprinkle with more Parmesan.

Fettuccine Sweet Corn Alfredo

We love to get the most out of corn season. Here is our version of the famous fettucine Alfredo, one of the top ten most requested pasta dishes ever. The "gloss" in Alfredo sauce is an emulsion of starchy pasta water, cheese, and butter. Sweet corn is an epic summer vegetable to go alongside cheese and butter. We add cream to make this dish even more silky, decadent, rich, and memorable. This pasta dish is perfect served with a big bowl of salad greens dressed in Our House Vinaigrette (page 178) that is lovely and lemony.

SERVES 4 TO 6

1 pound (450 g) fettuccini
3 tablespoons unsalted butter, divided
1 tablespoon olive oil
1 small yellow onion, finely diced
2 garlic cloves, finely chopped
½ cup water, more if needed
6 cups fresh sweet corn kernels (from about 6 cobs), divided
Salt and cracked black pepper
1 cup heavy (35%) cream
⅓ cup torn fresh basil leaves
½ cup grated Parmesan cheese, plus more for serving
Fresh lemon juice, for serving

1. Bring a large pot of salted water to a boil. When the water is boiling, add the pasta and cook until al dente, about 8 minutes. Drain the pasta, reserving ½ cup of the cooking liquid.

2. Meanwhile, melt 1 tablespoon of the butter with the olive oil in a large skillet over medium heat. Add the onions and garlic and cook, stirring occasionally, until soft, about 2 minutes. Add the water and 4 cups of the corn kernels. Cook until the corn is heated through and tender, about 5 minutes. Season to taste with salt and pepper.

3. Transfer the corn mixture to a high-speed blender and blend until a smooth pourable consistency, adding more water to thin if needed.

4. In the same skillet (no need to wipe it), melt the remaining 2 tablespoons butter over medium-high heat. Add the remaining 2 cups corn kernels and cook until tender, 2 minutes. Add the corn purée and cream, stir together, and cook until the sauce starts to bubble and thicken, about 5 minutes.

5. Reduce the heat to low. Add the pasta, the reserved cooking liquid, and the basil. Toss until the pasta is evenly coated and cook for another 1 to 2 minutes, until hot. Stir in the Parmesan and season well with salt and pepper.

6. Divide the pasta between warm pasta bowls and garnish with a sprinkling of lemon juice, more Parmesan, and pepper.

NOTE: Yes, this dish is rich, we won't deny that. You can eliminate the cream altogether and replace it with vegetable stock or water. Just use a little less of it so you get a good consistency in the sauce.

Mains

Spinach Ricotta Gnudi with Chive Butter Sauce

Making gnudi, or Italian ricotta dumplings, only sounds fancy. This is an easy pasta dinner anyone can pull off. Gnudi are made with ricotta, which makes them tender, soft, and pillowy, full of flavour, and every bit as comforting as pasta. A classic "beurre blanc" sauce preparation is enriched with chives but feel feel to use any fresh herb that you love to change the flavour profile of the sauce.

1. **Make the gnudi dough and shape:** Place a colander over a large bowl. Heat 1 tablespoon of the olive oil in a large skillet over medium heat. Add half of the spinach, cover with a lid, and cook until the spinach is wilted, 2 to 3 minutes. Drain the spinach in the colander. Repeat with the remaining 1 tablespoon olive oil and the remaining spinach. Let cool. Once the spinach is cool, squeeze it with your hands to remove excess water. Finely chopped the spinach, then squeeze again.

2. In a medium bowl, stir together the ricotta and cooked spinach until well combined. Add the Parmesan, eggs, all-purpose flour, and nutmeg, and season to taste with salt. Stir until combined; the dough should be soft but hold together in a ball (see Note).

3. Line a baking sheet with parchment paper. Sprinkle the paper with the semolina flour. Shape the ricotta mixture into 24 equal balls, rolling them between damp hands. Place the balls on the lined baking sheet and carefully roll in the semolina until coated on all sides. Cover the gnudi with plastic wrap and refrigerate for 1 hour or until ready to cook. (The gnudi can be stored in the refrigerator for a maximum of 4 hours before cooking.)

4. **Make the chive butter sauce:** In a medium saucepan, combine the white wine and white wine vinegar and bring to a boil. Add the shallots and season to taste with salt and pepper, then reduce the heat to a simmer and cook until most of the liquid has evaporated. Remove from the heat. Whisk the butter, a few pieces a time, into the reduction, allowing each piece to melt before adding more. Return the saucepan to low heat for a moment if necessary to help melt the butter. It is important to maintain a low heat and never let the sauce boil once the butter is added or the sauce will separate. When all of the butter has been incorporated, remove the sauce from the heat and whisk in the lemon juice and chives. Keep the butter sauce in a warm spot on the stove, off the heat.

5. **Cook the gnudi:** Remove the sheet of gnudi from the refrigerator. Bring a large pot of salted water to a boil. When the water is boiling, working in batches to avoid crowding the pot, add the gnudi to the boiling water, then reduce the heat to a simmer and cook until they rise to the surface, 5 to 7 minutes. Using a slotted spoon, carefully transfer the cooked gnudi to the butter sauce. Once all the gnudi are cooked, toss them in the butter sauce. Spoon into a serving dish or into warm shallow bowls.

SERVES 4 TO 6

SPINACH RICOTTA GNUDI

2 tablespoons olive oil, divided
2 pounds (900 g) baby spinach, divided
2½ cups ricotta cheese, drained
½ cup grated Parmesan cheese
2 eggs, lightly beaten
2 tablespoons all-purpose flour
¼ teaspoon ground nutmeg
Salt
¼ cup semolina flour, for coating

CHIVE BUTTER SAUCE

2 tablespoons dry white wine
2 tablespoons white wine vinegar
1 shallot, finely chopped
Salt and cracked black pepper
1 cup unsalted butter, diced
¼ teaspoon fresh lemon juice
2 teaspoons finely chopped fresh chives

———

NOTE: The dough can be very delicate. If it feels too wet, you can add more flour by the tablespoon (up to 2 tablespoons total) to make sure the dough stays together. Try not to do so, however, until you do a quick test shaping one. The beauty of this wonderful recipe is that the gnudi are so light and fluffy—too much flour can take away from that.

Eggplant Katsu with Caramelized Onion Tonkatsu Sauce and Red Cabbage and Green Onion Slaw

Katsu is a popular Japanese dish of fried cutlets, usually chicken or pork coated with panko breadcrumbs. Taking inspiration from this comforting dish, we coat thick slices of eggplant in panko and pan-fry them until crispy and golden brown to create the perfect vegetarian cutlet. The eggplant is served on a bed of rice, drizzled with an aromatic sweet and sour tonkatsu sauce made with caramelized onions and tart plums, and topped with vibrant red cabbage and green onion slaw.

SERVES 4

**CARAMELIZED ONION
TONKATSU SAUCE
(MAKES ABOUT 1½ CUPS)**

1 tablespoon unsalted butter

2 tablespoons olive oil

2 medium yellow onions, finely diced

2 garlic cloves, minced

1 (2-inch) piece fresh ginger, peeled and chopped

2 plums, pitted and roughly chopped

2 tablespoons brown sugar

½ cup ketchup

3 tablespoons Worcestershire sauce

3 tablespoons soy sauce

2 tablespoons mirin

2 teaspoons Dijon mustard

Pinch of ground allspice

Salt and cracked black pepper

**RED CABBAGE AND
GREEN ONION SLAW**

½ head red cabbage, finely shredded (about 4 cups)

2 green onions, thinly sliced

1 medium carrot, peeled and julienned

2 tablespoons olive oil

2 tablespoons soy sauce

2 tablespoons fresh lemon juice

1 tablespoon brown sugar

1 tablespoon grated peeled fresh ginger

1 tablespoon white vinegar

2 teaspoons sesame oil

Salt and cracked black pepper

EGGPLANT KATSU

1 large globe or graffiti eggplant, cut lengthwise into four ¾-inch-thick slices

3 teaspoons kosher salt, divided

1 cup all-purpose flour

2 eggs

2 cups panko breadcrumbs

⅓ cup grated Parmesan cheese

½ teaspoon black pepper

⅓ cup olive oil

Cooked rice, for serving

Shichimi togarashi, for garnish

— continued —

1. **Make the caramelized onion tonkatsu sauce:** Melt the butter with the olive oil in a medium saucepan over medium heat. Add the onions, garlic, and ginger and cook, stirring occasionally, until the onions are nicely caramelized, 8 to 10 minutes. Add the plums and brown sugar and cook until the plums soften, 2 to 3 minutes. Add the ketchup, Worcestershire sauce, soy sauce, mirin, mustard, and allspice and cook, stirring often, until the mixture has thickened, 6 to 8 minutes. Transfer the mixture to a blender and purée until smooth, adding a bit of water if too thick. Season to taste with salt and pepper. Set aside or store in an airtight container in the refrigerator for up to 1 month.

2. **Make the red cabbage and green onion slaw:** In a large bowl, combine the cabbage, green onions, and carrots. Toss together.

3. In a medium bowl, whisk together the olive oil, soy sauce, lemon juice, brown sugar, ginger, vinegar, and sesame oil. Season to taste with salt and pepper. Pour over the cabbage mixture and toss to combine. Set aside.

4. **Make the eggplant katsu:** Preheat the oven to 200°F (100°C). Line one baking sheet with parchment paper and line a second baking sheet with paper towel.

5. Place the eggplant slices on the paper towel. Sprinkle with 1 teaspoon of the kosher salt. Let sit for 20 minutes (see Note). After 20 minutes, blot the eggplant slices with paper towel to remove excess moisture.

6. Set out 3 medium shallow bowls. In the first bowl, stir together the flour and 1 teaspoon of the kosher salt. In the second bowl, beat the eggs. In the third bowl, stir together the panko, Parmesan, the remaining 1 teaspoon kosher salt, and pepper.

7. Heat the olive oil in a large skillet over medium-high heat until shimmering.

8. Working with one slice at a time, dredge the eggplant in the flour, turning to lightly coat. Place the eggplant in the egg, turning to coat. Finish with the seasoned panko, coating both sides. Press the coating into the eggplant to help the breading stick.

9. Working in batches of 2 pieces of eggplant at a time, fry the eggplant until golden brown, about 4 minutes per side. Using tongs, transfer the fried eggplant to the parchment-lined baking sheet and keep warm in the oven while you fry the remaining eggplant.

10. Meanwhile, reheat the caramelized onion tonkatsu sauce over medium heat until warmed through.

11. To serve, slice the eggplant into 2-inch pieces. Portion the rice onto plates. Top each with eggplant slices. Drizzle with the caramelized onion tonkatsu sauce. Scoop a generous portion of the red cabbage and green onion slaw on top. Garnish with a sprinkle of shichimi togarashi.

NOTE: Salting the eggplant before cooking draws out excess moisture so the eggplant has a stronger flavour and a softer, more tender texture.

Onion Bourguignon with Buttery Mashed Parsnips

This is one of our favourite dishes to make when autumn rolls around and all we want is a big bowl of comfort food. Meaty mushrooms are simmered with balsamic slow-roasted onions in a red wine sauce to make this Bourguignon-style stew. Sear the mushrooms well—the rich caramelized flavour adds so much depth to the delicious saucy goodness. Mushroom powder is a seasoning we use to give depth of flavour to a dish and add an extra punch of umami and fragrance. Buttery mashed parsnips are the perfect accompaniment to hold up to all of the deep savoury notes.

SERVES 4 TO 6

MUSHROOM POWDER
(MAKES ABOUT ¼ CUP)
2 ounces (55 g) dried mushrooms
    (such as a mix of porcini, shiitake,
    portobello)

ONION BOURGUIGNON
4 medium red onions
3 tablespoons balsamic vinegar
2 tablespoons olive oil
1 tablespoon chopped fresh oregano
2 teaspoons Dijon mustard
5 tablespoons unsalted butter, divided
1 pound (450 g) button mushrooms
2 large leeks (white and pale green
    parts only), cut into 1-inch pieces
2 medium carrots, peeled and thinly
    sliced
2 garlic cloves, minced
1 tablespoon tomato paste
3 tablespoons all-purpose flour
3 cups Vegetable Stock (page 162 or
    store-bought)
1 cup dry red wine
2 tablespoons soy sauce
3 sprigs fresh thyme
1 tablespoon Mushroom Powder
    (recipe at left)
Salt and cracked black pepper

BUTTERY MASHED PARSNIPS
6 cups peeled parsnips cut into 2-inch
    pieces
½ cup whole milk
4 tablespoons unsalted butter
Salt and cracked black pepper

Chopped fresh flat-leaf parsley, for
    garnish

— *continued* —

1. **Make the mushroom powder:** In a spice grinder or small food processor, grind the dried mushrooms to a fine powder. Set aside or store in an airtight container at room temperature for up to 3 months.

2. **Make the onion bourguignon:** Preheat the oven to 400°F (200°C).

3. Peel the red onions and cut in half from tip to root. Cut each half into 4 wedges, slicing through the root so that the wedges stay intact. Place the onions in a large baking pan.

4. In a small bowl, whisk together the balsamic vinegar, olive oil, oregano, and mustard. Pour over the onions and toss gently to coat. Cover with foil and roast for 20 minutes. Remove the foil and continue roasting for another 10 minutes or until the onions are tender. Remove from the oven.

5. While the onions are roasting, melt 2 tablespoons of the butter in a large pot over medium heat. Add half of the button mushrooms and cook, stirring frequently, until evenly browned, 3 to 4 minutes. Using a slotted spoon, transfer the mushrooms to a large bowl or plate. Repeat with 2 tablespoons of the butter and the remaining mushrooms. Transfer to the bowl with the cooked mushrooms.

6. In the same pan (no need to wipe it), melt the remaining 1 tablespoon butter over medium-low heat. Add the leeks and carrots and cook, stirring frequently, until the leeks start to soften, about 5 minutes. Add the garlic and cook for another minute. Stir in the tomato paste and cook for 1 minute. Add the flour and cook, stirring, for 1 minute. Add the vegetable stock, red wine, soy sauce, thyme, and mushroom powder, stirring and scraping up the browned bits from the bottom of the pot. Add the reserved cooked mushrooms and the roasted onions and bring to a simmer. Reduce the heat to low, cover with the lid slightly ajar, and simmer until the carrots and onions are tender and the sauce is thick, about 30 minutes. Season with salt and pepper.

7. **Meanwhile, make the buttery mashed parsnips:** Place the parsnips in a large pot and cover with cold water. Bring to a boil over high heat, then reduce the heat to medium and cook for 20 minutes or until the parsnips are tender. Drain the parsnips and return them to the pot. Add the milk and butter. Using a potato masher, mash the parsnips until smooth. Season to taste with salt and pepper.

8. Serve the onion bourguignon over the buttery mashed parsnips. Garnish with the parsley.

End-of-Summer Tomato Risotto

Our garden produces so many different varieties of tomatoes, and our family loves every single one. When it's time to harvest them, we grab the kids and some empty baskets and wander down to the garden, usually in the early evening when the sun isn't blazing. We have a race to see who can fill their basket the most before the sun sets.

The absolute best time to enjoy this dish is when you get your hands on ripe, juicy tomatoes just picked off the vine. The intense sweet and balanced flavour of summer tomatoes is off the charts. We all have those incredible warm memories of the smell and taste of summer tomatoes, and this recipe will for sure become one of your fondest.

1. Heat 2 tablespoons of the olive oil in a large skillet over medium heat. Add the shallots and garlic and cook, stirring, until softened, 2 to 3 minutes. Add the rice, stir to coat with the oil, and cook, stirring, for 2 minutes. Pour in the white wine (if using) and stir until absorbed. Reserve 1 cup of the tomatoes for garnish. Add the remaining tomatoes and their juices to the rice and stir until they begin to break down, 1 to 2 minutes. Season to taste with salt and pepper.

2. Pour in 2½ cups of the vegetable stock and cook, stirring, until absorbed. Add the remaining 2½ cups stock and cook, stirring, until the stock is absorbed and the rice is tender but still firm to the bite, about 18 minutes. The rice should be loose but not liquidy. Remove from the heat. Stir in the Parmesan, butter, and basil. Season to taste with salt and pepper.

3. In a medium bowl, toss together the fennel, the reserved 1 cup of tomatoes, the remaining 2 tablespoons olive oil, and salt and pepper to taste.

4. Serve the risotto in warm shallow bowls and garnish with the tomato fennel salad.

SERVES 4 TO 6

4 tablespoons olive oil, divided
2 shallots, finely chopped
1 garlic clove, minced
1½ cups arborio rice
½ cup dry white wine (optional)
1 pound (450 g) small tomatoes, halved or quartered and juices reserved, divided
Salt and cracked black pepper
5 cups hot Vegetable Stock (page 162 or store-bought), divided
½ cup grated Parmesan cheese
2 tablespoons unsalted butter
¼ cup loosely packed fresh basil leaves, chopped
1 small fennel bulb, thinly sliced crosswise

Harissa and Maple Roasted Carrot Tart with Carrot-Top Dill Cream Cheese

SERVES 4 TO 6

2 garlic cloves, minced

2 tablespoons pure maple syrup

1 tablespoon olive oil

1 teaspoon harissa powder

Salt and cracked black pepper

1 pound (450 g) carrots, scrubbed and sliced lengthwise into ¼-inch-thick pieces

1 sheet (8 ounces/225 g) frozen puff pastry, thawed

1 cup (8 ounces/225 g) cream cheese, at room temperature

¼ cup sour cream

2 tablespoons fresh lemon juice

2 tablespoons finely chopped fresh dill

1 tablespoon finely chopped fresh flat-leaf parsley

GARNISHES

Fresh dill sprigs, chopped

Flaky sea salt

In this tasty little tart, sweet and lightly spiced carrots show off their true colours and tasteful versatility. This tart comes together quickly and elevates the everyday carrot into a real showstopping main ingredient in a perfectly composed dish that is ideal for lunch, dinner, or brunch.

1. Preheat the oven to 450°F (230°C). Line a baking sheet with parchment paper.

2. In a large bowl, whisk together the garlic, maple syrup, olive oil, harissa, and salt and pepper to taste. Add the carrots and mix well to evenly coat. Spread out evenly on the lined baking sheet and roast, tossing occasionally, until the carrots are tender, 15 to 20 minutes. Remove from the oven and let cool.

3. On a lightly floured work surface, roll out the puff pastry into a 10 × 14-inch rectangle. Using a knife, lightly score a border around the sides (do not cut all the way through), about ¼ inch from the edge. Transfer the pastry to the lined baking sheet. Using a fork, prick the pastry all over, inside the border, to prevent it from puffing up while baking. Bake until lightly golden, about 20 minutes. Remove from the oven and let cool on the baking sheet, then transfer to a serving plate or cutting board.

4. In a food processor, combine the cream cheese, sour cream, and lemon juice. Blend until smooth. Season to taste with salt and pepper. Fold in the dill and parsley.

5. Spread the cream cheese mixture over the cooled puff pastry, staying within the border. Arrange the carrots in a single layer on top. Sprinkle with the dill and flaky sea salt.

NOTE: The puff pastry and savoury whipped herb cream cheese are the perfect canvas for a simple tart that loves an assortment of roasted veggies. Try caramelized onions and parsnips, roasted beets drizzled with Pecan Pesto (page 211), or zucchini with pine nuts and the Lemon Dill Vinaigrette (page 178). The tart is easily assembled and perfect served warm or at room temperature.

Savoy Cabbage with Borscht Trimmings

Most people only think about cabbage when they are about to make coleslaw or cabbage rolls. But cabbage has so many awesome qualities when roasted in big, hearty wedges. Searing the outside of the cabbage until blistered and charred gives it a wonderful smoky flavour, and the miso butter adds richness and enhances the sweetness of the braised leaves. The "borscht trimmings" are the perfect garnish, and we love how the earthiness of the beets, the cool creaminess of the horseradish sour cream, and the final shower of dill complement the cabbage in such a beautiful way.

1. **Prepare the cabbage:** Preheat the oven to 400°F (200°C).

2. Discard the outer leaves from the cabbage and trim the base. Cut the cabbage in half through the core, then cut each half into 4 wedges.

3. In a small bowl, combine the garlic, 4 tablespoons of the butter, miso, honey, ginger, thyme, smoked paprika, and lime zest and juice; stir until combined.

4. Heat the olive oil in a large ovenproof skillet over medium-high heat. Place the cabbage wedges cut side down in the hot oil and cook until nicely browned, 5 minutes per side. Spread the miso butter on both sides of the cut wedges. Reduce the heat to medium. Pour the vegetable stock into the skillet, then season to taste with salt and pepper. Cover, transfer to the oven, and roast for 20 minutes. Remove the lid and cook for another 10 minutes or until the cabbage is just fork-tender.

5. **Meanwhile, make the croutons:** Melt 1 tablespoon of the butter in a large sauté pan over medium heat. Add the bread cubes, season to taste with salt and pepper, and toss until lightly toasted, about 2 minutes. Transfer the croutons to a plate.

6. **Prepare the beets:** In a small saucepan over medium-high heat, combine the cubed beets and the remaining 1 tablespoon butter and cook, stirring, for 1 to 2 minutes, until the butter has melted. Add the tomato paste and cook, stirring occasionally, until combined, 1 to 2 minutes. Stir in the tomato sauce. Reduce the heat to medium-low, cover, and cook, stirring occasionally, until the beets are fork-tender, 12 to 15 minutes. Season to taste with salt and pepper and keep warm.

7. **Make the horseradish sour cream:** In a small bowl, stir together the sour cream, horseradish, lemon juice, and sugar until well combined. Season to taste with salt and pepper.

8. To serve, place a large spoonful of horseradish sour cream on each plate. Top with the roasted cabbage and beets. Garnish with the croutons and dill.

SERVES 4 TO 6

1 head savoy cabbage
1 garlic clove, minced
6 tablespoons unsalted butter, divided
2 tablespoons yellow miso
1 tablespoon liquid honey
2 teaspoons grated peeled fresh ginger
1 teaspoon fresh thyme leaves
½ teaspoon smoked paprika
Zest and juice of 1 lime
2 tablespoons olive oil
1 cup Vegetable Stock (page 162 or store-bought)
Salt and cracked black pepper
2 slices pumpernickel bread or Country Morning Loaf (page 77), cut into ½-inch cubes
2 cups peeled red beets cut into ½-inch cubes
2 teaspoons tomato paste
¾ cup tomato sauce

HORSERADISH SOUR CREAM

1 cup sour cream
2 tablespoons freshly grated or prepared horseradish
1 tablespoon fresh lemon juice
Pinch of granulated sugar
Salt and cracked black pepper

¼ cup fresh dill, roughly chopped, for garnish

Lentil Mushroom Shepherd's Pie with Buttery Rutabaga Potato Mash

Shepherd's pie was a dish that Lynn grew up on and brings back childhood memories of making this dish with her mother, who always put cornflakes on top of the casserole. Our hearty, flavour-packed lentil and mushroom version meets fluffy mashed rutabaga and potatoes crowned with that familiar cornflake topping for a bit of nostalgic laughter around the dinner table.

1. **Make the buttery rutabaga potato mash:** Place the rutabaga in a large pot of salted cold water. Bring to a simmer and cook until fork-tender, about 30 minutes. Drain the rutabaga and return to the pot. Mash the rutabaga.

2. Meanwhile, place the potatoes in a medium pot of salted cold water. Bring to a simmer and cook until fork-tender, 20 to 25 minutes. Drain the potatoes and return to the pot. Mash the potatoes.

3. Add the mashed potatoes to the pot of mashed rutabaga along with the butter and milk. Using the potato masher, mix together well, then season to taste with salt. Cover and set aside.

4. **Make the filling:** Preheat the oven to 350°F (180°C).

5. Melt the butter in a large skillet over medium-high heat. Add the mushrooms and cook, stirring often, until deep golden brown, 8 to 10 minutes. Reduce the heat to medium, add the leeks, carrots, celery, garlic, and thyme, and continue cooking until the vegetables are tender, another 10 minutes. Season to taste with salt and pepper. Add the tomato paste and cook, stirring, another 2 to 3 minutes, until well combined. Sprinkle the flour over the mixture and cook, stirring, for 1 minute. Add the lentils and vegetable stock and cook, stir constantly, for 3 to 4 minutes, until the sauce has thickened. Discard the thyme sprigs.

6. **Assemble and bake:** Transfer the lentil mixture to a 13 × 9-inch baking dish and spread in an even layer. Scoop the rutabaga potato mash over the filling and smooth the top. Bake until golden brown on top, 25 to 30 minutes.

7. Sprinkle the cornflakes over the casserole and bake for another 5 minutes. Remove from the oven and let sit for 10 minutes before serving.

SERVES 4 TO 6

BUTTERY RUTABAGA POTATO MASH
3 cups peeled rutabaga cut into 2-inch cubes
1 cup peeled Yukon Gold potatoes cut into 2-inch cubes
4 tablespoons unsalted butter
¾ cup whole milk
Salt

FILLING
4 tablespoons unsalted butter
2 cups thinly sliced mixed mushrooms (such as button, cremini, and shiitake)
1 leek (white part only), thinly sliced
1 large carrot, peeled and finely chopped
2 celery stalks, finely diced
2 garlic cloves, minced
2 sprigs fresh thyme
Salt and cracked black pepper
2 tablespoons tomato paste
3 tablespoons all-purpose flour
1 can (19 ounces/540 mL) lentils, rinsed and drained
2 cups Vegetable Stock (page 162 or store-bought)
1 cup cornflakes

Potato, Kale, and Chickpea Korma

The ever-popular korma curry has its roots in the Mughlai cuisine of India, and features meat or vegetables braised in a cream or yogurt sauce. We skip the meat in this vegetarian korma that comes together quickly for a perfect weeknight dinner. It's comforting and satisfying and can be adapted to use up whatever vegetables you have in your kitchen.

1. **Make the raita:** In a small bowl, stir together the yogurt, cucumber, cilantro, lemon juice, and cumin. Season to taste with salt and pepper. Set aside or store in an airtight container in the refrigerator for up to 3 days.

2. **Make the potato, kale, and chickpea korma:** Heat the olive oil in a large skillet over medium heat. Add the onions and cook, stirring, until translucent, about 5 minutes. Add the ginger and garlic and cook, stirring, for 1 minute. Add the jalapeño, curry powder, and turmeric and cook, stirring, for 1 to 2 minutes, until the spices are fragrant.

3. Stir in the potatoes and vegetable stock. Increase the heat to medium-high and cook for 15 minutes or until the potatoes are tender, stirring frequently. Add the chickpeas, ground almonds, kale, and coconut milk and stir together. Reduce the heat to low, cover, and simmer until the vegetables are tender, 20 to 25 minutes. Stir in the cilantro and season well with salt and pepper.

4. Scoop the curry over bowls of basmati rice. Top with the raita, a few cucumber slices (if using), and a sprinkle of cilantro. Serve with warm garlic herb naan.

SERVES 4 TO 6

RAITA
(MAKES ABOUT 1 CUP)
½ cup plain full-fat yogurt
½ cup finely diced cucumber
Leaves from 4 sprigs fresh cilantro, roughly chopped
2 teaspoons fresh lemon juice
¼ teaspoon ground cumin
Salt and freshly ground black pepper

POTATO, KALE, AND
CHICKPEA KORMA
2 tablespoons olive oil
2 yellow onions, diced
1 tablespoon grated peeled fresh ginger
3 garlic cloves, minced
1 jalapeño pepper, seeded and minced
2 tablespoons curry powder
½ teaspoon ground turmeric
6 medium Yukon Gold potatoes, peeled and cubed
2 cups Vegetable Stock (page 162 or store-bought)
1 can (19 ounces/540 mL) chickpeas, rinsed and drained
¼ cup ground almonds
2 cups chopped lacinato kale
1 can (14 ounces/400 mL) full-fat coconut milk
½ cup chopped fresh cilantro, plus more for garnish
Salt and cracked black pepper

FOR SERVING
Cooked basmati rice
Cucumber slices (optional)
Garlic Herb Naan (page 86) or 4 to 6 store-bought naan, warmed

Spicy Orange Sesame Cauliflower

Cauliflower is an incredible vegetable that you can turn into so many amazing dishes. In this fun plant-based take on a popular takeout dish, crispy cauliflower nuggets are tossed in a tasty orange sauce that is a little sweet and a little spicy with such great flavour. This is best served over steamed rice with a scattering of toasted sesame seeds and green onions on top.

1. In a large bowl, whisk the egg white until frothy. Add 1 tablespoon of the soy sauce and 1 tablespoon of the orange zest, season with salt and pepper to taste, and whisk to combine. Add the cauliflower florets and toss well to evenly coat.

2. In a small bowl, whisk together the orange juice, the remaining 2 table-spoons orange zest, vegetable stock, the remaining ⅓ cup soy sauce, honey, and rice vinegar. Set aside.

3. Put the cornstarch in a large bowl. Dredge the cauliflower through the cornstarch to coat. Transfer to a plate.

4. Heat the vegetable oil in a large skillet over medium heat. Working in batches, carefully place the cauliflower in the hot oil and fry until golden brown all over, 3 to 5 minutes. Using a slotted spoon, transfer the cauli-flower to a plate lined with paper towel to absorb excess oil.

5. Once all the cauliflower has been fried, in the same skillet (no need wipe it) over medium heat, add the garlic, ginger, and chili flakes and cook, stirring, until soft, 1 to 2 minutes. Pour in the reserved orange sauce, bring to a boil, and cook until the sauce starts to thicken, 5 to 8 minutes. Toss in the cooked cauliflower and mix to evenly coat in the orange sauce. Season to taste with salt and pepper.

6. Serve the cauliflower over rice. Garnish with the toasted sesame seeds and green onions.

SERVES 4 TO 6

1 egg white

⅓ cup + 1 tablespoon soy sauce, divided

3 tablespoons orange zest, divided

Salt and cracked black pepper

1 head cauliflower, cut into florets (about 6 cups)

1 cup fresh orange juice

⅓ cup Vegetable Stock (page 162 or store-bought)

3 tablespoons wildflower honey

2 tablespoons seasoned rice vinegar

⅓ cup cornstarch

⅓ cup vegetable oil, for frying

4 garlic cloves, minced

1 tablespoon grated peeled fresh ginger

1 teaspoon red chili flakes

FOR SERVING

Cooked long-grain or jasmine rice

2 tablespoons sesame seeds, toasted, for garnish

Green onions, thinly sliced, for garnish

Moroccan-Spiced Pumpkin Tagine with Pumpkin Yogurt

A tagine, sometimes spelled tajine, is a traditional Moroccan cooking vessel make of ceramic or unglazed clay. Tagine is also the name of a North African stew that is cooked in a tagine pot. This rustic and warming vegetable tagine with pumpkin and chickpeas has a wonderful blend of aromatic Moroccan spices in a rich and vibrant tomato sauce and is topped with pumpkin yogurt. Enjoy with the herb couscous or crusty bread. If you don't have a tagine pot, you can use a Dutch oven.

SERVES 4 TO 6

PUMPKIN YOGURT
(MAKES 1¼ CUPS)
¾ cup plain full-fat Greek yogurt
½ cup pure pumpkin purée
1 tablespoon fresh lemon juice
Salt and cracked black pepper

MOROCCAN-SPICED
PUMPKIN TAGINE
2 tablespoons olive oil
1 medium yellow onion, diced
4 garlic cloves, minced
1 tablespoon grated peeled fresh
    ginger
1 fresh red chili, seeded and chopped
1 red bell pepper, diced

1 tablespoon ground cumin
1 tablespoon smoked paprika
2 teaspoons cinnamon
2 teaspoons ground turmeric
2 teaspoons red chili flakes
2 Medjool dates, pitted and finely
    diced
2 tablespoons tomato paste
1 tablespoon brown sugar
3 cups Vegetable Stock (page 162 or
    store-bought)
1 can (28 ounces/796 mL) diced
    tomatoes
3 cups peeled pumpkin or butternut
    squash cut into ¾-inch cubes
Salt and cracked black pepper

1 can (19 ounces/540 mL) chickpeas,
    rinsed and drained
2 tablespoons fresh lemon juice
2 tablespoons chopped fresh cilantro
1 tablespoon chopped fresh mint

HERB COUSCOUS
2 tablespoons unsalted butter
1 tablespoon extra-virgin olive oil
2¼ cups water
2 teaspoons kosher salt
2 cups couscous
1 tablespoon chopped fresh flat-leaf
    parsley
1 tablespoon chopped fresh mint

1. **Make the pumpkin yogurt:** In a small bowl, stir together the yogurt, pumpkin purée, and lemon juice until combined. Season to taste with salt and pepper. Set aside or store in an airtight container in the refrigerator for up to 1 week.

2. **Make the Moroccan-spiced pumpkin tagine:** In a large tagine or Dutch oven, heat the olive oil over medium heat. Add the onions, garlic, ginger, red chili, and bell peppers and cook, stirring, until the onions are soft and translucent, 4 minutes. Add the cumin, smoked paprika, cinnamon, turmeric, and chili flakes. Stir for 2 minutes, until fragrant. Add the dates, tomato paste, and brown sugar. Stir to combine well and cook for another minute.

3. Add the vegetable stock, tomatoes, and pumpkin, then season to taste with salt and pepper. Bring to a boil, then cover, reduce the heat to a simmer, and cook for 30 minutes or until the pumpkin is tender. Stir in the chickpeas and lemon juice and simmer, uncovered, for 5 minutes. Add the cilantro and mint.

4. **Meanwhile make the herb couscous:** Melt the butter with the olive oil in a medium saucepan over medium-high heat. Add the water and kosher salt and bring to a boil. Once the water is boiling, add the couscous, stir once, cover, and remove the pot from the heat. Let sit for 10 minutes. Remove the lid and fluff the couscous with a fork, separating any lumps. Stir in the parsley and mint. Cover and keep warm until ready to use.

5. Divide the herb couscous between shallow bowls. Scoop the stew over the couscous. Serve with the pumpkin yogurt.

Sweet Potato and Black Bean Chili

We love how this chili recipe comes together in record time and packs so much flavour from all the spices and those smoky, spicy chipotle peppers in adobo sauce.

SERVES 4 TO 6

**QUICK-PICKLED RED ONIONS
(MAKES ABOUT 1 CUP)**
Juice of 3 limes
1 tablespoon apple cider vinegar
½ teaspoon granulated sugar
½ teaspoon salt
1 medium red onion, thinly sliced

**SWEET POTATO AND
BLACK BEAN CHILI**
2 tablespoons olive oil
1 medium yellow onion, cut into
    ½-inch cubes
3 garlic cloves, minced
2 tablespoons chili powder
1 tablespoon unsweetened cocoa
    powder

2 teaspoons smoked paprika
2 teaspoons ground cumin
1 teaspoon dried oregano
2 tablespoons tomato paste
2 to 3 chipotle peppers in adobo
    sauce, finely chopped, plus 2 to
    3 tablespoons adobo sauce
2 large sweet potatoes, peeled and
    cut into 1-inch cubes
1 can (28 ounces/796 mL) diced
    tomatoes
1 can (19 ounces/540 mL) black beans,
    rinsed and drained
2 red or yellow bell peppers, cut into
    ½-inch pieces
Salt and cracked black pepper

CRISPY TORTILLA CHIPS
4 cups canola oil, for deep-frying
20 Corn Tortillas (page 124 or store-
    bought), cut into quarters
Kosher salt

GARNISHES
1 cup cherry tomatoes, halved
2 green onions, thinly sliced
½ cup crumbled queso fresco or feta
    cheese
Fresh cilantro sprigs
3 limes (1 for squeezing, 2 cut into
    wedges)

1. **Make the quick-pickled red onions:** In a medium bowl, stir together the lime juice, apple cider vinegar, sugar, and salt until the sugar is dissolved. Add the sliced red onions. Use a spoon to press the onions down into the liquid. Let sit for 30 minutes before using. Store in an airtight container in the refrigerator for up to 3 days.

2. **Make the sweet potato and black bean chili:** Heat the olive oil in a large skillet over medium-high heat. Add the onions and cook, stirring occasionally, until they begin to soften, 3 to 4 minutes. Add the garlic, chili powder, cocoa powder, smoked paprika, cumin, and oregano and cook, stirring, until the spices are fragrant, 1 to 2 minutes. Stir in the tomato paste, chipotle peppers, and adobo sauce. Add the sweet potatoes, diced tomatoes, black beans, bell peppers, and salt and pepper to taste. Stir to mix. Reduce the heat to low and simmer, uncovered, until the vegetables are tender, 20 to 25 minutes. Remove from

the heat. The chili can be cooled and stored in an airtight container in the refrigerator for up to 4 days.

3. **Meanwhile, make the crispy tortilla chips:** Heat the canola oil in a large, heavy pot until it reaches 350°F (180°C) on a deep-fry thermometer. Working in batches, carefully drop 3 or 4 tortillas into the hot oil and fry for 1 to 2 minutes, until golden. Using tongs, turn the tortillas and fry for another minute or until golden brown and crisp. Transfer to a plate lined with paper towel to absorb excess oil and sprinkle with salt.

4. **Finish the chili and serve:** Spoon the chili into warm bowls and garnish with the cherry tomatoes, green onions, queso fresco, and cilantro sprigs. Squeeze the juice of 1 lime over top. Serve with extra lime wedges on the side, crispy tortilla chips, and quick-pickled red onions.

NOTE: Feel free to add more of your favourite veggies or different types of beans to the chili pot. Butternut squash, celery, sweet corn, and zucchini all like to join the chili party.

Sweet Potato and Spinach Enchiladas

Enchiladas are super fun to eat and great for a crowd. All the work goes into the production—tasty tortillas filled with sweet potato and lots of spinach, smothered with homemade enchilada sauce and cheese, all baked until bubbly—but the dish takes no time at all to heat up. Make a big bowl of Simple Salad (page 177) and a pitcher of ice-cold margaritas and you're all set for a great night.

SERVES 4

ENCHILADA SAUCE

3 tablespoons olive oil

1 medium yellow onion, finely diced

3 garlic cloves, minced

1 can (5.5 ounces/156 mL) tomato paste

1 chipotle pepper in adobo sauce, finely chopped, plus 2 to 3 tablespoons adobo sauce

1 tablespoon ground cumin

2 teaspoons chili powder

2 teaspoons garlic powder

2 teaspoons chopped fresh oregano

2 teaspoons kosher salt

3 cups Vegetable Stock (page 162 or store-bought)

SWEET POTATO AND SPINACH ENCHILADAS

2 tablespoons olive oil

1 yellow onion, finely chopped

2 garlic cloves, finely chopped

2 sweet potatoes, peeled and cut into ½-inch dice

2 teaspoons chili powder

½ teaspoon ground cumin

Salt and cracked black pepper

4 cups baby spinach

1 can (19 ounces/540 mL) black beans, rinsed and drained

½ cup chopped fresh cilantro, plus more for garnish

1½ cups grated cheddar cheese, divided

¼ cup canola oil, for frying

8 small Corn Tortillas (page 124 or store-bought)

FOR SERVING

Sour cream

½ cup crumbled queso fresco or feta cheese

Sliced avocado

1 jalapeño pepper, seeded and thinly sliced

2 radishes, thinly sliced

— *continued* —

1. **Make the enchilada sauce:** Heat the olive oil in a large saucepan over medium heat. Add the onions and cook, stirring occasionally, for 5 minutes, until slightly caramelized. Add the garlic and cook, stirring, for 1 minute. Stir in the tomato paste, chipotle pepper, adobo sauce, cumin, chili powder, garlic powder, oregano, and kosher salt. Add the vegetable stock and simmer for 15 minutes, stirring occasionally.

2. Transfer the mixture to a blender and blend until smooth. Set aside or let cool to room temperature, then store in an airtight container in the refrigerator for up to 2 weeks or in the freezer for up to 6 months.

3. **Make the sweet potato and spinach filling:** Preheat the oven to 375°F (190°C).

4. Heat the olive oil in a large saucepan over medium heat. Add the onions and cook, stirring occasionally, until softened, 2 to 3 minutes. Add the garlic and cook for another minute. Add the sweet potatoes, chili powder, cumin, 1 cup of the enchilada sauce, and salt and pepper to taste. Cook, stirring occasionally, until the sweet potatoes are tender, 12 to 15 minutes. Fold in the spinach, black beans, and cilantro, and stir until the spinach wilts. Add another ½ cup of the enchilada sauce, then season to taste with salt and pepper. Remove from the heat and stir in ¾ cup of the cheddar.

5. **Fry the tortillas, assemble, and bake the enchiladas:** Heat the canola oil in a large skillet over medium-high heat. Once the oil is hot, fry the tortillas, one at a time and carefully turning once with tongs, for about 1 minute, until golden. Transfer to a plate lined with paper towel to absorb excess oil and season with salt.

6. Spoon 3 tablespoons of the enchilada sauce into a shallow bowl. Working with one fried tortilla at a time, dredge both sides in the sauce to coat. Spoon ½ cup of the sweet potato and spinach filling across the centre of the tortilla, fold one half of the tortilla over the filling, tuck it in, and roll up tightly. Place the enchiladas seam side down in a rectangular casserole dish. Cover the tortillas with the remaining enchilada sauce and sprinkle with the remaining ¾ cup cheddar.

7. Bake until the cheese is golden brown and the sauce is bubbling, about 20 minutes. To serve, garnish the enchiladas with sour cream, queso fresco, avocado, jalapeños, radishes, and cilantro.

NOTE: Making your own enchiladas sauce is the only way to go because it's the best and we promise it's easy to make. You can even make it in advance. It freezes well.

Chili Oil

Makes about 1½ cups

A tongue-tingling chili oil with earthy and floral notes thanks to the dance of dried chilies, Szechuan peppercorns, star anise, and cinnamon.

  1½ cups canola oil
  6 star anise
  1 cinnamon stick
  2 tablespoons Szechuan peppercorns
  ¾ cup red chili flakes
  1 teaspoon sea salt

1. Heat the canola oil in a small saucepan over medium-high heat. When the oil is hot, add the star anise, cinnamon stick, and Szechuan peppercorns. When the oil starts to bubble slightly, reduce the heat to medium-low. The oil temperature should be 225°F (110°C) so the spices do not burn. Let the spices cook in the oil, without stirring, until the seeds and pods are darker, about 20 minutes. Remove from the heat and let cool for 5 minutes.

2. In a medium bowl, combine the chili flakes and salt. Set a fine-mesh sieve over the bowl and pour the oil through the sieve to remove the aromatics. Stir the oil well. Let cool completely, then transfer to a jar with a lid and store in the refrigerator for up to 6 months.

Celery Stir-Fry with Crispy Tofu and Sesame Honey Chili Sauce

Crispy tofu seasoned with five-spice powder is delicious on its own. But when tossed with the robust flavour and crunch of celery dressed in sesame honey chili oil, it becomes a dish that will definitely make regular appearances on your dinner table.

1. **Make the sesame honey chili sauce:** In a small bowl, combine the honey, soy sauce, chili oil, and sesame oil. Stir to mix well. Set aside.

2. **Make the celery stir-fry with crispy tofu:** In a medium bowl, stir together the cornstarch, five-spice powder, and salt and pepper to taste.

3. Cut the tofu into 2-inch-long strips, ¼ inch thick. Gently toss the tofu strips in the cornstarch mixture to evenly coat.

4. Heat the vegetable oil in a small deep pot over medium-high heat until it reaches 375°F (190°C) on a deep-fry thermometer. Working in batches, fry the coated tofu until golden brown, 2 to 3 minutes per side. Using tongs, transfer the tofu to a plate lined with paper towel to absorb excess oil.

5. Heat the olive oil in a large skillet over medium-high heat. Add the ginger and garlic and cook, stirring, until softened, 1 to 2 minutes. Add the celery and cook until it starts to soften, about 2 minutes. Pour in some of the sesame honey chili sauce, stir to combine, and cook for another 2 to 3 minutes, until the celery is well coated.

6. To serve, arrange the celery stir-fry and crispy tofu on a serving plate or individual plates. Spoon a little more sesame honey chili sauce over top. Garnish with the celery leaves.

SERVES 4

SESAME HONEY CHILI SAUCE

3 tablespoons liquid honey
2 tablespoons soy sauce
1 tablespoon Chili Oil (page 257 or store-bought)
½ teaspoon sesame oil

CELERY STIR-FRY WITH CRISPY TOFU

1 cup cornstarch
¼ teaspoon five-spice powder
Salt and cracked black pepper
8 ounces (225 g) firm tofu
1 cup vegetable oil, for frying
2 tablespoons olive oil, for frying
1 (2-inch) piece fresh ginger, peeled and finely julienned
4 garlic cloves, minced
6 celery stalks, cut into 2-inch × ¼-inch sticks

Celery leaves, for garnish

Beet Falafel with Lemony Tzatziki

**MAKES 8 FALAFEL PATTIES,
SERVES 4**

**LEMONY TZATZIKI
(MAKES ABOUT 1 CUP)**

½ cup finely grated English cucumber
1 cup plain full-fat Greek yogurt
1 tablespoon fresh lemon juice
1½ teaspoons olive oil
2 teaspoons Confit Garlic Purée
    (page 89)
1 tablespoon chopped fresh dill
1 tablespoon chopped fresh mint
Salt and cracked black pepper

BEET FALAFEL

1½ cups canned chickpeas, rinsed
    and drained
4 garlic cloves
½ cup fresh flat-leaf parsley leaves
¼ cup walnuts, toasted
2 medium red beets, peeled and
    grated (about 1½ cups)
¾ cup panko breadcrumbs
1 tablespoon tahini
1 tablespoon ground coriander
2 teaspoons ground cumin
2 teaspoons olive oil, more for
    brushing
Salt and cracked black pepper

MIXED GREEN SALAD

2 cups mixed baby greens
2 mini cucumbers, thinly sliced
1 tablespoon hemp seeds
Lemon Dill Vinaigrette (page 178)
Salt and cracked black pepper

Beets are one of the tastiest vegetables that we grow in our garden. They have an earthy sweetness that is beyond compare. Falafel, often considered fast food or street food in Middle Eastern cuisine, are very versatile. The classic deep-fried version is what's typically found, but there's no reason they can't be baked. Beets add a sweet flavour and plenty of nutrition and help to keep the falafel moist.

1. **Make the lemony tzatziki:** Place the cucumber on a clean kitchen towel and gently squeeze to release excess water.

2. In a medium bowl, mix together the cucumber, yogurt, lemon juice, olive oil, confit garlic purée, dill, and mint. Season to taste with salt and pepper. Refrigerate until ready to use or store in an airtight container in the refrigerator for up to 1 week.

3. **Make the beet falafel:** Preheat the oven to 375°F (190°C). Line a baking sheet with parchment paper.

4. Evenly spread out the chickpeas on the lined baking sheet. Bake until slightly cracked and dried out, 10 to 12 minutes. Set aside; leave the oven on.

5. In a food processor, combine the garlic, parsley, and walnuts and pulse into small pieces. Add the baked chickpeas (set aside the baking sheet with parchment paper), grated beets, panko, tahini, coriander, cumin, and olive oil, then season well with salt and pepper. Pulse until a loose, coarse mixture forms, about 30 seconds.

6. Scoop ½ cup of the chickpea mixture per falafel, using your hands to form patties, about ¾ inch thick, and arranging the patties evenly spaced on the lined baking sheet. (You should have 8 patties.) Brush with olive oil and bake until crispy on the outside, 15 to 20 minutes, turning halfway through.

7. **Make the mixed green salad:** In a medium bowl, toss together the baby greens and sliced cucumbers. Sprinkle the hemp seeds over top, then toss with some of the lemon dill vinaigrette. Season to taste with salt and pepper.

8. **Assemble:** Spoon some lemony tzatziki onto plates. Top each with beet falafel and serve with the mixed green salad.

Celery Root Steaks with Sautéed Mushrooms and Café de Paris Butter

Café de Paris butter is the perfect flavoured compound butter for these roasted celery root steaks. Celery root (or celeriac) delivers a nutty, slightly sweet flavour, and softens to a scrumptious meaty texture when cooked. As the butter melts all over the celery root and mushrooms, it brings a tantalizing mix of herbs, spices, and savoury notes to this French bistro favourite.

1. **Make the café de Paris butter:** Put the butter in a medium bowl. Add the garlic, shallots, Worcestershire sauce, curry powder, mustard, lemon juice, parsley, thyme, and Parmesan. Mix well. Season well with salt and pepper. Set aside or store in an airtight container in the refrigerator for up to 1 week.

2. **Make the celery root steaks with sautéed mushrooms:** Preheat the oven to 400°F (200°C).

3. Cut the celery root crosswise into four 1-inch-thick slices. Season well with salt and pepper.

4. Heat 2 tablespoons of the olive oil in a large ovenproof skillet over medium-high heat. Place the celery root steaks in the pan and cook until golden brown, about 4 minutes per side. Transfer the skillet to the oven and roast the celery root until tender, 8 to 10 minutes. Transfer to a plate and cover with foil to keep warm.

5. In the same skillet (no need to wipe it), heat the remaining 2 tablespoons olive oil over medium heat. Add the shallots and cook, stirring, until softened, 2 to 3 minutes. Add the mushrooms and cook, stirring often, until the mushrooms have started to caramelize, about 3 minutes. Add the garlic and cook, stirring, until fragrant, 30 to 60 seconds. Season to taste with salt and pepper. Remove from the heat. Add 2 tablespoons of the café de Paris butter, swirling in the pan until just melted.

6. Place the celery root steaks on a large serving platter. Spread the remaining 2 tablespoons café de Paris butter evenly over the celery root. Spoon the sautéed mushroom mixture over top and season with pepper and flaky sea salt. Place the lemon halves on the platter for squeezing over the steaks. Serve with extra café de Paris butter on the side, along with the fondant potatoes and sautéed green vegetables.

SERVES 4

**CAFÉ DE PARIS BUTTER
(MAKES ABOUT ½ CUP)**

8 tablespoons unsalted butter, at room temperature
1 garlic clove, minced
2 teaspoons shallots, finely chopped
2 teaspoons Worcestershire sauce
1 teaspoon curry powder
1 teaspoon Dijon mustard
1 teaspoon fresh lemon juice
2 tablespoons finely chopped fresh flat-leaf parsley
2 teaspoons finely chopped fresh thyme
1 tablespoon grated Parmesan cheese
Salt and cracked black pepper

CELERY ROOT STEAKS WITH SAUTÉED MUSHROOMS

1 large celery root, peeled
Salt and cracked black pepper
4 tablespoons olive oil, divided
2 small shallots, minced
2 cups quartered cremini mushrooms
2 garlic cloves, minced
4 tablespoons Café de Paris Butter (recipe above), divided
Flaky sea salt, for finishing

FOR SERVING

1 lemon, cut in half, for squeezing
1 batch Fondant Potatoes (page 300)
Sautéed green vegetables (such as green beans, asparagus, broccoli florets)

Grilled Cajun Zucchini and Summer Corn Salad with Avocado

SERVES 4 TO 6

**CAJUN SPICE BLEND
(MAKES ABOUT ½ CUP)**

2 tablespoons smoked paprika

2 tablespoons cracked black pepper

1 tablespoon kosher salt

2 teaspoons brown sugar

2 teaspoons dried oregano

2 teaspoons dried thyme

1 teaspoon cayenne pepper

**GRILLED CAJUN ZUCCHINI AND
SUMMER CORN SALAD**

6 tablespoons olive oil, divided

2 tablespoons fresh lemon juice

2 garlic cloves, minced

2 sweet corn cobs, shucked

4 medium green zucchini, halved
    lengthwise

1 to 2 teaspoons Cajun Spice Blend
    (recipe above)

2 tablespoons finely chopped fresh
    basil, plus more for garnish

2 tablespoons grated Parmesan
    cheese

1 can (19 ounces/540 mL) black
    beans, rinsed and drained

1 red bell pepper, finely diced

2 cups mixed red and yellow cherry
    tomatoes, halved

½ teaspoon lime zest

2 tablespoons fresh lime juice

2 teaspoons granulated sugar

1 teaspoon Dijon mustard

Salt and cracked black pepper

GARNISHES

1 to 2 avocados, pitted, peeled, and
    cut into thick slices

1 Jalapeño pepper, thinly sliced

2 limes, halved

When it's time to fire up the grill, this zucchini and corn marinated in Cajun spice is such a perfect recipe for a casual, fast, and flavourful platter. The Cajun spice blend will become your go-to when cooking on the grill—there is nothing better than spiced-up veggies hot off the grill for a light entrée on a warm summer night.

1. **Make the Cajun spice blend:** In a small bowl, whisk together the smoked paprika, black pepper, salt, brown sugar, oregano, thyme, and cayenne pepper until well combined. Set aside or store in an airtight container at room temperature for up to 6 months.

2. **Grill the corn and zucchini:** In a large baking dish, whisk together 3 tablespoons of the olive oil, lemon juice, and garlic. Add the corn and zucchini and season well with the Cajun spice blend to taste. Turn the corn and zucchini to coat well. Let marinate for 30 minutes.

3. Meanwhile, preheat the grill to medium-high heat.

4. Place the corn on the grill, close the lid, and grill, turning often, until lightly browned on all sides, 8 to 10 minutes. Transfer to a plate. Place the zucchini cut side down on the grill and cook until tender, 4 to 5 minutes per side. Transfer the zucchini to a serving platter and sprinkle with the basil and Parmesan.

5. **Assemble the salad:** Cut the corn kernels off the cobs in a large bowl. Add the black beans, bell peppers, and tomatoes.

6. In a small bowl, whisk together the lime zest, lime juice, sugar, mustard, and the remaining 3 tablespoons olive oil. Drizzle over the corn salad. Season to taste with salt and pepper. Mix well.

7. Spoon the corn salad over the grilled zucchini. Garnish with basil, avocado, jalapeños, and lime halves for squeezing.

Butternut Squash Scallopini with Apples, Sage, and Hazelnut Dukkha

The ever-popular butternut squash has a creamy, pale orange exterior. The more orange the skin, the riper and sweeter the flesh will taste. In this recipe, butternut squash basted in brown butter is made extra special with the addition of heat from harissa, sweetness from maple syrup, and a sprinkle of crunchy hazelnut dukkha for great texture.

1. **Make the hazelnut dukkha spice:** Heat a large, heavy skillet over medium heat. When the skillet is hot, add the hazelnuts and toast, stirring frequently, until fragrant, about 3 minutes. Add the sesame seeds and continue cooking, stirring often, until the sesame seeds start to turn golden brown, about 2 minutes. Transfer the mixture to a small food processor.

2. Add the coriander, cumin, allspice, sea salt, and pepper. Pulse until the nuts are broken down and the mixture resembles coarse sand. Store cooled dukkha spice in an airtight container at room temperature for up to 1 month.

3. **Make the butternut squash scallopini:** Melt 2 tablespoons of the butter in a large, heavy skillet over medium-high heat. Add the apples, maple syrup, and harissa and cook, stirring occasionally, until the apples are tender, 5 to 7 minutes. Add the apple cider vinegar and cook for another minute. Transfer the apples and the liquid to a small bowl. Set aside and keep warm.

4. In the same skillet (no need to wipe it), heat the olive oil over medium heat. Working in batches if needed, add the squash rounds and cook until deeply browned and fork-tender, 3 to 4 minutes per side. Add the remaining 1 tablespoon butter and the sage, tilt the pan toward you so the butter pools on one side, and use a large spoon to continually baste the squash with butter until the butter is no longer bubbling, smells nutty, and is starting to brown, about 1 minute. Remove from the heat and season well with salt and pepper. (Reserve the fried sage leaves for garnish.)

5. Transfer the squash rounds to a serving platter. Wipe the skillet.

6. In the same skillet, warm the apples and the liquid, then pour over the squash. Garnish with the fried sage and sprinkle with hazelnut dukkha spice.

SERVES 4

HAZELNUT DUKKHA SPICE (MAKES 1 CUP)

1 cup blanched hazelnuts
¼ cup sesame seeds
1 teaspoon ground coriander
1 teaspoon ground cumin
⅛ teaspoon ground allspice
1 teaspoon sea salt
½ teaspoon ground black pepper

BUTTERNUT SQUASH SCALLOPINI

3 tablespoons unsalted butter, divided
2 Gala apples, each cored and cut into 8 wedges
¼ cup pure maple syrup
1 teaspoon harissa powder
2 tablespoons apple cider vinegar
2 tablespoons olive oil
1 large butternut squash, peeled and cut crosswise into eight ½-inch-thick slices
4 fresh sage leaves
Salt and cracked black pepper
2 tablespoons Hazelnut Dukkha Spice (recipe above)

Buffalo Fried Cauliflower

SERVES 4 TO 6

FRIED CAULIFLOWER

2½ cups all-purpose flour

2½ tablespoons cayenne pepper

1½ tablespoons smoked paprika

2 teaspoons garlic powder

1½ teaspoons salt

½ teaspoon brown sugar

2 heads cauliflower, cut into large
    florets

2 cups buttermilk

3 tablespoons Frank's Red Hot sauce

Canola oil, for deep-frying

Salt and cracked black pepper

**BUFFALO HOT SAUCE
(MAKES ABOUT 1¼ CUPS)**

⅔ cup Frank's Red Hot sauce

½ cup cold unsalted butter

1 tablespoon white vinegar

1 tablespoon liquid honey

¼ teaspoon Worcestershire sauce

½ teaspoon cayenne pepper

⅛ teaspoon garlic powder

Salt and cracked black pepper

FOR SERVING

Sliced bread

Bread and butter pickles

We can't get enough of this recipe. Nashville hot cauliflower is everything the name promises—it's sticky and juicy, with the perfect amount of spice to light up your taste buds. Crispy fried cauliflower dredged in spicy hot sauce—our version of a buffalo hot sauce that is finger-licking good. Dive in—it really is that good!

1. **Prepare the cauliflower:** Set a rack over a baking sheet. In a large bowl, stir together the flour, cayenne pepper, smoked paprika, garlic powder, salt, and brown sugar. Toss the cauliflower in the spiced flour, lightly coating the florets.

2. In another large bowl, whisk together the buttermilk and hot sauce.

3. Shake off most of the flour from the cauliflower florets back into the bowl, then transfer the florets to the buttermilk mixture and toss to coat well.

4. Working with one floret at a time, dredge the florets through the spiced flour and place on the rack.

5. **Make the buffalo hot sauce:** In a small saucepan, combine the hot sauce, butter, vinegar, honey, Worcestershire sauce, cayenne pepper, and garlic powder. Bring to a simmer over medium heat while stirring with a whisk. As soon as the sauce begins to bubble around the sides of the pot, remove from the heat. Season to taste with salt and pepper. Set aside or let cool completely, then store in an airtight container in the refrigerator for up to 2 months.

6. **Deep-fry the cauliflower:** In a large, deep skillet or Dutch oven, heat 4 inches of canola oil over medium-high heat until it reaches 350°F (180°C) on a deep-fry thermometer. Working in batches, fry the cauliflower in the hot oil until golden brown and crispy, 4 to 5 minutes, turning halfway through. Using tongs, transfer the cauliflower to a large bowl. Drizzle with buffalo hot sauce to taste and toss to coat. Season to taste with salt and pepper.

7. Serve with sliced bread, bread and butter pickles, and more buffalo sauce on the side for dipping.

Sides

Sweet Corn on the Cob with Coconut and Lime

When sweet corn comes into season it's time to bring out the big pot to boil up some corn on the cob. If you're like us, corn on the cob is served with dinner almost every night. Adding coconut milk to the pot brings just enough sweetness and creaminess to the corn, but really, it's all about the butter. Corn loves butter, and you'll love the one and only butter hit you'll ever need to make the tastiest corn on the cob you've ever tasted.

1. In a large saucepan, combine the water and coconut milk, then season well with salt. Bring to a boil over medium heat, then add the corn and cook until tender, 4 to 5 minutes. Using tongs, transfer the corn to a large bowl.

2. Toss the corn with the one-hit butter and season with salt and pepper to taste. Sprinkle with the toasted coconut and cilantro. Serve with lime wedges.

SERVES 4

4 cups water

1 can (14 ounces/400 mL) full-fat coconut milk

4 sweet corn cobs, shucked and cut in half

2 to 3 heaping tablespoons One-Hit Butter (page 62)

Salt and cracked black pepper

¼ cup unsweetened shredded coconut, toasted

3 tablespoons chopped fresh cilantro

Lime wedges, for serving

Braised New Potatoes with Shallots, Garlic, Rosemary, and Thyme

SERVES 4

1½ pounds (675 g) new potatoes, washed and halved

2 shallots, thinly sliced

4 garlic cloves, thinly sliced

2 sprigs fresh thyme

1 sprig fresh rosemary

1 teaspoon thinly sliced fresh red finger chili

3 tablespoons olive oil

1 cup Vegetable Stock (page 162 or store-bought)

Salt and cracked black pepper

3 tablespoons One-Hit Butter (page 62) or unsalted butter, at room temperature

New potatoes are not a variety; they are any potato that is harvested early in the season. We dig them up early before they get too big, so they can be enjoyed for their delicate thin skins, sweet flavour, and fluffy texture. These braised potatoes are melt-in-your-mouth delicious—buttery, garlicky, and so tender. We could eat them every day.

1.   Preheat the oven to 325°F (160°C).

2.   Place the potatoes in a single layer in a large baking pan. Evenly sprinkle with the shallots, garlic, thyme, rosemary, and chilies. Pour the olive oil and vegetable stock over the potatoes, then season to taste with salt and pepper. Cover with foil and bake until the potatoes are fork-tender, 45 to 60 minutes.

3.   To serve, transfer the potatoes to a serving dish. Add the butter and toss until melted. Season to taste with salt and pepper.

Spaghetti Squash Gratin with Leeks and Spinach

Spaghetti squash is an incredible veggie to cook with. When roasted, it turns into pasta-like strands, perfect for mixing with cheese and sauce. The hollowed-out squash halves become bowls you can fill with that cheesy squash mixture. Crispy breadcrumbs with toasted pumpkin seeds add delicious crunch on top.

1.   Preheat the oven to 400°F (200°C).

2.   Cut the squash in half lengthwise. Use a spoon to scoop out the seeds. Discard the seeds. Rub the cut sides with a little olive oil, then place the squash cut side down in a shallow baking dish. Bake for about 40 minutes, until tender and a paring knife easily pierces the skin. Remove from the oven, turn the squash halves cut side up, and let cool slightly. Leave the oven on.

3.   When the squash is cool enough to handle, use a fork to gently scrape strands from the shells into a bowl, loosening and fluffing the strands so they look like spaghetti. Place the empty shells on a baking sheet lined with parchment paper.

4.   Melt the butter in a large skillet over medium-high heat. Add the leeks and onions and sauté until the vegetables are starting to soften, 4 to 5 minutes. Add the garlic and thyme and cook for another 1 to 2 minutes. Pour in the white wine and simmer, stirring occasionally, until the leeks are tender, 4 to 5 minutes.

5.   Reduce the heat to low. Add the mozzarella and cream cheese and simmer for 2 to 3 minutes to melt the cheese and thicken the sauce. Add the spinach and cook until wilted. Add the spaghetti squash and mix well. Remove from the heat and season to taste with salt and pepper.

6.   Divide the mixture between the squash halves.

7.   In a small bowl, stir together the pumpkin seeds, panko, Parmesan, and parsley. Evenly top the stuffed squash with the breadcrumb mixture. Return the squash to the oven and bake until hot and golden brown, 10 to 12 minutes.

SERVES 4 TO 6

1 spaghetti squash

Olive oil, for rubbing

2 tablespoons unsalted butter

2 cups chopped leeks (white and light green parts only)

1 cup finely diced yellow onions

2 garlic cloves, minced

1 teaspoon fresh thyme leaves

½ cup dry white wine

½ cup grated mozzarella cheese

¼ cup (2 ounces/55 g) cream cheese, at room temperature

3 cups baby spinach

Salt and cracked black pepper

¼ cup pumpkin seeds, chopped

¼ cup panko breadcrumbs

¼ cup grated Parmesan cheese

1 tablespoon finely chopped fresh flat-leaf parsley

Pan-Roasted Asparagus with Sage, Shallot Cream, and Crispy Parmesan

SERVES 4 TO 6

CRISPY PARMESAN

1 cup grated Parmesan cheese

PAN-ROASTED ASPARAGUS WITH SAGE AND SHALLOT CREAM

2 cups thinly sliced shallots

½ cup heavy (35%) cream

4 tablespoons unsalted butter, divided

Salt and cracked black pepper

1 lemon, halved

2 tablespoons olive oil

4 garlic cloves, very thinly sliced

6 to 8 fresh sage leaves

1½ pounds (675 g) asparagus spears, trimmed

This is one of our favourite ways to enjoy asparagus when it's at the peak of its season. Asparagus is prized for a buttery, sweet flavour with a hint of earthy bitterness, and it pairs beautifully with the creamy shallots and the crispy Parmesan. We love that there is wild asparagus growing all over our property and we enjoy the long hike down to the duck pond to forage for those tender spears. Lucky us!

1. **Make the crispy Parmesan:** Preheat the oven to 350°F (180°C). Line a baking sheet with parchment paper.

2. Spoon 2-tablespoon portions of the Parmesan 2 inches apart on the lined baking sheet, and using the back of a spoon, spread into 3-inch circles. Take care to give them a little room to spread without touching. Bake until melting and very slightly browned, 8 to 12 minutes. Remove from the oven and let cool completely on the baking sheet.

3. **Make the pan-roasted asparagus with sage and shallot cream:** In a small saucepan, combine the shallots and cream. Cook over medium heat, stirring occasionally, until the shallots are tender, 8 to 10 minutes. Strain into a small bowl; reserve the cream.

4. In a blender, combine the cooked shallots and 2 tablespoons of the butter. With the blender running, drizzle in enough of the reserved cream to make a smooth and creamy mixture. Season to taste with salt and pepper.

5. Heat a large skillet over medium-high heat. Place the lemon halves cut sides down in the hot pan and sear for 2 to 3 minutes, until caramelized. Transfer the lemons to a plate. Add the olive oil and garlic to the skillet and cook, stirring, until the garlic is light golden brown and crispy, 2 to 3 minutes. Add the sage and cook for another 30 seconds, until the leaves turn bright green. Transfer the garlic and sage to a plate lined with paper towel to absorb excess oil. Season to taste with salt and pepper.

6. Add the asparagus and the remaining 2 tablespoons butter to the skillet and cook over medium-high heat, turning the asparagus often to ensure even cooking, until fork-tender, 4 to 5 minutes. Return the fried garlic and sage leaves to the skillet and toss together.

7. **Assemble:** Spoon the shallot cream onto a serving platter, then arrange the asparagus on top. Squeeze the juice from the charred lemon all over the asparagus and garnish with the crispy Parmesan.

Roasted Cauliflower and Tomatoes with Mint Chimichurri Sauce

Lots of cauliflower florets roasted until golden and caramelized with crispy edges, tossed with capers and tomatoes, and topped with a zesty mint chimichurri sauce is a wonderful side dish. It always amazes us how just a few simple ingredients can work together to create such a brilliant taste explosion.

1. **Make the mint chimichurri sauce:** In a medium bowl, stir together the garlic, mint, parsley, oregano, red wine vinegar, and lemon juice. Season with the salt, pepper, and chili flakes. Slowly whisk in the olive oil until well combined. Cover with plastic wrap and let sit for 1 hour at room temperature. Set aside or store in an airtight container in the refrigerator for up to 3 days.

2. **Prepare the roasted cauliflower with capers and tomatoes:** Preheat the oven to 475°F (240°C). Line a baking sheet with parchment paper.

3. In a large bowl, toss the cauliflower with the olive oil. Season to taste with salt and pepper. Spread out evenly on the lined baking sheet and roast until the cauliflower is tender and starting to brown in spots, about 15 minutes. Add the teardrop and cherry tomatoes, capers, and garlic and stir to mix evenly. Roast until the tomatoes start to wilt, another 5 to 7 minutes. Transfer the roasted vegetable mixture to a serving bowl. Spoon the mint chimichurri sauce over the cauliflower.

SERVES 4

MINT CHIMICHURRI SAUCE

2 garlic cloves, minced

½ cup fresh mint, finely chopped

¼ cup fresh flat-leaf parsley, finely chopped

1 tablespoon finely chopped fresh oregano

¼ cup red wine vinegar

2 tablespoons fresh lemon juice

1 teaspoon kosher salt

⅛ teaspoon black pepper

¼ teaspoon red chili flakes

½ cup extra-virgin olive oil

ROASTED CAULIFLOWER WITH CAPERS AND TOMATOES

6 cups medium cauliflower florets (from 1 large head of cauliflower)

3 tablespoons olive oil

Salt and cracked black pepper

½ cup yellow teardrop tomatoes, halved

½ cup red cherry tomatoes, halved

1 tablespoon drained capers

2 garlic cloves, minced

Curried Acorn Squash with Golden Raisins, Honey, and Pine Nuts

SERVES 4 TO 6

2 acorn squash, halved, seeded, and cut into ½-inch wedges

3 tablespoons olive oil

2 teaspoons curry powder

1 teaspoon ground turmeric

⅛ teaspoon red chili flakes

Salt and cracked black pepper

½ cup golden raisins

3 tablespoons liquid honey

3 tablespoons unsalted butter

1 tablespoon brown sugar

Leaves from 1 sprig fresh rosemary

2 tablespoons pine nuts, toasted

Curry-roasted acorn squash is the perfect autumn side dish. Your house will fill up with the delicious smells of the curry spices and the sweet smell of the roasting acorn squash. This is a very easy dish that comes together in minutes, and the honey butter glaze with rosemary, toasty pine nuts, and raisins pulls everything together.

1. Preheat the oven to 375°F (190°C). Line a baking sheet with parchment paper.

2. In a large bowl, combine the squash wedges, olive oil, curry powder, turmeric, and chili flakes and toss to coat. Season well with salt and pepper. Arrange the squash cut side down in a single layer on the lined baking sheet. Roast for 15 minutes, then turn the squash wedges over and bake until caramelized and soft, another 15 to 20 minutes.

3. Put the golden raisins in a small bowl, cover with boiling water, and let sit for 5 minutes to rehydrate and plump up. Drain the raisins and set aside.

4. In a small saucepan over medium heat, stir the honey with a wooden spoon until it starts to caramelize, 2 to 3 minutes. Add the butter, brown sugar, and rosemary leaves and stir until the butter is melted. Remove from the heat. Stir in the pine nuts and raisins.

5. To serve, arrange the roasted squash on a serving platter. Drizzle the honey raisin mixture over the squash.

Charred Broccoli Spears with Confit Garlic Butter, Chickpeas, and Kale

In this recipe, the broccoli spears come out perfectly browned and tender, while the stalks keep a nice al dente bite. This side dish is so simple, flavourful, and good for you. It's on constant repeat in our home, and once you've tasted it, we're sure you'll think the same way too.

1. Fill a large bowl with ice water. Bring a large saucepan of salted water to a boil. Add the broccoli and blanch until just slightly tender, 2 minutes. Using a slotted spoon, remove the broccoli from the boiling water and plunge it into the ice bath. When the broccoli is cooled, drain and pat dry with paper towel.

2. Melt the butter with the olive oil in a large skillet over medium heat. Add the broccoli and cook until lightly browned, 1 to 2 minutes per side. Add the confit garlic purée, chickpeas, and kale and cook, stirring occasionally, until the kale is just wilted, 3 to 4 minutes. Add the one-hit butter and cook until melted, 1 to 2 minutes. Season to taste with salt and pepper.

3. Transfer the mixture to a serving platter. Drizzle any extra melted butter in the pan over the broccoli. Sprinkle with the nutritional yeast.

SERVES 4 TO 6

1 bunch broccoli, trimmed and cut into medium spears (about 3½ cups)

1 tablespoon unsalted butter

3 tablespoons olive oil

2 tablespoons Confit Garlic Purée (page 89)

1 cup canned chickpeas, rinsed and drained

2 cups torn lacinato kale

2 tablespoons One-Hit Butter (page 62)

Salt and cracked black pepper

2 tablespoons nutritional yeast

NOTE: Swap the broccoli for sliced carrots or sweet potatoes, cauliflower florets, broccoli rabe, or green beans. They all love that garlic slow-cooked in olive oil and the flavoured compound butter.

Roasted Rainbow Carrots with Honey Miso Glaze and Carrot-Top Green Goddess Dip

SERVES 4 TO 6

CARROT-TOP GREEN GODDESS DIP

1 avocado, pitted and peeled
1 cup mayonnaise
½ cup sour cream
1 shallot, minced
1 garlic clove
½ cup loosely packed carrot tops (from Roasted Rainbow Carrots, below)
2 tablespoons chopped fresh chives
2 tablespoons fresh lemon juice
Salt and cracked black pepper

ROASTED RAINBOW CARROTS WITH HONEY MISO GLAZE

1 bunch rainbow carrots, peeled
2 tablespoons olive oil
Salt and cracked black pepper
2 tablespoons unsalted butter, melted
2 tablespoons yellow miso
2 tablespoons liquid honey
2 teaspoons grated peeled fresh ginger
2 teaspoons soy sauce
2 teaspoons fresh lime juice
1 teaspoon sambal oelek
2 teaspoons sesame seeds, toasted, for garnish

Rainbow carrots start out being simply roasted in the oven with a little olive oil, but then they get a makeover: a perfectly balanced sweet and savoury honey miso glaze drenches the carrots and caramelizes them while they finish roasting. The honey in the glaze enhances the carrots' natural sweetness, while the miso adds incredible warm caramel-like notes. You will want to keep this glaze on hand to try on squash, parsnips, sweet potatoes, and more. It's a game changer.

Utilizing the carrot tops in the dip is a great way to use the whole carrot and it adds great herbaceous flavour.

1. **Make the carrot-top green goddess dip:** In a blender, combine the avocado, mayonnaise, sour cream, shallot, garlic, carrot tops, chives, and lemon juice. Blend until smooth. Season to taste with salt and pepper. Transfer to a small bowl, cover, and refrigerate until ready to use.

2. **Make the roasted rainbow carrots with honey miso glaze:** Preheat the oven to 400°F (200°C). Line a baking sheet with parchment paper.

3. Place the carrots in a large bowl, toss with the olive oil, then season to taste with salt and pepper. Spread evenly on the lined baking sheet and roast until golden brown, 10 to 15 minutes.

4. **Meanwhile, make the honey miso glaze:** In a small bowl, combine the melted butter, miso, honey, ginger, soy sauce, lime juice, and sambal oelek. Whisk until smooth.

5. Remove the carrots from the oven and pour about three-quarters of the honey miso glaze over them. Continue roasting the carrots, stirring occasionally, until tender, another 10 to 12 minutes.

6. Transfer the carrots to a serving platter and drizzle with the remaining glaze. Sprinkle with the sesame seeds. Serve with the carrot-top green goddess dip.

Thai Green Bean Curry

Our daughter Gemma requests curry practically every day. We've never met a kid who loves curry more than Gem! There are a few weeks when our garden is producing more beans than we can eat in one day, and that's when we came up with this recipe to satisfy Gemma's curry craving. Once you learn how to make your own curry paste from scratch, you'll never buy it again. This recipe makes a good amount and we will sometimes freeze half for the next time Gemma's in the mood for a Thai curry.

1. **Make the green curry paste:** In a food processor, combine the garlic, lemongrass, ginger, shallots, chilies, soy sauce, cumin, and coriander. Process until almost smooth. Set aside or store in an airtight container in the refrigerator for up to 2 weeks or in the freezer for up to 4 months.

2. **Make the Thai green bean curry:** Heat the olive oil in a large sauté pan over medium-low heat. Add the shallots, garlic, ginger, and chili flakes and sauté, stirring frequently, until the shallots are softened and just starting to turn golden brown, 5 to 6 minutes. Increase the heat to medium. Add the green beans and bell pepper, stir to coat with oil, and sauté for another 2 minutes.

3. Stir in the coconut milk, water, green curry paste, brown sugar, and salt and pepper to taste. Bring to a simmer and cook, stirring occasionally, until the beans are tender, 5 to 7 minutes.

4. To serve, transfer the beans and sauce to a serving dish. Sprinkle the sunflower seeds over top.

SERVES 4

GREEN CURRY PASTE (MAKES 1 CUP)

4 garlic cloves
3 lemongrass stalks, outer leaves removed, cut into 1-inch pieces
1 (2-inch) piece fresh ginger, peeled
2 shallots
4 fresh green Thai or serrano chilies
2 tablespoons soy sauce
2 teaspoons ground cumin
1 cup fresh coriander leaves

THAI GREEN BEAN CURRY

2 tablespoons olive oil
4 shallots, thinly sliced
2 garlic cloves, thinly sliced
2 teaspoons grated peeled fresh ginger
¼ teaspoon red chili flakes
1 pound (450 g) green beans, trimmed
1 red bell pepper, julienned
1 cup full-fat coconut milk
¼ cup water
2 teaspoons Green Curry Paste (recipe above or store-bought)
2 teaspoons firmly packed brown sugar
Salt and cracked black pepper
2 tablespoons sunflower seeds, toasted

Sweet-and-Sour Glazed Golden Beets with Walnuts and Black Pepper Mascarpone

SERVES 4 TO 6

SWEET-AND-SOUR GLAZED GOLDEN BEETS

6 small golden beets, peeled and cut into thick wedges
2 cups water
¼ cup apple cider vinegar
Zest and juice of 1 orange
2 tablespoons brown sugar
1 teaspoon ground turmeric
¼ teaspoon red chili flakes
Salt

BLACK PEPPER MASCARPONE

½ cup mascarpone cheese
1 teaspoon orange zest
2 tablespoons fresh orange juice
1 tablespoon liquid honey
Salt and cracked black pepper

GARNISHES

¼ cup walnuts, toasted
Microgreens (optional)

Golden beets are slightly sweeter and milder than classic red beets, but nutritionally the two are practically identical. Cooking golden beets in this sweet-and-sour glaze results in tender and juicy beets with a translucent, sunshine-yellow colour that makes them so exciting and appealing. Thanks to their sweet, earthy flavour, these beets are delicious on their own, but we love them even more when they're paired with the creaminess of mascarpone, and topped with toasted walnuts for crunch.

1. **Make the sweet-and-sour glazed golden beets:** In a medium saucepan, combine the beets, water, apple cider vinegar, orange zest and juice, brown sugar, turmeric, and chili flakes. Season with salt. Bring to a boil over high heat, then reduce the heat to medium and simmer, uncovered, until the beets are soft when pierced with a fork or paring knife, 20 to 30 minutes. Remove from the heat and let the beets cool in the cooking liquid.

2. Once cooled, transfer the beets to a bowl. Strain the cooking liquid and return it to the saucepan. Over medium-high heat, reduce the cooking liquid by a third or until it is syrupy. Remove from the heat. Return the beets to the saucepan and toss to evenly coat.

3. **Make the black pepper mascarpone and assemble:** In a small bowl, combine the mascarpone, orange zest, orange juice, and honey. Season well with salt and pepper. Mix until well combined.

4. To serve, spoon the mascarpone in the centre of a serving plate. Arrange the glazed beets on top of the mascarpone. Garnish with the walnuts and some microgreens, if using. Drizzle with some of the beet glaze.

Sesame Cucumber Salad with Lime, Cilantro, and Pickled Shallots

Cool as a cool cucumber salad. This simple, refreshing, bright summer salad has just the right amount of ginger spice and lime. Serve with any spicy dish for putting out the fire.

1. In a large bowl, combine the cucumbers, radishes, cilantro, and pickled shallots and toss together.

2. In a medium bowl, whisk together the rice vinegar, olive oil, lime juice, soy sauce, miso, garlic, ginger, brown sugar, and sesame oil. Pour over the salad and toss to evenly coat. Cover with plastic wrap and let marinate in the refrigerator for about 20 minutes.

3. Just before serving, sprinkle with the sesame seeds.

SERVES 4

2 English cucumbers, thinly sliced

6 radishes, cut into quarters

½ cup fresh cilantro leaves, roughly chopped

2 tablespoons Pickled Shallots (page 203)

3 tablespoons seasoned rice vinegar

2 tablespoons olive oil

1 tablespoon fresh lime juice

1 tablespoon soy sauce

2 teaspoons yellow miso

1 small garlic clove, minced

1 teaspoon grated peeled fresh ginger

1 teaspoon brown sugar

1 teaspoon sesame oil

1 tablespoon sesame seeds, toasted

NOTE: For a fun presentation, try using your vegetable peeler to make long noodle-like strands of cucumber.

Savoury Bread Pudding with Swiss Chard and Cheddar

SERVES 4 TO 6

8 tablespoons unsalted butter

2 large yellow onions, thinly sliced

3 garlic cloves, minced

4 celery stalks, halved lengthwise and finely chopped

2 cups finely chopped Swiss chard leaves and stems

Salt and cracked black pepper

2 large eggs

2 cups Vegetable Stock (page 162 or store-bought)

¼ cup finely chopped fresh flat-leaf parsley

1 teaspoon finely chopped fresh rosemary

1 teaspoon finely chopped fresh sage

1 teaspoon finely chopped fresh thyme

¼ cup grated Parmesan cheese

1 cup grated cheddar cheese, divided

1 baguette, cut into 1-inch cubes and toasted

An easy cheesy, golden-topped casserole layered with all the classic flavours of a really good stuffing—nuggets of toasty bread, butter, onions, celery, and lots of herbs. We've added Swiss chard (kale or spinach work equally well) and lots of cheese. If you have leftovers, this makes an incredible savoury French toast, sliced and seared, and served with fried eggs.

1. Preheat the oven to 400°F (200°C). Butter a 13 × 9-inch baking dish.

2. Melt the butter in large skillet over medium-high heat. When the butter is foaming, add the onions, garlic, and celery and sauté until translucent, 7 to 8 minutes. Add the Swiss chard and sauté until wilted, about 5 minutes. Remove from the heat and season well with salt and pepper.

3. Whisk the eggs in a large bowl. Stir in the vegetable stock, parsley, rosemary, sage, thyme, Parmesan, and ½ cup of the cheddar. Season to taste with salt and pepper. Add the Swiss chard mixture and stir together. Add the toasted bread and toss to combine.

4. Transfer the mixture to the prepared baking dish. Evenly scatter the remaining ½ cup cheddar over the top. Cover with foil and bake until heated through, about 25 minutes. Remove the foil and bake until crispy around the edges and the cheese is golden brown, about another 15 minutes.

Butternut Squash Bravas with Basil Aioli

Served in tapas bars throughout Spain, patatas bravas are fried potato cubes tossed in a smoky, fiery tomato sauce and served with a garlicy aioli that makes the dish insanely delicious. In our version, we use butternut squash instead of potato. When you roast butternut squash cubes in a hot oven, they become extra crispy and caramelized on the outside and have a super-fluffy and buttery texture on the inside. Grab a fork, grab a drink, and dig in.

1. **Make the basil aioli:** In a food processor, combine the mayonnaise, basil, lemon juice, mustard, and garlic. Process until smooth. Season to taste with salt and pepper. Set aside or store in an airtight container in the refrigerator for up to 2 weeks.

2. **Make the butternut squash bravas:** Preheat the oven to 400°F (200°C). Line a baking sheet with parchment paper.

3. Put the squash cubes on the lined baking sheet and toss with 2 tablespoons of the olive oil, then season to taste with salt and pepper. Spread in an even layer and roast until golden brown around the edges and fork-tender, 30 to 35 minutes.

4. Meanwhile, heat the remaining 2 tablespoons olive oil in a small saucepan over medium heat. Add the onions and garlic and cook, stirring frequently, until the onions are soft and translucent, 3 to 4 minutes. Add the tomato sauce, cherry tomatoes, sherry vinegar, sugar, smoked paprika, and chili flakes; stir together. Simmer, uncovered and stirring occasionally, for 20 minutes or until thickened.

5. When the squash is cooked, transfer it to a large bowl. Pour the tomato sauce over the squash and toss to coat. Adjust the seasoning as needed.

6. Spoon the basil aioli across a serving platter. Spoon the coated squash over top. Garnish with the green onions and sea salt.

SERVES 4 TO 6

**BASIL AIOLI
(MAKES ABOUT 1½ CUPS)**

¾ cup mayonnaise
1 cup packed fresh basil leaves
2 tablespoons fresh lemon juice
1 tablespoon Dijon mustard
2 garlic cloves
Salt and cracked black pepper

BUTTERNUT SQUASH BRAVAS

1 butternut squash, peeled and cut
    into 1-inch cubes
4 tablespoons olive oil, divided
Salt and cracked black pepper
1 small yellow onion, finely chopped
3 garlic cloves, minced
1 cup tomato sauce
1 cup cherry tomatoes, quartered
2 tablespoons sherry vinegar
1 teaspoon granulated sugar
1 teaspoon smoked paprika
½ teaspoon red chili flakes

FOR SERVING

2 green onions, thinly sliced
Sea salt, for finishing

Spice Market Fried Rice

SERVES 4 TO 6

4 tablespoons olive oil, divided

½ cup thinly sliced yellow onion

2 garlic cloves, minced

1 teaspoon grated peeled fresh
    ginger

2 cups finely chopped rainbow or
    Swiss chard leaves and stems

1 cup snap peas, trimmed

Salt and cracked black pepper

10 to 12 fresh curry leaves

2 teaspoons curry powder

1 teaspoon black mustard seeds

½ teaspoon cumin seeds

¼ teaspoon red chili flakes

3 cups cooled cooked basmati rice
    (see Note)

1 teaspoon ground turmeric

½ teaspoon ground coriander

GARNISHES

½ cup salted roasted peanuts

2 tablespoons chopped fresh mint

If you want to make a gorgeous, intensely vibrant vegetable fried rice dish packed with lots of toasted spices, zippy ginger, and aromatic curry leaves, look no further. It may look like a lot of ingredients and seem complicated to make, but it's not. Just measure out your ingredients before you start cooking. You will instantly experience the multi-layered aroma of the incredible flavour base that is waiting to meet the basmati rice and fresh garden veggies.

1. Heat 2 tablespoons of the olive oil in a large nonstick skillet over medium heat. Add the onions, garlic, and ginger and cook, stirring occasionally, until fragrant and the onions have softened, about 2 minutes. Increase the heat to medium-high, add the chard and snap peas, and continue cooking, stirring constantly, for 2 minutes, until the vegetables are just tender. Season to taste with salt and pepper. Transfer the vegetable mixture to a large plate.

2. In the same skillet (no need to wipe it) over medium heat, add the remaining 2 tablespoons olive oil, curry leaves, curry powder, mustard seeds, cumin seeds, and chili flakes. Stir until the mustard seeds begin to pop, about 30 seconds. Add the cooked rice and stir to combine. Add the turmeric, coriander, and salt and pepper to taste. Fold in the sautéed vegetables and cook until heated through.

3. Serve in a large bowl or on a serving platter, garnished with the peanuts and mint.

NOTE: Use cold leftover rice, or rice that you made ahead and chilled. Not only is it much easier to stir-fry, but the finished dish will have a better texture than if you use fresh rice, which is too soft and can turn mushy during the frying.
Feel free to use any rice you like, short or long grain, white or brown.

Fondant Potatoes

SERVES 4

4 large russet potatoes
2 tablespoons olive oil
4 tablespoons unsalted butter, diced
2 garlic cloves, sliced
2 sprigs fresh rosemary
2 sprigs fresh thyme
1 cup Vegetable Stock (page 162 or
    store-bought)
Salt and cracked black pepper

Chefs often call these "melting potatoes," and once you taste them, you'll understand why. Fondant potatoes are something special. They are one of the first potato preparations to be mastered at culinary school. With a bit of practice you will find out that this method will give you the most flavourful potato because you've taken the time to baste them with lots of stock, butter and garlic. The potatoes become coated in a decadent glaze with a fluffy interior and a slightly crispy top.

1. Preheat the oven to 400°F (200°C).

2. Peel the potatoes. Slice off the ends, then cut each potato in half crosswise, to form 2 flat-sided barrel shapes each about 2 inches high.

3. Heat the olive oil in a large ovenproof skillet over medium-high heat. Place the potatoes cut side down in the pan and cook until browned, 5 to 7 minutes per side. Remove from the heat. Add the butter, garlic, rosemary, and thyme. Pour the vegetable stock over the potatoes. Season to taste with salt and pepper. Transfer to the oven and bake until the potatoes are tender, 20 to 25 minutes. Spoon the butter mixture over the cooked potatoes.

Cheesy Corn Casserole

This easy corn casserole is a rich, creamy, decadent side dish. With each bite, sweet corn kernels pop against the light, delicate texture and flavour of the cheesy cornbread filling.

1. Preheat the oven to 350°F (180°C). Lightly spray a 9-inch square baking dish with nonstick cooking spray.

2. Heat the olive oil in a large skillet over medium-high heat. Add the onions, garlic, and celery and cook, stirring occasionally, until softened and golden brown, 3 to 4 minutes. Add the jalapeño, bell peppers, and corn kernels and cook for 3 to 4 minutes, until the corn is tender. Season well with salt and pepper. Remove from the heat. Add the parsley, thyme, and cream cheese and stir together.

3. In a large bowl, whisk together the eggs and milk. Add the cornmeal, flour, baking powder, and salt. Mix until well combined, then add the corn mixture.

4. Add 1 cup of the cheddar to the cooked vegetable mixture and stir well to combine. Spoon into the prepared baking dish and smooth the top. Evenly sprinkle the remaining ¼ cup cheddar over the casserole. Bake until a knife inserted into the centre of the casserole comes out clean, 35 to 45 minutes.

SERVES 4 TO 6

2 tablespoons olive oil
1 medium yellow onion, finely diced
2 garlic cloves, minced
2 celery stalks, finely diced
1 jalapeño pepper, seeded and finely diced
1 red bell pepper, finely diced
3 cups fresh sweet corn kernels (from about 4 cobs)
Salt and cracked black pepper
1 teaspoon chopped fresh flat-leaf parsley
1 teaspoon chopped fresh thyme
½ cup (4 ounces/115 g) cream cheese, at room temperature
3 eggs
½ cup whole milk
⅓ cup cornmeal
3 tablespoons all-purpose flour
½ teaspoon baking powder
¼ teaspoon salt
1¼ cups grated aged cheddar cheese, divided

Cauliflower Gratin with Caramelized Onions and Gruyère

SERVES 4 TO 6

1 large cauliflower, cut into florets

4 tablespoons olive oil, divided

Salt and cracked black pepper

1 medium yellow onion, thinly sliced

2 garlic cloves, minced

1 tablespoon finely chopped fresh sage

5 tablespoons unsalted butter, divided

3 tablespoons all-purpose flour

2 cups warm whole milk

¾ cup grated Gruyère cheese

2 teaspoons honey mustard

¼ cup panko breadcrumbs

¼ cup grated Parmesan cheese

Perfectly roasted cauliflower and caramelized onions are doused with a creamy sauce made with Gruyère cheese. This classic Mornay sauce is outrageously rich but so very satisfying.

1. Position the racks in the upper and lower thirds of the oven and preheat to 400°F (200°C). Line 2 baking sheets with parchment paper.

2. In a large bowl, toss the cauliflower florets with 3 tablespoons of the olive oil, then season to taste with salt and pepper. Spread out evenly in a single layer on the lined baking sheets and roast until the cauliflower is fork-tender and golden brown, 20 to 25 minutes. Remove from the oven; lower the oven temperature to 375°F (190°C).

3. Meanwhile, heat the remaining 1 tablespoon olive oil in a large skillet over medium heat. Add the onions and cook, stirring occasionally, until caramelized, about 10 minutes. Add the garlic and sage and continue cooking until fragrant, another 2 to 3 minutes. Spread the onion mixture over the roasted cauliflower. Set aside.

4. Melt 2 tablespoons of the butter in a small saucepan over medium heat, whisking until the butter just begins to become golden and smell nutty. Add the flour and cook, stirring constantly with a wooden spoon, for 2 minutes. Add the milk in a steady stream, whisking constantly until it comes to a boil, then continue whisking for another minute or until the sauce thickens. Remove from the heat and stir in the Gruyère cheese and mustard. Season to taste with salt and pepper.

5. Melt the remaining 3 tablespoons butter in a separate small saucepan, then remove from the heat. Brush a large baking dish with some of the melted butter. Stir the panko and Parmesan into the remaining melted butter and season to taste with salt and pepper.

6. In a large bowl, toss the roasted cauliflower and onion mixture with the cheese sauce. Pour the mixture into the prepared baking dish. Evenly top with the panko mixture. Bake until golden brown and bubbly, 20 to 25 minutes.

Roasted Brussels Sprouts with Maple Cashew Caramel

Brussels sprouts roasted simply with olive oil and seasoned with salt and pepper are delicious, but if you want something more interesting, toss them in this savoury-sweet sauce. Maple syrup, butter, and soy sauce combine to make a caramel shellac that coats each crispy sprout for an intense cherry pop that is quite unexpected and totally adds to the dish.

1. Preheat the oven to 400°F (200°C). Line a baking sheet with parchment paper (see Note).

2. In a large bowl, toss the brussels sprouts with the olive oil, then season to taste with salt and pepper. Arrange in a single layer on the lined baking sheet and roast until golden brown, crispy, and fork-tender, 20 to 25 minutes. Transfer to a large bowl.

3. In a medium saucepan, heat the maple syrup over medium heat, stirring occasionally, until bubbling, about 3 minutes. Carefully whisk in the butter, then add the cream, soy sauce, and sambal oelek and cook, whisking constantly, until the caramel sauce is bubbling and thick enough to coat the back of a spoon, about 1 minute. Immediately pour the sauce over the roasted brussels sprouts.

4. Add the green onions, sun-dried cherries, and cashews and toss together. Season to taste with salt and pepper. Transfer the brussels sprouts to a serving platter.

SERVES 4 TO 6

1½ pounds (675 g) brussels sprouts, trimmed and halved

2 tablespoons olive oil

Salt and cracked black pepper

¼ cup pure maple syrup

1½ tablespoons unsalted butter

2 tablespoons heavy (35%) cream

1 tablespoon soy sauce

½ teaspoon sambal oelek

2 green onions, thinly sliced

¼ cup sun-dried cherries

¼ cup cashews, toasted and chopped

NOTE: If you want your brussels sprouts to be perfectly crispy, don't crowd the baking sheet. This can cause them to steam. Make sure you give them plenty of room to cook. Roast on 2 baking sheets or in batches if needed.

Orange-Braised Leeks with Horseradish and Pine Nuts

SERVES 4 TO 6

4 medium leeks

1 orange, thinly sliced into rounds

2 teaspoons drained capers, roughly chopped

1 teaspoon thinly sliced fresh red finger chili

1 garlic clove, minced

½ cup fresh orange juice

¼ cup olive oil

1 cup Vegetable Stock (page 162 or store-bought)

Salt and cracked black pepper

3 tablespoons panko breadcrumbs, toasted

3 tablespoons pine nuts, toasted and chopped

3 tablespoons finely chopped fresh chives

1 tablespoon coarsely grated fresh horseradish

1 teaspoon lemon zest

Leeks are such a pleasure to cook with. Here, we showcase leeks in a starring role, and they get the biggest award for their performance! Braised leeks, simple and elegant and always a star in our kitchen.

1. Preheat the oven to 350°F (180°C).

2. Trim and discard the root end, dark green leaves, and outer layers from the leeks, then slice in half lengthwise. Slice the halves into 3-inch pieces. Arrange cut side up in a single layer in a 2-quart baking dish. Arrange the orange slices over the leeks and sprinkle with the capers, chili, and garlic. Pour the orange juice, olive oil, and vegetable stock over the leeks, then season to taste with salt and pepper. Cover with foil and bake until the leeks are fork-tender, about 1 hour. Remove from the oven, remove the foil, and let cool slightly in the pan.

3. In a small bowl, stir together the panko, pine nuts, chives, horseradish, and lemon zest. Season to taste with salt and pepper.

4. Just before serving, spoon the seasoned panko over the leeks.

Confit Garlic Potato Cakes

Seasoning fluffy mashed potatoes with lots of mellow confit garlic, salty Parmesan, and fresh herbs makes the interior of these cakes really tasty. We love that we can make these in advance and keep them in the refrigerator until we are ready to cook them up. They make a great side for dinner, but they are also a favourite at breakfast or brunch.

1. Place the potatoes and 1 tablespoon salt in a large pot, then add enough water to cover by 1 inch. Bring to a boil, then reduce the heat to medium-low and cook until the potatoes are just tender all the way through when pierced with a paring knife, 8 to 10 minutes. Drain, then return the potatoes to the pot.

2. Add the Parmesan, butter, egg yolks, confit garlic purée, chives, and parsley. Using a potato masher, mash until smooth and well combined. Season well with salt and pepper. Transfer the potato mixture to a large bowl and let cool completely.

3. Preheat the oven to 375°F (190°C). Line a baking sheet with parchment paper.

4. Set out 2 shallow bowls. In the first bowl, beat the eggs. Put the semolina flour in the second bowl.

5. Divide the potato mixture into 8 equal portions (about ½ cup per portion) and shape into 3-inch cakes, about ¾ inch thick. Working with one cake at a time, carefully dip the cake in the egg, turning to coat both sides and allowing excess to drip off; then coat with semolina flour, pressing gently to adhere. Transfer to a plate and let sit for 5 minutes.

6. Heat 2 to 3 tablespoons of canola oil in a large nonstick skillet over medium-high heat. Working in batches, place the potato cakes in the skillet and cook until deep golden brown, about 3 minutes per side. Transfer to the lined baking sheet. Discard the oil and wipe out the skillet with paper towel. Repeat with more canola oil and the remaining potato cakes.

7. Once all the potato cakes are browned, transfer to the oven and bake until heated through, 10 to 15 minutes. Transfer to a serving platter and garnish with flaky sea salt. Serve with sour cream.

SERVES 4 TO 6

2½ pounds (1.125 kg) russet potatoes, peeled and small diced

½ cup grated Parmesan cheese

3 tablespoons unsalted butter, at room temperature

2 egg yolks

2 tablespoons Confit Garlic Purée (page 89), plus more for garnish

2 tablespoons chopped fresh chives

2 tablespoons chopped fresh flat-leaf parsley

Salt and cracked black pepper

2 eggs

2 cups semolina flour

Canola oil, for frying

Flaky sea salt, for garnish

Sour cream, for serving

Desserts

Sweet Potato Pie with Maple Meringue

Years ago, Lora's grandmother gave her this recipe for her sweet potato pie that always took top billing at every Thanksgiving and Christmas dessert buffet. Fluffy and smooth, with plenty of sweet potato flavour, and topped off with snowy maple meringue peaks, this beautiful pie is the best.

1. **Make the pastry dough:** In a food processor, combine the flour, sugar, salt, and butter. Pulse until the mixture resembles wet sand. While pulsing, slowly drizzle in the water and continue to pulse until the dough comes together. Gather the dough into a ball. (Wipe the food processor bowl clean and set aside.) At this stage the dough can be flattened into a disc, wrapped in plastic wrap, and stored in the refrigerator for up to 2 days.

2. On a lightly floured work surface, use a rolling pin to roll out the dough into an 11-inch circle, ⅛ inch thick. Gently lift the dough into a 9-inch tart pan with removable bottom and press the dough onto the bottom and up the sides (but not into the creases) of the pan.

3. With a sharp knife, cut excess pastry from the top of the pan. Chill in the refrigerator for 15 minutes.

4. **Make the filling and bake:** Preheat the oven to 375°F (190°C).

5. In the food processor, combine the sweet potatoes, brown sugar, eggs, butter, milk, cinnamon, and nutmeg. Process until smooth. Pour the filling into the chilled pie shell. Bake until the filling is set and a knife inserted into the centre of the pie comes out clean, 60 to 65 minutes. Transfer the pie to a rack to cool completely before piping the maple meringue.

6. **Make the maple meringue and finish:** In the bowl of a stand mixer fitted with the whisk attachment, combine the egg whites, maple syrup, maple extract, cream of tartar, and salt. Whip on low speed until the mixture is foamy, then increase to medium-high and continue whipping until stiff peaks form, about 3 minutes.

7. Spoon the meringue into a piping bag fitted with a plain medium tip. Pipe 3-inch peaks of meringue over the filling. (Alternatively, spoon dollops of meringue over the filling and use a spoon to shape peaks.) Use a kitchen torch to lightly toast the meringue evenly until golden brown. Let the pie cool completely, uncovered, in the refrigerator before slicing.

8. When ready to serve, release the sides of the pan. This pie is best served the day it is made but can be refrigerated for up to 2 days.

MAKES ONE 9-INCH PIE

PASTRY DOUGH

1¼ cups all-purpose flour
1 teaspoon granulated sugar
½ teaspoon salt
½ cup cold unsalted butter, diced
¼ cup cold water

FILLING

3 large sweet potatoes, baked, peeled, and smashed
1 cup packed brown sugar
3 eggs
5 tablespoons unsalted butter, at room temperature
½ cup whole milk
1 teaspoon cinnamon
½ teaspoon ground nutmeg

MAPLE MERINGUE

3 egg whites
⅓ cup pure maple syrup
1 teaspoon maple extract
¼ teaspoon cream of tartar
Pinch of salt

NOTE: Homemade pie is a labour of love that requires a full morning or afternoon. Make the pie dough in advance so it's ready when you are. Give yourself even more time by baking and prepping the sweet potatoes the day before.

Summer Berry Spoon Cake with Vanilla Sauce

MAKES ONE 8-INCH SQUARE OR OVAL CAKE

VANILLA SAUCE
(MAKES 1 CUP)

½ cup whole milk

½ cup heavy (35%) cream

1 (2-inch) piece vanilla bean, split in half lengthwise

3 large egg yolks

3 tablespoons granulated sugar

CAKE

3 cups mixed fresh berries (strawberries, blueberries, raspberries, blackberries)

3 tablespoons granulated sugar

Zest and juice of 1 lemon

½ cup all-purpose flour

½ cup almond flour

½ cup granulated sugar

1 teaspoon baking powder

½ teaspoon salt

1 egg

¼ cup whole milk

8 tablespoons unsalted butter, melted

1 teaspoon pure vanilla extract

This warm, buttery almond cake surrounds juicy summer berries and is doused with a rich and decadent vanilla sauce—it's made for sharing! The batter comes together quickly using simple pantry ingredients. This is one of those outstanding desserts that will make everyone really, truly happy.

1. **Make the vanilla sauce:** Combine the milk and cream in a heavy medium saucepan. Scrape the seeds from the vanilla bean and add to the milk mixture along with the bean. Slowly bring to a boil over medium-high heat, stirring to allow the flavour of the vanilla to infuse into the milk. Once boiling, remove from the heat.

2. In a large bowl, use a wooden spoon to beat together the egg yolks and sugar until pale and thick. While stirring, slowly pour the hot milk into the egg yolk mixture and mix well. Rinse out and dry the saucepan. Pour the yolk mixture into the saucepan and cook over low heat, stirring constantly, until it begins to thicken and coats the back of a spoon, about 5 minutes. Do not let the custard boil. If the custard is getting too hot, remove the pan from the heat for a few seconds and continue to stir. Strain the custard into a medium bowl. Discard the vanilla bean. If serving cold, let the custard cool before chilling in the refrigerator. Store in an airtight container in the refrigerator for up to 4 days.

3. **Make the cake:** Preheat the oven to 350°F (180°C). Spray an 8-inch square or 2-quart baking dish with nonstick cooking spray or brush with melted butter.

4. In a medium bowl, gently mix the berries with the sugar and lemon zest and juice. Let sit until the berries start to release their juices, 15 to 20 minutes.

5. In a large bowl, whisk together the all-purpose flour, almond flour, sugar, baking powder, and salt.

6. In a small bowl, whisk together the egg, milk, melted butter, and vanilla. Add the wet ingredients to the dry ingredients and whisk until blended and smooth. Pour the batter into the prepared baking dish and smooth the top. Gently spoon the macerated fruit and their juices over the batter.

7. Bake until the cake is golden brown and puffed up, 30 to 35 minutes. Serve warm with the vanilla sauce. Store the cake, without the vanilla sauce, wrapped with plastic wrap at room temperature for up to 2 days.

NOTE: This summertime recipe showcases ripe summer berries in the best way possible, but it also works well with any ripe summer fruit. We've made it with peaches and blueberries, rhubarb, plums, and cherries.

Almond Coconut Plum Cake with Coconut Whipped Cream

MAKES ONE 9-INCH ROUND CAKE

COCONUT WHIPPED CREAM (MAKES ABOUT 1½ CUPS)

1 cup cold heavy (35%) cream

2 tablespoons granulated sugar

½ teaspoon pure vanilla extract

¼ cup sweetened shredded coconut, toasted

ALMOND COCONUT PLUM CAKE

1½ cups almond flour

⅓ cup all-purpose flour

½ cup granulated sugar

⅓ cup lightly packed brown sugar

½ cup sweetened shredded coconut

½ teaspoon cinnamon

½ teaspoon ground ginger

¼ teaspoon salt

3 eggs

¾ cup butter, melted and cooled slightly, more for greasing the pan

1 teaspoon pure vanilla extract

2 cups thinly sliced pitted plums

Since moving back to the area where Lora grew up, we now only live one country road away from her aunt Joyce and uncle Rick's home. They have a beautiful vegetable garden and flower garden with berry bushes and fruit trees. This recipe was inspired by a wonderful gift they gave us one sunny summer afternoon—a big basket of the most deliciously juicy plums you've ever tasted just picked from their plum trees. Fresh plums at their peak in summertime are a pleasure to bake with. Slightly tart, they bring lots of flavour, and they work beautifully here with the flavours of almond and sweet coconut.

1. **Make the coconut whipped cream:** In a large bowl, whisk the cream by hand until soft peaks form, about 2 minutes. Add the sugar and vanilla and whisk until incorporated. Fold in the toasted coconut. Store in an airtight container in the refrigerator until ready to use or up to 3 days.

2. **Make the almond coconut plum cake:** Preheat the oven to 375°F (190°C). Lightly grease a 9-inch round cake pan with melted butter.

3. In a large bowl, stir together the almond flour, all-purpose flour, granulated sugar, brown sugar, coconut, cinnamon, ginger, and salt.

4. In a medium bowl, whisk together the eggs, melted butter, and vanilla. Add the wet ingredients to the dry ingredients and mix until smooth. Spoon the batter into the prepared pan.

5. Arrange the sliced plums in concentric circles to mostly cover the batter, leaving a gap between slices. Bake until the plums are golden and a cake tester inserted into the centre of the cake comes out clean, 35 to 40 minutes. Let the cake cool in the pan set on a rack for 30 minutes.

6. Run a knife around the edge of the pan, then turn out the cake onto a baking sheet or cutting board, then invert onto a serving plate. Serve with the coconut whipped cream. Store the cake, without the coconut whipped cream, in an airtight container in the refrigerator for up to 2 days.

Chocolate Sheet Cake with Raspberries and Buttercream Frosting

The combination of chocolate and raspberries is always a winner. When you want to indulge in a rich, moist chocolate cake that everyone will request for every celebration, this is it. It's the kind of chocolate cake you dream about.

1. **Make the chocolate sheet cake:** Preheat the oven to 350°F (180°C). Lightly spray a 13 × 9-inch baking pan with nonstick cooking spray.

2. In a large bowl, whisk together the flour, cocoa powder, baking powder, baking soda, salt, and instant coffee.

3. In a medium bowl, whisk together the eggs, granulated sugar, milk, vegetable oil, and vanilla. Add the wet ingredients to the dry ingredients and whisk until smooth. The batter will be quite thick. Pour in the boiling water and whisk again until smooth.

4. Pour the batter into the prepared baking dish and bake until a cake tester inserted into the centre of the cake comes out clean, 25 to 30 minutes. Let the cake cool completely in the pan set on a rack.

5. **Meanwhile, make the buttercream frosting:** In a stand mixer fitted with the paddle attachment, beat the butter and salt on high speed until smooth, about 1 minute. Sift in the icing sugar, ½ cup at a time, beating on low speed after each addition until incorporated. Add the cream and vanilla and beat on high speed until light and fluffy. If you prefer a thinner consistency, add a little more cream or milk.

6. Turn out the cake onto a serving platter. (You can leave the cake in the pan.) Evenly spread the buttercream frosting over the cooled cake. Garnish with the raspberries and rainbow sprinkles. Store, covered with plastic wrap, in the refrigerator for up to 2 days.

SERVES 12

CHOCOLATE SHEET CAKE

2 cups all-purpose flour
¾ cup unsweetened cocoa powder
2 teaspoons baking powder
1½ teaspoons baking soda
1 teaspoon salt
1 teaspoon instant coffee granules
2 eggs
2 cups granulated sugar
1 cup whole milk
½ cup vegetable oil
2 teaspoons pure vanilla extract
1 cup boiling water

BUTTERCREAM FROSTING

1 cup unsalted butter, at room temperature
½ teaspoon salt
4 cups icing sugar
3 tablespoons heavy (35%) cream
1 tablespoon pure vanilla extract

GARNISHES

3 cups fresh raspberries
¼ cup rainbow sprinkles

Toffee Pecan Peach Crisp

SERVES 6 TO 8

FILLING

5 to 6 peaches, peeled, pitted, and
    cut into thick slices (about 5 cups)

1 cup pecans, roughly chopped

⅓ cup lightly packed brown sugar

2 tablespoons cornstarch

2 tablespoons fresh lemon juice

2 teaspoons pure vanilla extract

1 teaspoon cinnamon

½ teaspoon salt

STREUSEL TOPPING

⅔ cup all-purpose flour

⅔ cup old-fashioned rolled oats

⅔ cup lightly packed brown sugar

½ cup pecans, roughly chopped

¼ cup toffee bits

½ teaspoon salt

½ cup cold unsalted butter, diced

Vanilla ice cream or whipped cream,
    for serving

Bursting with juicy peaches and topped with oats, pecans, and toffee bits, this crisp is a breeze to put together with a handful of simple ingredients. When peaches are at their peak, they don't need much to shine—although a scoop of ice cream or whipped cream is highly encouraged!

1. **Make the filling:** Preheat the oven to 350°F (180°C). Grease a 9-inch square baking dish (or similar size dish) with 2 tablespoons unsalted butter.

2. In a large bowl, combine the peaches, pecans, brown sugar, cornstarch, lemon juice, vanilla, cinnamon, and salt. Toss gently until combined and the peaches are coated. Scrape the peaches and their juices into the prepared baking dish.

3. **Prepare the streusel topping:** In a large bowl, stir together the flour, oats, brown sugar, pecans, toffee bits, and salt. Add the diced butter and stir with a wooden spoon to break up the butter until the mixture is crumbly. Evenly sprinkle the topping over the peaches.

4. Bake until the streusel topping is golden brown and the filling is bubbling around the edges, 40 to 45 minutes. Let the crisp cool slightly in the pan set on a rack before serving. Serve warm with vanilla ice cream or whipped cream. Store, covered with plastic wrap, in the refrigerator for up to 4 days.

NOTE: You can assemble the crisp the night before, then just pop it in the oven and bake it when you're ready.

Ginger Rhubarb Custard Tarts

When Lora worked at the Connaught in London, there was a Portuguese pastry shop just around the corner from where she caught her bus in the morning. On her way to work she could smell that glorious scent of baking pastry wafting over and she would have to make a mad dash run to buy a half-dozen of their specialty, custard tarts, before her bus arrived. That amazing cinnamon-scented egg custard nestled in a flaky puff pastry crust is one of her fondest food memories. The bakery always topped theirs off with some variety of fruit compote. Here is Lora's version.

MAKES 12 TARTS

PASTRY DOUGH

2 cups all-purpose flour

¼ teaspoon salt

¾ cup + 2 tablespoons water

1 cup unsalted butter, at room temperature and stirred until smooth

GINGER RHUBARB TOPPING

2 cups rhubarb cut into ½-inch pieces

¼ cup liquid honey

¼ cup water

1 tablespoon grated peeled fresh ginger

1 teaspoon pure vanilla extract

CINNAMON CUSTARD

3 tablespoons all-purpose flour

1¼ cups whole milk, divided

1⅓ cups granulated sugar

1 cinnamon stick

⅔ cup water

½ teaspoon pure vanilla extract

6 egg yolks

1. **Make the pastry dough:** In the bowl of a stand mixer fitted with the dough hook, combine the flour, salt, and water. Mix on medium speed until a soft and pillowy dough forms and pulls away from the sides of the bowl, about 2 minutes.

2. Turn the dough out onto a generously floured work surface. Using a rolling pin, flatten the dough into a 6-inch square. Sprinkle the dough with flour, cover with a kitchen towel, and let rest for 15 minutes.

3. Roll the dough out into an 18-inch square. Using a small offset spatula, evenly spread one-third of the butter over the left two-thirds of the dough, leaving a 1-inch border on the sides. Carefully fold the right side of the dough over to the left by a third, brushing off any excess flour, and then again by another third. Gently pat the dough with your hand from top to bottom to release any air bubbles, then pinch the seam to seal. Turn the dough so the folded side is facing you. Lift the dough and dust the work surface with flour to prevent sticking.

4. Again roll out the dough into an 18-inch square. Evenly spread another one-third of the butter over the left two-thirds of the dough, leaving a 1-inch border on the sides. Carefully fold the right side of the dough over to the left by a third, brushing off any excess flour, and then again by another third. Gently pat the dough from top to bottom to release any air bubbles, then pinch the edges closed. Turn the dough so the folded side is facing you.

— continued —

5. Roll out the dough into a 21 × 18-inch rectangle, with a short side facing you. Evenly spread the remaining one-third butter all the way to the edges of the dough. Starting at the short edge closest to you, roll up the dough into a tight log, brushing off excess flour while rolling. Pinch the seam to seal. Using a sharp knife, trim the ends, then cut the log in half crosswise. Wrap each piece in plastic wrap and chill in the refrigerator for at least 2 hours or overnight.

6. **Make the ginger rhubarb topping:** Preheat the oven to 375°F (190°C).

7. Spread the rhubarb in a single layer in a shallow baking dish. In a small saucepan, combine the honey, water, ginger, and vanilla. Bring to a boil, then pour over the rhubarb. Bake until the rhubarb is just tender, 8 to 10 minutes. Remove from the oven and let cool.

8. **Make the cinnamon custard:** In a medium bowl, whisk together the flour and ¼ cup of the milk until smooth.

9. In a small saucepan, combine the sugar, cinnamon, and water. Bring to a boil over medium heat. Do not stir. Cook until the syrup reaches 220°F (105°C) on an instant-read thermometer. Remove from the heat and discard the cinnamon stick.

10. In a separate small saucepan over high heat, bring the remaining 1 cup of milk just to a boil. Whisk the scalded milk into the flour mixture. While whisking, pour the hot syrup in a thin stream into the hot milk mixture. Add the vanilla and stir until the mixture is very warm but not hot, 1 to 2 minutes. Whisk in the egg yolks. Strain the mixture into a large bowl. Cover with plastic wrap and set aside while you assemble the pastry.

11. **Assemble the tarts and bake:** Preheat the oven to 550°F (290°C). Butter a 12-cup muffin tin.

12. With the seam side down, cut each dough log crosswise into 6 equal pieces. Place the dough cut side down in the wells of the muffin tin and let sit for a few minutes until the dough is soft and pliable.

13. Have ready a small bowl of cold water. Dip your thumbs in the water, then press them into the centre of the dough. Flatten the dough against the bottom of the muffin tin to a thickness of about ⅛ inch, then smooth the dough up the sides to about ⅛ inch above the edge of the pan. The pastry sides should be thinner than the bottom.

14. Fill each pastry cup three-quarters full with the slightly warm cinnamon custard. Bake the tarts until the edges of the pastry are frilled and brown and the filling has set, 10 to 12 minutes. Let the tarts cool slightly in the pan before carefully transferring them to a rack. Top the cooled tarts with the ginger rhubarb mixture. Store in an airtight container in the refrigerator for up to 2 days. Serve at room temperature.

Apple Turnovers

These quick apple turnovers are so easy to make with store-bought puff pastry sheets and a flavourful from-scratch apple filling. They're light, flaky, and delicious. Even better, they take only a few minutes to prepare, making for the perfect dessert or lunch box treat.

1. **Make the apple filling:** Melt the butter in a large skillet over medium heat. Add the apples and cook, stirring, for 2 minutes, until well coated with the butter. Add the brown sugar, lemon juice, vanilla, cinnamon, nutmeg, and salt. Cook, stirring, until the apples are soft and syrupy.

2. In a measuring cup, stir together the cornstarch and 2 tablespoons of the water until smooth with no lumps.

3. Reduce the heat to low and stir the cornstarch mixture into the apples. Cook, stirring, until the mixture thickens slightly. Remove from the heat and let cool. Store in the refrigerator until ready to use or up to 2 days.

4. **Assemble and bake the turnovers:** Position the oven racks in the upper and lower thirds of the oven and preheat to 400°F (200°C). Line 2 baking sheets with parchment paper.

5. On a lightly floured work surface and working with one sheet of puff pastry at a time, roll out the pastry into a 12-inch square. Cut each sheet into 4 equal squares. Place 4 pastry squares evenly spaced on each lined baking sheet. Spoon an equal portion of apple mixture on the centre of each square. Lift the four corners of the pastry over the filling, allowing the corner points to overlap in the centre.

6. In a small bowl, whisk together the egg and the remaining 1 teaspoon water. Brush the tops of each turnover with the egg wash.

7. Sprinkle the demerara sugar over the turnovers and bake for 15 minutes or until golden brown. Transfer to a rack and let cool completely before drizzling with the glaze.

8. **Make the glaze and finish:** In a small bowl, mix together the icing sugar, milk, and vanilla until smooth.

9. Drizzle the glaze over the cooled apple turnovers. Store in an airtight container at room temperature for up to 2 days.

MAKES 8 TURNOVERS

APPLE TURNOVERS

1 tablespoon unsalted butter
2 cups finely diced peeled Granny Smith apples (about 4 apples)
¼ cup packed brown sugar
1 tablespoon fresh lemon juice
1 teaspoon pure vanilla extract
½ teaspoon cinnamon
¼ teaspoon ground nutmeg
¼ teaspoon salt
2 tablespoons cornstarch
2 tablespoons + 1 teaspoon water, divided
2 sheets (8 ounces/225 g each) frozen puff pastry, thawed
1 egg
¼ cup demerara sugar

GLAZE

1 cup icing sugar, sifted
1 tablespoon whole milk
½ teaspoon pure vanilla extract

Pumpkin Cheesecake with Chai Caramel Sauce

This New York-style pumpkin cheesecake with a chocolate crust is perfect for those times when you want true pumpkin flavour but also need a little chocolate and a whole lot of caramel sauce. Making your own pumpkin purée gives the best flavour, but you can use canned purée to save time. See the Note about using room-temperature ingredients.

SERVES 12

PUMPKIN PURÉE

1 Sugar Pie pumpkin or large squash such as butternut or kabocha (1½ pounds/675 g)

CRUST

1½ cups chocolate cookie crumbs
¼ cup packed light brown sugar
6 tablespoons unsalted butter, melted

FILLING

3 packages (8 ounces/225 g each) cream cheese, at room temperature
1½ cups lightly packed dark brown sugar
2 cups Pumpkin Purée (recipe at left or store-bought)
4 eggs, at room temperature
¼ cup sour cream, at room temperature
2 tablespoons all-purpose flour
1 tablespoon pure vanilla extract
¼ teaspoon salt

CHAI CARAMEL SAUCE (MAKES 2 CUPS)

2 cups fresh apple cider
1 cup packed light brown sugar
5 tablespoons unsalted butter
¾ cup heavy (35%) cream
2 teaspoons cinnamon
1 teaspoon ground allspice
1 teaspoon ground cardamom
1 teaspoon ground ginger
½ teaspoon ground cloves
¼ teaspoon ground nutmeg
1 teaspoon pure vanilla extract
Pinch of sea salt

1. **Make the pumpkin purée:** Preheat the oven to 400°F (200°C). Line a baking sheet with parchment paper.

2. Slice the pumpkin in half crosswise and scoop out the seeds. Place the halves cut side down on the lined baking sheet. Roast for 50 to 60 minutes or until the flesh is fork-tender. Remove from the oven, turn the pumpkin halves over, and let cool for about 30 minutes. Lower the oven temperature to 325°F (160°C).

3. Scoop out the cooked pumpkin flesh and transfer to a food processor. Purée until smooth, stopping to scrape down the sides of the bowl as needed. Set aside or store in an airtight container in the refrigerator for up to 4 days or in the freezer for up to 4 months.

4. **Make the crust:** Line the bottom of a 9-inch springform pan with parchment paper and grease the sides with butter.

5. In a small bowl, combine the cookie crumbs, brown sugar, and melted butter and stir with a wooden spoon until combined. Scatter the mixture in the prepared pan and press it evenly into the bottom and up the sides of the pan. Bake the crust for 10 minutes. Set aside to cool.

6. **Meanwhile, make the filling:** In a stand mixer fitted with the paddle attachment, beat the cream cheese with the brown sugar on medium speed until smooth, light, and fluffy, about 4 minutes, stopping to scrape down the sides of the bowl as needed.

NOTE: Remove the eggs, cream cheese, and sour cream from the refrigerator at least an hour before you begin making the cheesecake filling. Room-temperature ingredients will combine more evenly, resulting in a uniform batter and reducing the risk of cracks in your cheesecake.

7. In a large bowl, combine the pumpkin purée, eggs, sour cream, flour, vanilla, and salt. Mix until well combined. Add the pumpkin mixture to the cream cheese mixture and beat on low speed just until well combined and smooth, about 3 minutes, stopping to scrape down the sides of the bowl as needed.

8. Pour the filling into the baked crust and bake for 1 hour. Turn off the heat, prop the oven door open slightly, and let the cheesecake sit in the warm oven for another 45 minutes. Transfer to a rack and let cool completely in the pan.

9. **Meanwhile, make the chai caramel sauce:** In a medium saucepan, bring the apple cider to a boil over medium-high heat and cook until reduced to about ⅓ cup. Reduce the heat to medium and add the brown sugar, butter, cream, cinnamon, allspice, cardamom, ginger, cloves, and nutmeg. Continue cooking, stirring constantly, until the sauce thickens and darkens, about 2 minutes. Remove from the heat, add the vanilla and salt, and stir to combine. Set aside to cool; the chai caramel sauce will thicken a little more as it cools. Once cooled, the sauce can be stored in an airtight container in the refrigerator for up to 1 week.

10. When ready to serve, release the sides of the pan and carefully transfer the cheesecake to a large serving plate. Serve with the chai caramel sauce. Store the cheesecake, without the sauce, in an airtight container in the refrigerator for up to 4 days.

Cherry Ruffled Milk Pie

Lora has been making this cherry millk pie, or galatopita, for years. She first learned how to make the famous phyllo dessert while working in a tiny café on Saint-Laurent Boulevard in Montreal. The chef-owner was a passionate pastry chef who would bring her grandmother to the café to help out on busy weekends. Mrs. Kokkinos would come to the rescue and whip up a dozen or more of these delightful Greek ruffled milk pies in no time at all. She always made it look so easy! Lora could barely keep up with her, so her job was pitting the cherries.

1. Preheat the oven to 350°F (180°C). Line the bottom and sides of a 9-inch round cake pan with parchment paper.

2. In a medium bowl, toss the cherries with the flour to evenly coat.

3. Place the phyllo pastry on a work surface and cover with a damp kitchen towel so it doesn't dry out. Working with one sheet of phyllo at a time, brush the top with melted butter. Place another sheet of phyllo on top and brush with butter. Arrange about ⅓ cup of the cherries along the bottom third of the pastry. Tuck in the sides of the pastry and roll the dough up to enclose the cherries. Roll the log into a coil and place in the centre of the lined cake pan. Repeat with the remaining phyllo, butter, and cherries, placing the coils around the one in the centre of the pan. You should have 9 rolls. Brush the tops of the rolls with the remaining butter.

4. Bake until golden brown, 20 to 25 minutes. Remove from the oven; leave the oven on.

5. In a medium bowl, whisk together the eggs, milk, brown sugar, and vanilla. Pour the custard evenly over the pastry and bake until set in the centre, 20 to 25 minutes. Transfer to a rack and let cool for 15 minutes before serving. Serve warm, dusted with icing sugar.

MAKES ONE 9-INCH PIE

3 cups sweet cherries, pitted and halved

2 tablespoons all-purpose flour

18 sheets frozen phyllo pastry, thawed

6 tablespoons unsalted butter, melted

3 large eggs

1½ cups whole milk

½ cup packed brown sugar

1 tablespoon pure vanilla extract

Icing sugar, for dusting

Chocolate Swirl Meringue with Strawberries, Hazelnuts, and Sweet Cream

SERVES 6 TO 8

VANILLA WHIPPED CREAM (MAKES 1 CUP)

1 cup cold heavy (35%) cream

2 tablespoons icing sugar

½ teaspoon pure vanilla extract

CHOCOLATE SWIRL MERINGUE

3 large egg whites (about ⅓ cup)

¾ cup granulated sugar

1½ teaspoons cornstarch

1 teaspoon pure vanilla extract

1 cup semisweet chocolate chips

2 tablespoons heavy (35%) cream

GARNISHES

2 cups quartered hulled fresh strawberries

½ cup hazelnuts, toasted and roughly chopped

Fresh mint leaves

This is one of our family's favourite summertime desserts. When we go strawberry picking, we let the girls pick their own berries, which usually means they get a chance to eat their weight in fresh strawberries. With the few pints we usually end up taking home, we make this chocolate swirled meringue. It is crispy around the edges yet puffy, light, and cloud-like in the centre. We top it with our freshly picked strawberries, hazelnuts, and whipped sweet cream.

1. **Make the vanilla whipped cream:** In a medium bowl, combine the cream, icing sugar, and vanilla and whisk until medium peaks form, 3 to 4 minutes. Store in an airtight container in the refrigerator for up to 3 days.

2. **Make the chocolate swirl meringue:** Preheat the oven to 225°F (110°C). Line a baking sheet with parchment paper.

3. In a stand mixer fitted with the whisk attachment, whisk the egg whites on medium-high speed until frothy.

4. In a small bowl, stir together the sugar and cornstarch. Add the sugar mixture in a slow, steady stream to the egg whites and continue beating on medium-high speed until glossy and firm peaks form. Stir in the vanilla.

5. Melt the chocolate with the cream in a double boiler or in the microwave. Stir until the chocolate is completely melted and smooth. Let the chocolate mixture cool slightly so it is not hot, then using a spatula gently swirl it into the meringue, leaving visible streaks of chocolate. Spread the meringue onto the lined baking sheet in an even layer, about 1½ inches thick.

6. Bake for 1 hour, then turn off the oven and leave the meringue inside the oven, with the door closed, for another hour.

7. Remove from oven and tranfer the meringue to a serving platter or cutting board. Let the meringue cool completely. Just before serving, spread the vanilla whipped cream over the meringue. Garnish with the strawberries, hazelnuts, and mint.

Chocolate Almond Tart with Pears

This French-inspired tart is a beautiful centrepiece—sweet tart pastry filled with chocolaty almond frangipane and pears basted with vanilla, brown sugar, and butter. It's the perfect tart to wow your guests—or yourself!

1. **Make the pastry dough:** In a food processor, combine the flour, sugar, butter, and egg. Pulse until a dough starts to form and pulls away from the sides of the bowl, 15 to 20 seconds.

2. Turn the dough out onto a lightly floured work surface and shape it into a ball. Flatten the ball slightly with your hands to form a thick disc. Wrap the dough in plastic wrap and refrigerate for at least 30 minutes or overnight. Clean the processor bowl.

3. **Make the almond filling:** In the food processor, combine the almond flour, sugar, cocoa powder, all-purpose flour, salt, eggs, and butter. Process until the mixture is a paste-like consistency. Set aside at room temperature.

4. **Prepare the pears:** Melt the butter with the brown sugar and vanilla in a medium skillet over medium heat. Add the pears and cook, turning, until well glazed, 2 to 3 minutes per side. Remove from the heat and let the pears cool in the pan.

5. **Prepare the crust, assemble, and bake:** Preheat the oven to 375°F (190°C). Place a 9-inch tart pan with a removable bottom on a baking sheet.

6. On a lightly floured work surface, use a rolling pin to roll out the dough to an 11-inch circle, ⅛ inch thick. Transfer the pastry to the tart pan. Press the pastry into the bottom and up the sides of the pan. Trim the edges.

7. Spread the almond filling in the pastry shell.

8. Using a sharp knife, thinly slice the quartered pears without cutting through the stem end. Press slightly on the pears to fan the slices. Arrange the fanned pears over the almond filling, with the stem end in the centre. Bake until golden brown, 35 to 40 minutes. Let cool to room temperature before serving. Store in an airtight container in the refrigerator for up to 3 days.

MAKES ONE 9-INCH TART

SWEET PASTRY DOUGH

1⅓ cups all-purpose flour

½ cup granulated sugar

½ cup cold unsalted butter, cut into ½-inch cubes

1 large egg

ALMOND FILLING

1 cup almond flour

½ cup granulated sugar

2 tablespoons unsweetened cocoa powder

1 tablespoon all-purpose flour

¼ teaspoon salt

2 large eggs

8 tablespoons unsalted butter, at room temperature

PEAR LAYER

1 tablespoon unsalted butter

2 tablespoons brown sugar

1 teaspoon pure vanilla extract

3 large pears, peeled, cored, and cut into quarters

Acknowledgments

THANK YOU, PENGUIN RANDOM HOUSE CANADA TEAM, for your steadfast devotion in creating beautiful cookbooks for the world to enjoy. We are truly honoured to be part of your family.

To Andrea Magyar, our unbelievably talented, awesome, encouraging, and always so supportive publishing director and editor, for always being there for us. Words cannot express what it means to the both of us to always have you on our side, believing in us, in our ideas, and allowing us to do what we love to do—cook with all our hearts.

To Shaun Oakey, our patient copy editor: your razor-sharp editing skills and attention to detail are greatly appreciated, and we can't thank you enough for working on this book. You are amazing and exceptionally talented. Thank you!

To our book designer, Terri Nimmo, thank you for visualizing something so beautiful.

So, so, so many thanks to our new friend Ash Nayler. You are an extraordinarily talented photographer. We are indebted to you for the expertise and enthusiasm that you brought to this book. It could not have come together so effortlessly without your talent, passion, commitment, and humour! We loved every minute hanging out with you. We are very lucky to have you in our lives.

A very special thanks to Heather Brown, who helped to keep the calm, organization, and positive energy going in our kitchen during our many cooking days during the photo shoots. We appreciate all of your help to make the days go smoothly. You are our dream weaver.

To our two incredible daughters, Addie and Gemma, who are always up to playing in the dirt with us and helping grow and harvest our family garden. Thank you both so much for allowing us to see food through your eyes with such excitement and love and for constantly showing us new ways to have fun in the kitchen. We love you with all of our hearts.

And finally, many thanks to you. Words cannot express our gratitude for the readers and friends who always support us. Thank you for allowing us to garden, cook, create, and inspire.

Index